CRITICAL
INSIGHTS

Roberto Bolaño

CRITICAL INSIGHTS

Roberto Bolaño

Editor
Ignacio López-Calvo
University of California, Merced

SALEM PRESS
A Division of EBSCO Information Services, Inc.
Ipswich, Massachusetts

GREY HOUSE PUBLISHING

Publisher's Cataloging-In-Publication Data
(Prepared by The Donohue Group, Inc.)

Roberto Bolaño / editor, Ignacio López-Calvo, University of California, Merced. -- [First edition].

    pages ; cm. -- (Critical insights)

    Edition statement supplied by publisher.
    Includes bibliographical references and index.
    ISBN: 978-1-61925-834-1 (hardcover)

    1. Bolaño, Roberto, 1953-2003--Criticism and interpretation. 2. Chilean literature--20th century--History and criticism. I. López-Calvo, Ignacio. II. Series: Critical insights.

PQ8098.12.O38 Z65 2015
863/.64

First Printing

PRINTED IN THE UNITED STATES OF AMERICA

Contents

Resources

Dedication

To Alfonso and Álvaro López Rodríguez

About This Volume

Ignacio Lopez-Calvo

In spite of the interest generated by the Chilean Roberto Bolaño's works both in the United States and worldwide, to my knowledge, this is only the second English-language volume of essays on his works, after the one I edited in 2015, titled *Roberto Bolaño, a Less Distant Star*. Yet the interest in Bolaño's oeuvre continues to grow in the non-Spanish-speaking world, making English-language criticism a necessary complement to the literary criticism and biographies already published in Spanish. Thankfully, Chris Andrews' recent book, *Roberto Bolaño's Fiction: An Expanding Universe* (2014), has greatly contributed to filling in some of these gaps, as will other forthcoming English-language book-length studies. The essays in this volume address numerous topics, including filmic adaptations of Bolaño's works, the relations between his poetry and his prose, and the influence of infrarealism and US literature in Bolaño's writing. They also approach his literature from different theoretical angles, including Marxism, historicism, and queer theory. The first two articles study the historical background and critical reception of Bolaño's works. The third offers an approach from a Marxist perspective and the fourth, a comparative study with Elena Poniatowska. The rest are topical essays that include close readings of some of Bolaño's works.

Juliet Lynd opens this collection of essays on Bolaño's opus with an essay devoted to the historical background that influenced Bolaño's writing. As Lynd explains, Bolaño's literature is deeply marked by the authoritarian repression of revolutionary idealism throughout the twentieth-century and throughout the globe, but particularly in the countries where he lived: Chile, Mexico, and Spain. Bolaño spent his childhood in Chile (1953–1968), his adolescence and early adulthood in Mexico (1968–1977), and then moved to Spain, where he lived until his untimely death in 2003. Her essay explores the impact of the September 11, 1973 military coup on Bolaño and his work, and examines the parallels that Bolaño himself drew between struggles with revolution, dictatorship, and democracy in Chile and in Mexico, as well as the recurring references to the Spanish Civil War and World War II as early scenarios for the battles between right and left. For an undergraduate audience, this essay will offer succinct summaries of relevant historical markers that recur throughout the author's work, and it will unpack the complex relationship between Roberto Bolaño the author and the experiences of his fictional alter ego, Arturo Belano, whose literary persona frequently provides the lens through which these seminal historical moments are explored. Bolaño's innovative literary representations of the twentieth-century struggles between right and left have renewed and reinvigorated debates about the relationship between literature and politics. Moreover, Bolaño's complex interweaving of different national histories in his novels has challenged tired notions about the very category of national literatures, looking toward the transnational and the global, while still seriously engaging the importance of national histories.

In the second essay of the collection, Nicholas Birns looks at the critical reception of Bolaño's works. Bolaño's reputation, explains Birns, blossomed in the Spanish-speaking world with his receipt of the Premio Rómulo Gallegos in 1999, but, after his death in 2003, it rapidly spread globally, especially to the English-speaking countries. Yet there were notable differences in the publication history and reception of his books: the shorter and knottier works went to the independent publisher New Directions, while the longer and splashier works went to Farrar, Straus & Giroux. The presence of a marketing element in Bolaño's reception led to some worries that the author was being overexposed and had peaked too soon. It could be argued, though, that Bolaño, in *2666*, previews and helps construct a posthumous reception of his book that, at the time of the novel's writing, he knew was coming.

In the third essay, David Lau offers a close reading of Bolaño's Rómulo Gallegos-winning novel, *The Savage Detectives*, from a Marxist-historicist theoretical perspective. As Lau explains, in both the long diary entry that bookends *The Savage Detectives* and the deposition-like entries that form the labyrinth of the novel's central section, we learn the stories, hearsay, and gossip about the visceral realist poets and their chief instigators, Arturo Belano and Ulises Lima (the fictionalized names of Roberto Bolaño and Mario Santiago Papasquiaro). A kind of last avant-garde, the visceral realists both extend and retain traces of distinctively Mexican revolutionary literature, art, and politics (emanating from the 1910 revolution) as all three of these traditions are partly subsumed into the postwar Mexican state. The visceral realists also notably connect to several Mexican revolution-era avant-gardists who formed the defunct Stridentists. Otherwise, adds Lau, the visceral realists encounter a contemporary poetic culture (beginning in the mid-1970s), overseen by an increasingly conservative Octavio Paz and his many adherents and devotees, the novel's much-derided "peasant poets." Developing some ideas from Georg Lukács's *The Historical Novel* (refracted through Fredric Jameson, Perry Anderson, and Franco Moretti), Lau reveals how Bolaño's examination of literary history canvases an obscure convolution of the Mexican left under the twin forces of political repression during the 1970s-era dirty wars and the coming of state economic insolvency during the third-world debt crisis of the 1980s. The action of the novel takes place against the background of the emergence of the extra-legal, state-criminal nexus in Mexico.

In turn, Salvador Oropesa opts for a comparative analysis of Bolaño's short novel *Amuleto* (1999) in the light of *Paseo de la Reforma* (1996), a work by the Mexican Elena Poniatowska. In Oropesa's view, both represent the change of paradigm in Mexican literature, when the country accepted the defeat of leftist revolutionary policies and embraced neoliberalism. Different characters, members of the Spanish exile, the more recent Latin American exile, and lumpenproletariat characters are used to convey the idea that, by the new millennium, a political and cultural change had occurred. Both novels, according to Oropesa, resort to "hauntology" and the presence of ghosts of the past to represent a reflective nostalgia about the loss of a utopian future and the condemnation to live in the present. And both effectively use the cultural map of the city to reinforce their main message: Mexico City is one more character in which places of culture resist internal reactionary forces to become a dystopia.

Moving on to the topical essays, Ignacio López-Vicuña's article discusses how Bolaño's posthumous novel *Woes of the True Policeman* may be read as a work that complements Bolaño's better-known novels, in particular *2666*. Although it is an unfinished and fragmentary novel, it echoes and emphasizes themes that will become crucial in Bolaño's major works. Among these themes are the coexistence of idealism and melancholia, the trope of barbarism as anarchic rejection of the status quo, and literature as the voyage of life in the face of illness and death. López-Vicuña's essay explores how these aesthetic tropes reveal strong continuities in Bolaño's ethical and artistic preoccupations, while at the same time providing interesting variations, notably by bringing to the surface questions such as the closeness to poetry and poetic voice in Bolaño's narrative style, the origins of ethical questions in political disenchantment, and the aesthetic possibilities of queer sexuality as a form of dissidence.

Brantley Nicholson, in his chapter, argues that the trope of much of Bolaño's most ambitious and critically acclaimed works, *Los detectives salvajes* (1998) and *2666* (2004), turns on the interplay between a hypothetical pure aesthetics that glorifies the Latin American experience in and of itself and the disarticulation of this local idealism when it enters into world systems. Nicholson claims that Bolaño's emphasis on the dissonance between imagined and real cosmopolitan centers falls in line with what Mariano Siskind has recently defined as the traditional "deseo de mundo," or "desire for the world," among the Latin American literati. With Bolaño, he claims, we witness the realization of this desire, though the result is not the promised empowerment, but a deflating letdown. The "desire for the world" is only an affective cultural variable insofar as it does not give way to what he refers to as the *actual experience of the world*, under the terms of which the fantasy of cosmopolitanism cannot sustain the weight of material metropolitan experience. In this chapter, Nicholson analyzes the awkward presence European academics at the US-Mexico border during a spate of feminicides, the high and popular cultural misunderstandings that occur under the terms of transnationalism, and the persistent undertones of peripatetic disjointedness that fill the pages of Bolaño's most acclaimed novels.

José Javier Fernández Díaz explores the influence of US literature in Bolaño's opus, establishing a literary map of the dialogue between these authors and texts. Fernández Díaz analyzes more than one hundred citations from Bolaño's most acclaimed works to determine Bolaño's most significant features in conjunction with some of his influences, including Mark Twain, Jack Kerouac, and William S. Burroughs.

In the next chapter, Ryan Long elucidates connections among different texts by Bolaño that share queer themes, including the development of gay male characters and associations of poetry with homosexuality. He argues that attention to queer themes makes clearer a critique in Bolaño's work of the ways in which resistant politics—most consistently associated with the Chilean left in the years following Pinochet's coup—reproduce discriminatory and exclusive discourse and action. With this goal in mind, Long conducts close readings of the novel *Amulet* (1999) and the short story "Mauricio (The Eye) Silva" (2001), and then considers more broadly two additional texts, the novels *The Savage Detectives* (1998) and *Woes of the True Policeman* (2011). His analysis concludes that queer affinities in Bolaño's texts function as a way of negotiating past political failures.

Rubén Medina, a founding member—along with Bolaño—of infrarealism in Mexico City in the mid-seventies, looks at the early historical moment in which Bolaño emerges as a writer, addressing his relationship to infrarealism, the neo-avant-garde movement he cofounded, and how this movement turned politics into ethics. In Medina's view, everyday ethics, a key notion to infrarealism, is also key to understand Bolaño's writing.

My essay focuses on Bolaño's assertion that *Amberes* was the only one of his works that did not embarrass him. In this light, I consider this work a reification of the anti-realism he defended in his essays and interviews. At the same time, I use the sociologist Pierre Bourdieu's theories about writers' interest in disinterestedness to argue that it is not always wise to try to separate the author (or alter his egos) in his texts from real-life Bolaño himself, as Bolaño often invites his readers to construct a mental image of himself as a Latin American bohemian or *poète maudit*, hoping that the marginality that marked many years of his life will add to his credibility as a "pure" and "disinterested" writer.

The next two chapters are devoted to contrasting Bolaño's *Una novelita lumpen* (2002) and the Chilean filmmaker Alicia Scherson's film adaptation *Il futuro* (2013). Both novel and film, explains Traci Roberts-Camps, follow Bianca and her brother, Tomas, after the death of their parents in a car accident. Both express a shifted perception of reality after the accident, including continuous light and no distinction between night and day. They spend their time watching television, leaving it on even while sleeping. When Tomas's friends come to stay, they suggest a plan in which Bianca seduces a rich, older man, Maciste [Rutger Hauer], so they can rob him. The themes of film, television, and popular culture reappear when Maciste tells Bianca stories of his time as a movie star, playing in such films as *Maciste Against the Living Dead*. Throughout the cinematic version, Scherson incorporates scenes from several of Maciste's films, further underscoring the importance of film and television to the narrative. In fact, there is a direct connection made in both novel and film between popular culture and what Jeffrey Arnett has termed emerging adulthood. Roberts-Camps's essay examines specific scenes in the two texts that focus on Bianca's liminal position between adolescence and adulthood and the prevalence of popular culture in her life.

Along these lines, Alicia Ramos Jordán and Marco Valesi's chapter compares the novel and its cinematographic adaptation, underlining the complex relations between past and future. According to them, both cultural productions are suspended in time and have Rome as background in order to describe anonymous lives. They use an epic sword-and-sandal movie's hero (Maciste), Pasolinian realism (bodybuilders, hair-dressers), magic realism (the sun that never sets), Fellini-esque surrealism (escapes into desert), as a neo-mythological point of departure hoping for a new future. This essay delimits the precarious balance that Bolaño creates between posthumous past and uncertain future.

Closing the volume as a sort of epilogue, Ignacio Padilla offers his recollection of a gathering of twelve relatively young Latin American writers and godfathered by Roberto Bolaño and Guillermo Cabrera Infante, in Seville in 2003 (ten days before Bolaño's passing), which he considers a point of inflection in the history of Latin American literature. In Padilla's view, on that day, Bolaño was revealed as the missing link between the Latin American Boom and his own generation, an assertion that has been questioned by several critics. Padilla also sees Bolaño as the last of his kind: the last Latin American writer.

With these essays, we hope to bring Bolaño's opus closer to the English-speaking reader and to promote the work of one of the most important and influential Latin American writers of the last decades.

CAREER, LIFE, AND INFLUENCE

On Roberto Bolaño: Poet and Vagabond_____

Ignacio López-Calvo

In 1976, upon his return from a trip throughout Latin America, Roberto Bolaño co-founded the infrarrealist movement in Mexico City, at the house of a Chilean friend, poet Bruno Montané. In the same year, he penned an infrarealist manifesto with a title that rewrote a poem by André Breton, the father of surrealism: *Déjenlo todo, nuevamente* (*Give It All Up Again*). This manifesto already voices Bolaño's refusal to separate poetry, literature, and art from revolution and life in general, one of the keystones of his worldview: "Our ethic is the Revolution, our aesthetics is Life: one-and-the-same."[1] In an interview with his friend, Mexican writer Carmen Boullosa, he actually claims that the movement only had two members, his best friend, Mario Santiago Papasquiaro (1953–1998) and himself:

> Infrarealism was a kind of *Dada á la Mexicana*. At one point there were many people, not only poets, but also painters and especially loafers and hangers-on, who considered themselves Infrarealists. Actually there were only two members, Mario Santiago and I. We both went to Europe in 1977. One night, in Rosellón, France, at the Port Vendres train station (which is very close to Perpignan), after having suffered a few disastrous adventures, we decided that the movement, such as it was, had come to an end. (n.p.)

However, Rubén Medina, another infrarrealist poet and critic, has denied the veracity of this statement: "in public declarations he even reduces Infrarealism to a movement constituted only by Mario and him and as an event from the past, when in the mid-1990s he publishes *El último salvaje* in Mexico City and is aware of the existence of an infrarrealist contingent."[2] In fact, in his anthology *Perros habitados por las voces del desierto: Poesía infrarrealista entre dos siglos* (*Dogs Inhabited by the Voices of the Desert: Infrarealist Poetry Between Two Centuries*, 2014), Medina includes, besides Bolaño, Mario Santiago Papasquiaro and himself, numerous others writers and artists.[3] Some of these poets published their works in photocopies, journals, and anthologies, such as *Pájaro de calor* (*Bird of Heat*; Mexico City, 1976), *Correspondencia infra* (*Infra Correspondence*; Mexico City, 1977), *Rimbaud vuelve a casa* (*Rimbaud Returns Home*; Barcelona, 1977), or *Berthe Trépat* (Barcelona-Mexico City, 1978–1983).

Although the infrarealists have been considered a neo-avant-garde movement, Bolaño's writing, as the Spanish novelist and journalist Javier Cercas points out, is far from the hermeticism and linguistic experimentalism that was typical of the avant-garde; on the contrary, his texts are, for the most part, reader friendly and characterized by a plain, conversational prose that avoids superfluous ornamentation. In the words of Cercas, Bolaño was "a writer who was allergic to any form of logomaquia, a compulsively legible narrator."[4] Indeed, perhaps with the exception of *Amberes* (*Antwerp*, 2002), his prose tends to be easily readable and lacks the irrationalism, incoherence, and free association of images that characterized avant-garde literature.

Determined to focus on poetry, during his infrarealist years, Bolaño burned, in his friend Bruno Montané's presence, the approximately seven hundred pages of drama he had written, claiming they were of poor quality. Some of Bolaño's poems were published in 1978 in the anthologies *Algunos poetas en Barcelona* (*Some Poets in Barcelona*) and *La novísima poesía latinoamericana* (*The Newest Latin American Poetry*). The following year, his poetry would be included in the anthology *Muchachos desnudos bajo el arcoíris de fuego. Once jóvenes poetas latinoamericanos* (*Naked Youngsters under the Fire Rainbow: Eleven Young Latin American Poets*). Even though Bolaño's true passion was poetry (during his first years in Spain, he would give away visiting cards that read "Roberto Bolaño, Poet and Vagabond"), he allegedly switched to prose in order to support his family. However, Valerie Miles has suggested that "Contrary to what has been repeatedly claimed about Bolaño the poet versus Bolaño the prose writer, his notebooks show that he had every intention of becoming a novelist" (Locascio n.p.). At any rate, this decision, after the birth of his son Lautaro in 1990, turned a marginal, outcast poet into an iconic novelist, a cult figure in the world republic of letters (including in the United States, were less than four percent of the literature published is translated fiction), and the most influential Latin American writer of his generation. Bolaño changed the map of Spanish-language literature to the point where the impact of the publication of his novel *Los detectives salvajes* has been compared to that of Julio Cortázar's *Rayuela* (*Hopscotch*) in 1963 or Gabriel García Márquez's *Cien años de soledad* (*One Hundred Years of Solitude*) in 1967. Many young Latin American writers and readers saw in Bolaño's literature a definitive break with the Boom writers of the 1960s, as well as an originality in both style and themes that had been lacking in Spanish-language fiction for some time. Cercas, however, has astutely pointed out that Bolaño never rejected nor was a detractor of the Boom; rather, his prose was a continuation of his masters' writing:

> Not only is his oeuvre unimaginable without a hard-fought reading of Borges, but also without that colloquial transparence of Cortázar's prose or without that narrative astuteness and the novelistic architecture of Vargas Llosa, undoubtedly the living Spanish-language novelist whom Bolaño admired the most, and one of those whom he assimilated more carefully.[5]

Still within the framework of his originality, Bolaño's fiction is often populated by unsuccessful and sometimes mediocre writers whose actions are sprinkled with literary intertextualities and cultural references. And it is not uncommon to find a lack of closure or denouement in his narrative; rather than having an open ending, however, many of his stories suddenly end or just seem to fade away. Bolaño also blends aesthetics and politics, and recreates minor individual struggles where utopian projects have already failed. As Juan de Castro points out,

> Bolaño has provided other writers with an example of how to write about politics in a post-political manner. Throughout his novels Bolaño replaces political commitment with ethical evaluation. If the image of the Latin American writer as necessarily radical was

a caricature drawn up by both conservatives and leftists during the 1960s . . . most contemporary novelists judge politics from a position akin to that of Bolaño: ethical and beyond any identifiable political current or position. (Varn n.p.)

Among Bolaño's twenty publications (most of them published in the last decade of his life), his most critically acclaimed works published while still alive were the novel *Los detectives salvajes* (*The Savage Detectives*, 1998)—for which he won the Herralde Award, the Rómulo Gallegos Award, and the Chilean Consejo Nacional del Libro Award in 1999—and the novellas *Estrella distante* (*Distant Star*, 1996) and *Nocturno de Chile* (*By Night in Chile*, 2000). His posthumous novel *2666* (2004) finally established him as an international literary star, winning the National Book Critics Circle Award for Fiction in 2008. His short story collections, *Llamadas telefónicas* (1997), *Putas asesinas* (2001), *El gaucho insufrible* (*The Insufferable Gaucho*; 2003, his first posthumous work), and the posthumous *El secreto del mal* (*The Secret of Evil*, 2012) were also awarded literary prizes. English translations of some of these short stories were later included in the collections *Last Evenings on Earth* (2007) and *The Return* (2010). Several other works were extracted from Bolaño's unpublished archive of 14,374 pages and published posthumously, such as the novels *El Tercer Reich* (*The Third Reich*, 2010) and *Los sinsabores del verdadero policía* (*Woes of the True Policeman*, 2011), which have received mixed reviews. It is not entirely clear, however, whether or not the Chilean author intended to publish them. The nonfiction that was published in the Catalan journal *Diari de Girona* and later in the Chilean journal *Las últimas noticias*, much of it dealing with Bolaño's views on world literature, was later compiled by his friend Ignacio Echevarría in the 2004 volume *Entre paréntesis. Ensayos, artículos y discursos (1998–2003)* (*Between Parentheses. Essays, Articles, and Speeches, [1998–2003]*).

Rather than his poetry, therefore, it was his fiction (novels, novellas, short story collections) that improved his reputation as a writer. Bolaño's first published novel was *Consejos de un discípulo de Morrison a un fanático de Joyce* (*Advice for a Morrison Disciple from a Joyce* Fanatic, 1984), which he wrote in collaboration with the Catalan writer Antoni García Porta. Although they were awarded the Ámbito Literario de Narrativa Prize in Barcelona, this work would not propel Bolaño to fame and prestige yet. His second published novel was *La senda de los elefantes* (1984, published again in 1999 under the title *Monsieur Pain*), and his third was *La pista de hielo* (*The Skating Rink*), which was initially published in 1993. All three are generally considered minor works. In the last one, three male narrators, a Chilean, a Mexican, and a Spaniard, tell, each in separate chapters, their own version of the story of Nuria Martí, a beautiful figure-skating champion who, after being dropped from the Olympic team, gets involved in a strange crime scene at a skating rink secretly built by a civil servant in an abandoned mansion. As witnesses to the crime, they recall the events, and the reader has to come to her own conclusions, as in a detective story.

Bolaño reached a point of inflection in his literary career with the publication in 1996 of *La literatura nazi en América* (*Nazi Literature in the Americas*), a parodic and disturbing catalog— inspired, among other works, by Jorge Luis Borges's *Historia universal de la infamia* (*A Universal History of Iniquity*, 1935)—of fictional, unhappy, mediocre, and fascist North American and Latin American writers and critics who dream in vain of reaching fame and glory. Although the book was well received by Hispanic critics, to Bolaño's dismay, very few copies were sold at the time of its first edition. As the author stated in a television interview in Chile, it was ironically inspired by his realization that many of his peers— other Latin American writers—seemed completely unaware of the fact that their work was not going to survive the passing of time. In this same interview, he also clarified that the main reason so many of his characters are writers was simply because that he was most comfortable writing about what he knew best. *La literatura nazi en América* blends the world of literature with evil, crime and politics, one of the leitmotifs of Bolaño's oeuvre. He would later expand its epilogue, titled "Carlos Ramírez Hoffman," into the novel *Estrella distante* (*Distant Star*, 1996). Bolaño's prologue to *Estrella distante* explicitly mentions Jorge Luis Borges's "Pierre Menard, autor del Quijote" ("Pierre Menard, author of the Quixote"), from the 1944 collection *Ficciones*, as a literary precedent. Indeed, the Chilean implements Borges's theories in this story about the role of repetition in writing.[6]

Bolaño devoted numerous pages of his fiction to the exploration of human attraction to violence and evil. This lucubration about the possible sources of pure evil is often set in violent Latin American societies, such as the fictional rendering of Ciudad Juárez or General Augusto Pinochet's Chile, where murder, terror, and impunity have become a part of the country's daily life, including those of its writers. As Cercas astutely reveals, in Bolaño's works "literature or literary life is only a metaphor for life itself, and one of Bolaño's main merits is having given literary gossip an almost epic dimension in which all the passions, vertigos, and perplexities of human beings find a new and torn dimension."[7] From this perspective, Bolaño sets his novella *Estrella distante* (*Distant Star*), also published in 1996, in his native Chile, during Pinochet's dictatorship, where, violence and evil are again blended with the world of literature, poetry workshops, and art. As in *Nocturno de Chile* and other works, in *Estrella distante*, Bolaño includes a villain or evil, fascist writer and explores how poets react to or interact with authoritarian regimes. Carlos Wieder (initially known as Alberto Ruiz-Tagle) is one of the few characters in Bolaño's works whose poetry is available to the reader (typically, the author is more interested in recreating how poets "live" poetry than in how they write it). Within the world of the government-run death squads and the Chilean *desaparecidos*, this seemingly normal poet turns out to be a lieutenant in the Chilean air forces who writes fascist-sounding poetry lines ("Death is friendship," "Death is Chile," "Death is cleansing") in the air with his plane's exhaust pipe. He is also a serial killer who photographs mostly female, "disappeared," Chilean victims to exhibit them at a party. It is insinuated that some of these murders may have been motivated in part by mere literary jealousy, but, in any case, Wieder is the embodiment of absolute evil, a topic that will later be greatly amplified with the serial femicides in *2666*. As Chris Andrews explains, "The ending of *Distant Star* is haunted by the faint suggestion that the 'absolute evil' embodied by Wieder may not be simply an isolated freak of nature, an extreme form of sociopathy, but a metaphysical disease that has already spread by contagion, a kind of evil that is diabolical in the archaic sense of the word" (161).

The unnamed narrator, Carlos Wieder's former poetry workshop classmate, is haunted by the image of the fascist poet-pilot-assassin. In the end, as in a detective novel, he aids a detective to track Wieder in a Spanish apartment building. Once again, Bolaño resorts to the story of a writer who searches another missing writer, mixing literature and crime. In both *Distant Star* and *By Night in Chile*, the crimes are eventually solved, in contrast with the outcome of the numerous crimes that take place in *2666* and other novels.

Shortly before his death, Bolaño said half-jokingly, in an interview with Mónica Maristáin, that he would have liked to be a homicide detective rather than a writer. Perhaps for this reason, he was an avid reader of detective stories, which influenced his writing, as is evident even in the title of his first long novel and his most acclaimed work while still alive, *Los detectives salvajes* (*The Savage Detectives*).[8] In this sprawling and fragmentary novel, the "detectives" mentioned in the title are actually the marginal, but determined visceral realist (the fictional version of the infrarealists) poets Arturo Belano and Ulises Lima, stand-ins for the author himself and his best friend, Mario Santiago. Fifty-two different characters narrate the action, which takes place between 1975 and 1996 in different countries, but mostly in mid-1970s Mexico.[9] The first part, narrated by the seventeen-year-old aspiring poet Juan García Madero in his private diary entries, introduces the reader to his excitement about being initiated as a visceral realist and—as in a *Bildungsroman*—to the awakening of his sexual life. Toward the end of the first part, still in 1975, García Madero, Belano and Lima flee Mexico City to save a prostitute named Lupe from her violent pimp. They travel in a friend's car to the Sonora Desert in search for the elusive Cesárea Tinajero, their precursor and founder of the Mexican avant-garde movement "Real visceralismo"—just like the protagonist of Julio Cortázar's 1963 *Rayuela* (*Hopscotch*) looked for La Maga.[10] As is common in Bolaño's narrative, we find writers or people related to the literary trade looking for or writing about other missing writers, as well as characters that suddenly vanish, leaving their acquaintances to provide testimonies about them.

The second part of *Los detectives salvajes*, by far the longest, covers the years from 1976 through 1996 and includes a polyphonic, oral history formed by the testimonies of thirty-eight people from different countries who knew Belano and Lima. The narrators recall what happened to them after their trip to Sonora, during their international travels. While it is apparent that they never became successful writers, Belano and Lima are not seen as a failure; these young men without an oeuvre managed to *live*—rather than "write"—like poets. Like the real-life infrarealists, the two visceral realists conceived of poetry mostly as a way of life, rather than as a way to make a living. They were courageous enough to follow their own ideals regarding poetry, art, and life to the ultimate consequences, without fearing failure. In the third part, it is again García Madero who narrates the end of the story, beginning in 1976 (where it was left in the first part). Eventually, they manage to find Cesárea Tinajero in Sonora.

A literary guerrilla of young, antibourgeois and rebellious poets, modeled after the iconoclast infrarealists, mocks the pretentious literary world and cultural scene of the Mexico City of the 1970s, with their official cultural events. They also harass state-funded writers such as Octavio Paz (who, in real life, would become the first Mexican author to receive the Nobel Prize for Literature) and even conspire to kidnap him. Curiously, even though there is a tendency (inherited from Borges) in Bolaño's writing to summarize the plots of fictional writings, there are no samples of poems by the visceral realists in *Los detectectives salvajes*, other than one poem by Cesárea Tinajero. The reason for this, according to Rubén Medina, is that they "are poets with no oeuvre. The important thing in the account is not his poems, but the way in which they survive through the years in their eagerness to write; the important thing is the union between art and life, rather than ending (each of the infras in the novel) as a social climber, a coward, or a cannibal."[11]

Los detectives salvajes also deals with lost youth, a love letter to the young men and women of his generation (Latin Americans born in the 1950s) who sacrificed their lives for failed ideals and utopias. In this context, in his acceptance speech for the Rómulo Gallegos Prize, Bolaño stated:

> Everything that I've written is a love letter or a farewell letter to my own generation, those of us who were born in the 1950s and who at a certain moment chose military service, though in this case it would be more accurate to say "militancy," and gave the little we had—the great deal that we had, which was our youth—to a cause that we thought was the most generous cause in the world and in a certain way it was, but in reality it wasn't. It goes without saying that we fought our hardest, but we had corrupt leaders, cowardly leaders with a propaganda apparatus that was worse than a leper colony, we fought for parties that if they had won would have sent us straight to labor camps, we fought for and put all our generosity into an ideal that had been dead for more than fifty years, and some of us knew it, and how could we not when we'd read Trotsky or were Trotskyites, but we did it anyway, because we were stupid and generous, as young people are, giving everything and asking for nothing in return, and now those young people are gone, because those who didn't die in Bolivia died in Argentina or Peru, and those who survived went on to die in Chile or Mexico, and those who weren't killed there were killed later in Nicaragua, Colombia, or El Salvador. All of Latin America is sown with the bones of these forgot- ten youths. ("Caracas Address" 35)[12]

These melancholic, almost romantic, overtones permeate much of Bolaño's opus. In a mostly male world of bookish and intellectual characters that have lost all hope for utopian or revolutionary struggles, fleeting friendships are the only islands in an ocean of disillusion, nihilism, and evil. Now they are simply trying to forget (albeit some continue to fight until the end), while sailing adrift in their life.

Bolaño's next published work was the less celebrated novella *Amuleto* (*Amulet*, 1999), an expansion of the fourth chapter of part

II of *Los detectives salvajes*. In it, the middle-aged Uruguayan poet Auxilio Lacouture (modeled after the real-life Uruguayan teacher Alcira Soust Scaffo, Bolaño's mother's friend) narrates, from a first-person narrative perspective, how she hid for several days in a toilet stall during a violent military raid of the National Autonomous University of Mexico (UNAM) campus in 1968. She also tells the adventures of Arturo Belano and other Latin American writers and artists. Lacouture had briefly appeared in *Los detectives salvajes*, where she participated in the 1968 student revolt, describing herself as "Mother of Mexican Poetry."

As seen, the characters of aspiring, frustrated writers embody Bolaño's lucubration about the role of the literary world in society, particularly under authoritarian regimes. But perhaps nowhere in his opus is this more apparent than in the novella *Nocturno de Chile* (*By Night in Chile*, 2000), which he initially wanted to entitle "Tomenta de mierda" (*Shit Storm*). In it, we find the deathbed confession of the Chilean Sebastián Urrutia Lacroix, a failed poet, literary critic, corrupt priest, and member of Opus Dei. While Father Urrutia tries to find words to justify his actions (or lack thereof), he can hardly hide a sense of remorse and guilt for his passive complicity with the Junta's crimes. At the beginning of the story, we find out that the Church—through two allegorical characters named Odeim and Oido (Fear and Hate spelled backwards in Spanish)—has chosen him to study the preservation of cathedrals against pigeon droppings in Europe. As Urrutia finds out, hawks are being used in Europe to hunt the pigeons, plausibly a metaphor for the Chilean dictatorship's hunting of leftists. Fear and Hate are precisely two of the key topics in the novel. As Karim Benmiloud explains, "Ultimately, Odeim and Oido, Miedo and Odio, represent the narrator's feelings, in his deep soul, to the image and likeness of that 'aged youngster' . . . who is conceived of, toward the end of the novel, as another double of the narrator."[13]

Urrutia, an erudite man who admires art and literature, but ignores human rights abuses around him, will end up becoming a passive supporter and accomplice of the Pinochet regime through silence and acquiescence. In fact, he proudly teaches the main tenets of Marxism to Pinochet and other members of the Chilean military junta with the goal of understanding the enemy better (according to Bolaño, it is true that, after the coup, Pinochet took some courses on Marxism to learn about the enemy [Stolzmann 370]). At one point, Urrutia, who is often blinded by his attraction to famous and powerful people, finds out that he has been at parties in houses whose owners were torturing political prisoners in their basements. This episode in the novella is based on the real-life "Townley affair" in Chile, in which an American named Michael Townley, married to a Chilean wife who hosted a literary salon at her house, was exposed as one of the Junta's secret torturers. Like *Estrella distante* and other works, *Nocturno de Chile* returns to one of Bolaño's social obsessions: the relationship between art/literature and crime, between the artist/ writer and the totalitarian state.

Amberes (*Antwerp*, 2002), a text published both as fiction and as poetry, is a blend of prose and poetry in which, as I explain in the chapter included in this volume, we find many of Bolaño's topics, motifs, and obsessions (murders, corruptions, misfit, aspiring and failed poets). The work does not have a clearly defined plot, but rather a number of interrelated sketches.

As seen in the essay by Traci Roberts-Camps as well as in the one by Alicia Ramos Jordán and Marco Valesi in this volume, Bolaño's *Una novelita lumpen* (*A Little Lumpen Novelita*), also published in 2002, was turned into Alicia Scherson's film *Il futuro*. The novel, the only one he wrote under contract, deals with the adolescent Bianca who, along with her brother, becomes an orphan and has to choose between becoming a criminal or a prostitute.

Bolaño's posthumous novel *2666*, which he envisioned as his masterpiece, was highly anticipated, after the success of *Los detectives salvajes* and the common knowledge that he had been feverishly writing it against the clock of his impending death, while waiting for a liver transplant. A long and ambitious novel divided into five parts and with numerous characters, it was published in 2004 (a year after the author's death), even though there is speculation that it was left unintentionally unfinished, like several of his other posthumous works. The fourth and longest part (or novel) deals with serial femicides in the fictional town of Santa Teresa, in the northern state of Sonora, which is reminiscent of real-life Ciudad Juarez, Mexico. Bolaño, inspired by Sergio González Rodríguez's *Huesos en el desierto* (*The Femicide Machine*, 2002), presents these femicides as a microcosm of the horrors of contemporary violence and evil, an apocalyptic metaphor for humankind's fate. According to José Manuel López de Abiada, however, Santa Teresa represents political corruption in Mexico: "a metaphor and synecdoche of a failed rule of law in a state, of a state in a state (sorry for the redundancy) of partial exception, a state one could suspect it has abolished or derogated part of its juridical order."[14]

It was precisely the notorious femicides in Ciudad Juarez, in the Mexican state of Chihuahua—which have claimed the lives of more than seven hundred women, adolescent, and young girls since January 1993—that inspired Bolaño to write this novel. Most of the murdered women, in both the novel and real life, were between fifteen and twenty-two years old and from the working class. Many of them were raped, tortured, or both before being assassinated. There has been an international outrage over the passivity and negligence of local and national authorities. As reflected in Bolaño's novel, the impunity has been shocking: more than half of these murders have never resulted in a conviction.

While in *Los detectives salvajes* the protagonists looked for the poet Cesárea Tinajero, in *2666* the quest for vanished writers (so common in Bolaño's literary world) continues: now four European critics are determined, in the mid-1990s, to find the reclusive German writer Benno von Archimboldi in the state of Sonora. Along these lines, the possibly diabolic nature of Carlos Wieder in *Estrella distante* reappears in *2666* with full force: Bolaño suggests that the Santa Teresa femicides may be explained again by a supernatural conception of human evil.

El Tercer Reich (*The Third Reich*, 2010), also published posthumously, has a German protagonist, Udo Berger, who is a war game champion (Bolaño was a war game aficionado). Berger and his girlfriend Ingeborg spend their vacation in a small town on the Costa Brava, where they go to clubs with another German couple they have met at the beach. Berger teaches the board game "The Third Reich" to El Quemado (as he is known locally because of his burn scars), a local stranger who lives at the beach taking care of paddleboats. Because Berger is a German who tries to change the course of World War II history through the game, he gains a reputation as a Nazi, even though he considers himself an anti-Nazi. At one point, Berger's obsession with the Third Reich game begins to disrupt his relationship with Ingeborg.

Another posthumous novel, the unfinished *Los sinsabores del verdadero policía* (*Woes of the True Policeman*, 2011), offers variations of episodes appearing in *2666*. Although these latest posthumous publications have received mixed critical reviews, they will probably not affect Bolaño's reputation negatively, as it is unclear whether or not he intended to have them published.

As to Bolaño's short-story collections, his *Llamadas Telefónicas* is a collection of fourteen short stories, mostly dealing with writers and the literary world, narrated from a first-person perspective, often by the author's alter ego, "B." Another collection, titled *El Gaucho Insufrible* (*The Insufferable Gaucho*) includes five short stories and two essays. The title story is Bolaño's version of Jorge Luis Borges's "El sur" ("The South.") Several of these stories end abruptly, leaving the inconclusive narratives without a clearly defined end. *El Secreto del Mal* (*The Secret of Evil*, 2007) is a collection of twenty-one short stories and essays with characters such as Arturo Belano, who had appeared in previous narratives.

Regarding his favorite literary genre, Bolaño edited the poetry collection *Reinventar el amor* (*Reinventing Love*, 1976) and *Pájaro de calor. Ocho poetas infrarrealistas* (*Bird of Flames: Eight Infrarealist Poets*, 1976). His first published poetry collection was *Los perros románticos* (*The Romantic Dogs*, 1993) and his complete poetry was translated and published under the title *The Unknown University*.

Many critics see Bolaño's writing as a major break in Latin American literature, as he allegedly distanced himself from the Boom authors and their post-Boom epigones, rejecting, in particular, the tenets of magical realism. Along the way, he famously praised the writers of many Hispanic authors and criticized many others (Octavio Paz, Isabel Allende, Antonio Skármeta, Volodia Teitelboim, Luis Sepúlveda, Hernán Rivera Letelier, Diamela Eltit, Ángeles Mastretta, Marcela Serrano, Camino José Cela, Arturo Pérez-Reverte, Francisco Umbral) for different reasons, which gained him numerous enemies, particularly in his native Chile.[15] Throughout his fiction, essays, and interviews Bolaño—who saw the writing profession, particularly for poets, as courageous and stoic, if not masochistic—insists on his anti-literary establishment stance and rejects people he considers literary careerist and arrivistes. And he maintained this anti-establishment position even after becoming an international sensation, as Rubén Medina explains: "Bolaño is a marginal writer who is consistently against the literary institution. Even after entering the powerful publishing world and being acknowledged, he continued to behave as a marginal writer who was viscerally and visibly against the literary institution."[16] Proof of this, according to Medina, is the fact that the Chilean never created his own literary mafia, tried to obtain a position in a cultural institution, or helped his friends to become published authors.

As to his literary techniques, Chris Andrews explains Bolaño's impressive literary production through the processes of expansion, circulating characters, metarepresetation, and overinterpretation:

> Bolaño expanded and "exploded" his own published texts, blowing them up by adding new characters and episodes as well as circumstantial details. He also allowed characters to circulate or migrate from text to text, sometimes altering their names and properties. Within his novels and stories, he included representations of imagined texts and artworks, that is, metarepresentations. Finally, some of his characters and narrators are overinterpreters: they seize on details, invest them with significance, and invent stories to connect and explain them. (xii)

Bolaño's literature has also been described as postnational (or extraterritorial) fiction, since it was written and takes place mostly in Mexico and Chile, and sometimes in Spain, and tends to look beyond national borders. His uprootedness and self-identification as a Latin American (rather than just a Chilean), along with his impressive ability to have his characters use the Spanish dialects and slang from these three countries also contributed to a perception beyond the borders of his place of birth.

Bolaño's narratives often blend autobiographical sources with fiction. This has sometimes misled readers and critics into assuming that certain information is autobiographical. Along these lines, Bolaño's topics and characters (including his alter egos) reappear time and again in his works. In fact, he claimed to conceive of his oeuvre as a cohesive unit and saw his ideal reader as someone who would read all his works in order to have a holistic understanding of his literature.

Overall, Bolaño is today one of the most influential Spanish-language writers, as evidenced by the numerous publications about his works (particularly in Spanish), translations of his opus, and the constant praise that his major works receive from critics and other readers.

Notes

1. "Nuestra ética es la Revolución, nuestra estética la Vida: una-sola-cosa" (n.p.).

2. "En declaraciones públicas incluso reduzca el infrarrealismo a un movimiento únicamente constituido por Mario y él, y como un evento del pasado aun cuando a mediados de los noventa incluso publica *El último salvaje* en el DF, y sabe de la existencia de un contingente infrarrealista" (52).

3. Medina includes the writers Óscar Altamirano, Edgar Artaud Jarry, Pedro Damián Bautista, Rafael Catana, Mario Raúl Guzmán, Claudia Kerik, Ramón Méndez Estrada, Cuauhtémoc Méndez, Víctor Monjarás Ruiz, Bruno Montané Krebs, María Guadalupe Ochoa Ávila, José Peguero, José Rosas Ribeyro; the musicians Rafael Catana; the filmmakers Juan Esteban Harrington, Jorge Henández Piel Divina, Víctor Monjarás, and José Peguero; and the artists Jorge, Hernández Piel Divina, and Víctor Monjarás Ruiz.

4. "Un escritor alérgico a cualquier forma de logomaquia, un narrador compulsivamente legible" (n.p.).

5. "Su obra no es sólo inimaginable sin una lectura a brazo partido de Borges, sino también sin la transparencia coloquial de la

prosa de Cortázar o sin las astucias narrativas y las arquitecturas novelescas de Vargas Llosa, sin duda el novelista vivo en español a quien más admiró Bolaño, y uno de los que con más cuidado asimiló" (n.p.).

6. For more information on the role of repetition in Bolaño's opus, see my essay "Roberto Bolaño's Flower War: Memory, Melancholy, and Pierre Menard" (*Roberto Bolaño, a Less Distant Star: Critical Essays*. Ed. Ignacio López-Calvo. Palgrave Macmillan Publishing, 2015. 35–64).

7. "La literatura o la vida literaria es sólo una metáfora de la vida a secas, y uno de los principales méritos de Bolaño consiste en haber dotado al chisme literario de una dimensión casi épica en la que todas las pasiones, los vértigos y las perplejidades del ser humano hallan una expresión desgarrada y nueva" (n.p.).

8. He enjoyed reading science fiction as well.

9. Fernando Saucedo Lastra has studied the presence of Mexico in Bolaño's works in his 2015 book *México en la obra de Roberto Bolaño. Memoria y territorio*.

10. As Bolaño explained in a summary of the novel before he completed it, Tinajero, who disappeared from Mexico City in 1929, at age twenty-six, is a former member of the first Mexican avant-garde movement, the 1920s Estridentismo, who later founded her own avant-garde movement, also called visceral realism.

11. "Son poetas sin obra. Lo que importa en el relato no son sus poemas, sino el modo en que éstos sobreviven a través de los años en su afán de escribir; lo que importa es la unión arte y vida, y no terminar (cada uno de los infras en la novela) como un trepador social, un cobarde o un canibal" (53).

12. "Todo lo que he escrito es una carta de amor o de despedida a mi propia generación, los que nacimos en la década del cincuenta y los que escogimos en un momento dado el ejercicio de la milicia, en este caso sería más correcto decir la militancia, y entregamos lo poco que teníamos, lo mucho que teníamos, que era nuestra juventud, a una causa que creímos la más generosa de las causas del mundo y que en cierta forma lo era, pero que en la realidad no lo era. De más está decir que luchamos a brazo partido, pero tuvimos jefes corruptos, líderes cobardes, un aparato de propaganda que era peor que una leprosería, luchamos por partidos que de haber vencido nos habrían enviado de

inmediato a un campo de trabajos forzados, luchamos y pusimos toda nuestra generosidad en un ideal que hacía más de cincuenta años que estaba muerto, y algunos lo sabíamos, y cómo no lo íbamos a saber si habíamos leído a Trotski o éramos trotskistas, pero igual lo hicimos, porque fuimos estúpidos y generosos, como son los jóvenes, que todo lo entregan y no piden nada a cambio, y ahora de esos jóvenes ya no queda nada, los que no murieron en Bolivia murieron en Argentina o en Perú, y los que sobrevivieron se fueron a morir a Chile o a México, y a los que no mataron allí los mataron después en Nicaragua, en Colombia, en El Salvador. Toda Latinoamérica está sembrada con los huesos de estos jóvenes olvidados" (37–38).

13. "Odeim y Oido, Miedo y Odio, figuran en última instancia sentimientos que alberga el propio narrador, en su alma profunda, a imagen y semejanza de aquel *'joven envejecido'*. . . del que se entiende al final de la novela que también es un doble más del narrador" (n.p).

14. "Metáfora y sinécdoque de un Estado de derecho fallido, de un Estado (valga la redundancia) en estado de excepción parcial, un Estado del que se podría sospechar que ha abolido o derogado parte de su ordenamiento jurídico" (28).

15. Among the many authors whom Bolaño praised are the following: Jorge Luis Borges, Julio Cortázar, Nicanor Parra, Ernesto Sabato, Adolfo Bioy Casares, Enrique Lihn, Gonzalo Rojas, Jorge Edwards, José Donoso, Mario Santiago, Rodrigo Fresán, Daniel Sada, Juan Rulfo, Juan Villoro, Carmen Boullosa, Álvaro Enrigue, Mauricio Montiel, Jorge Volpi, Ignacio Padilla, Sergio Pitol, Carlos Monsiváis, Sergio González Rodríguez, Juan Goytisolo, Javier Marías, Olvido García Valdés, Álvaro Pombo, Eduardo Mendoza, Silvina Ocampo. Enrique Vila-Matas, César Aira, Rodrigo Rey Rosa, Pedro Lemebel, Rodolfo Wilcock, Ricardo Piglia, Manuel Puig, Osvado Lamborghini, and Juan Marsé.

16. "Bolaño es un escritor marginal y consistentemente en contra de la institución literaria, y al entrar al poderoso mundo editorial y recibir reconocimiento sigue comportándose como un escritor marginal, y visceral y visiblemente en contra de la institución literaria" (52).

Works Cited

Andrews, Chris. *Roberto Bolaño's Fiction: An Expanding Universe*. New York: Columbia UP, 2014.

Benmiloud, Karim. "Odeim y Oido en *Nocturno de Chile* de Roberto Bolaño." *Isthesis* 48 (Dec. 2010): 229–43. Web. 17 Jun 2015.

Boullosa, Carmen. "Roberto Bolaño by Carmen Boullosa." *Bomb* 78 (Winter 2002): n.p.

Bolaño, Roberto. *2666*. Barcelona: Anagrama, 2008.

_____. *Amberes*. Barcelona: Anagrama, 2002.

_____. *Amuleto*. Barcelona: Anagrama, 1999.

_____. *Antwerp*. Trans. Natasha Wimmer. New York: New Directions, 2002.

_____. "Caracas Address." *Between Parenthesis. Essays, Articles, and Speeches, 1998–2003*. Ed. Ignacio Echevarría. Trans. Natasha Wimmer. New York: New Directions, 2011. 28–37.

_____. "'Déjenlo todo, nuevamente.' Primer Manifiesto Infrarrealista." *Archivo Bolaño*. CA/Blogger.com, 7 Aug 2007. Web. 10 Jun 2015.

_____. *Los detectives salvajes*. New York: Vintage Español, 1998.

_____. *Distant Star*. Trans. Chris Andrews. New York: New Directions, 2004.

_____. *Estrella distante*. Barcelona: Anagrama, 1996.

_____. *La literatura nazi en América*. Barcelona: Seix Barral, 2005.

_____. *La pista de hielo*. Barcelona: Seix Barral, 2003.

_____. *The Romantic Dogs 1980–1998*. Trans. Laura Healy. New York: New Directions, 2008.

_____. *The Savage Detectives*. Trans. Natasha Wimmer. New York: Farrar, Straus & Grioux, 2007.

_____. *The Secret of Evil*. New York: New Directions, 2012.

_____. *El secreto del mal*. Barcelona: Anagrama, 2007.

_____. *Los sinsabores del verdadero policía*. Barcelona: Anagrama, 2011.

_____. *The Skating Rink*. New York: New Directions, 2009.

_____. *Tres*. Trans. Laura Healy. New York: New Directions, 2011.

_____. *Woes of the True Policeman*. New York: Farrar, Straus & Giroux, 2012.

González Rodríguez, Sergio. *Huesos en el desierto*. Barcelona: Anagrama, 2010.

_____. *The Femicide Machine*. Cambridge: MIT, 2012.

Locascio, Lisa. "My Bolaño Archive." *Los Angeles Review of Books*. Los Angeles Review of Books, 23 Jun 2013. Web 6 Jun 2015.

López de Abiada, José Manuel. "Hacia Bolaño. Una introducción." *Roberto Bolaño, estrella cercana. Ensayos sobre su obra*. Ed. Augusta López Bernasocchi & José Manuel López de Abiada. Madrid: Verbum, 2012. 11–40.

López-Calvo, Ignacio. "Roberto Bolaño's Flower War: Memory, Melancholy, and Pierre Menard." *Roberto Bolaño, a Less Distant Star: Critical Essays*. Ed. Ignacio López-Calvo. Palgrave Macmillan, 2015. 35–64.

Maristain, Mónica. *Bolaño: A Biography in Conversations*. New York: Melville House, 2014.

Medina, Rubén. *Perros habitados por las voces del desierto: Poesía infrarrealista entre dos siglos*. Mexico City: Aldus Biblioteca José Sordo, 2014.

Saucedo Lastra, Fernando. *México en la obra de Roberto Bolaño. Memoria y territorio*. Madrid, Mexico City: Iberoamericana Vervuerte/Bonilla, 2015.

Stolzmann, Uwe. "Entrevista a Roberto Bolaño." *Roberto Bolaño, estrella cercana. Ensayos sobre su obra*. Ed. Augusta López Bernasocchi & José Manuel López de Abiada. Madrid: Verbum, 2012. 364–77.

Varn, Derick. "Bolaño and Beyond: An Interview with Juan E. De Castro on Contemporary Spanish Language Literature." *Former People: A Journal of Bangs and Whimpers*. C. Derick Varn & Steven A. Michalkow/WordPress, 30 Nov 2013. Web. 16 Feb 2014.

From *Poète Maudit* to *Pater Familias*: Biography of Roberto Bolaño

Ignacio López-Calvo

The relevance of Roberto Bolaño's biography in understanding his works has been a topic of debate among his critics for years. Curiously, the new *Bolañismo* or Bolañomania has emulated Bolaño's masterpieces *2666* and *The Savage Detectives*, where poets or critics desperately try to find out the whereabouts of (or disambiguate the hidden truths about) writers who suddenly vanished, leaving no trace, such as the fictional Cesárea Tinajero or Benno von Archimboldi (pseudonym of Hans Reiter). This new interest in discerning the differences between the real-life Bolaño and his fictional alter egos (Arturo Belano, "Arturo B," "B"), as well as in finding additional information about the mysterious Chilean's biography has led to confusions between his fiction and his life. Thus, a cursory online search on Bolaño will yield several English-language articles "revealing" his addiction to heroin as well as many others either belying or affirming the veracity of his trips to El Salvador and Chile. These multiple perspectives and ambiguities respond in part to the fact that Bolaño enjoyed creating his own myth by playing with fake identities and autobiographical traps that may trick his readers, critics, and biographers. This is perhaps the case of the story "Playa" ("Beach"), which was first published in the Spanish newspaper *El País* in July 2000, in a series of mostly autobiographical essays, and was then included by Ignacio Echevarría in *Between Parentheses*, a book with the subtitle *Essays, Articles, and Speeches, 1998–2003*. The first line of the story reads: "I gave up heroin and went home and began the methadone treatment administered at the outpatient clinic" (260).[1] Not surprisingly, this led many readers and critics to assume that Bolaño was a heroin addict and that his untimely death was somewhat related to his addiction. As a result, his wife, Carolina López, had to explain in an interview that "Playa" was a fictional, rather than an autobiographical, text.

Along these lines, readers and critics have tried to label his political ideology. While Bolaño often mentioned his early sympathies with Trotskyism and anarchism while living in Mexico as well as his collaboration with a communist cell in post-coup Chile, his friend, the Spanish writer Javier Cercas, has described him as a moderate leftist. Bolaño himself has joked about the exaggerated interpretations of his brief incarceration in Chile after general Augusto Pinochet's coup—which nonetheless have added credibility and gravitas to *Estrella distante* and *Nocturno de Chile*, his novellas set in Pinochet's Chile. Some of Bolaño's Mexican acquaintances, however, have questioned whether he really returned to Chile or met Roque Dalton in El Salvador, suggesting instead that it was his remorse for not being in his native country at such a historic moment that moved the Chilean writer to make up a badge of honor that would add to his social capital. But Bolaño himself helped to create—through his self-characterization in writings and interviews—the legend about his *enfant terrible* and *poète maudit* reputation while living in Mexico City, as he perhaps invented part of his past and dreamt of turning his life into a work of art, just like Arthur Rimbaud, the French poet he admired, had done (Bolaño even took the libertine poet's name "Arturo" for his fictional alter ego Belano). Bolaño spoke and wrote candidly, for example, about the deprivation and hardships he endured while living in Spain. He also confessed his personal and social obsessions, such as his voracious reading habits, his fear of mortality, or his melancholy about the useless deaths of many among the utopian and idealist Latin American youth of his generation. In any case, all this speculation has added to the so-called Bolaño myth by increasing the bohemian and radical aura of an author who actually spent many years of his life as a devoted family man, quietly writing in his apartment in the Costa Brava.

Although he defined himself simply as a Latin American, Bolaño was born on April 28, 1953 in Santiago, Chile. In several interviews, he maintained a certain distance with his native country, which some critics have identified with resentment: "I do not feel Chilean, there's no doubt, but I am Chilean. And knowing that one is Chilean, at least in my case, is an act of humility,"[2] he averred in an interview with Uwe Stolzmann. His grandparents were illiterate Catalan immigrants, and he was born to a lower-middle class family: León Bolaño, a truck driver and champion amateur, heavy weight boxer, and Victoria Ávalos, a primary school teacher and avid reader of best-sellers who has been credited for Bolaño's love of poetry. Roberto Bolaño grew up in the southern coast of Chile, first in Cerro Placeres, Valparaíso, and then in Quilpué, Viña del Mar, Cauquenes, Mulchén, and Los Ángeles (in the province of Bío Bío).

In 1968, trying to improve Victoria's health (she had problems with chronic asthma), the Bolaño family moved to Mexico City. A year later, at age sixteen, the young, dyslexic Bolaño dropped out of high school and began his self-education through reading. Later, he worked as a journalist and became involved in left-wing politics, sympathizing with Trotskyism. According to the poet Jaime Quezada, Bolaño's friend, "As a teenager, Bolaño was a borderline agoraphobic, and he spent his first years in Mexico stuck at home, moving between the bedroom and the living room, smoking and writing" (Maristain n.p.). Victoria Soto, Bolaño's mother's friend, also explains that "He suffered terrible fits of depression. Sometimes it made me sad to see him. I came to see him and he didn't look at me, didn't greet me, or anything like that" (Maristain n.p.). This constant malaise is reflected in an interview with Stolzmann, where Bolaño admits that at age seventeen, he almost went mad (364). Avowedly, only literature provided a refuge for him during those years.

An episode that marked Bolaño's life and writing was his return to his native country in August 1973, one month before the September 11 coup d'etat. His dream was to help President Salvador Allende build the socialist revolution in Chile and then to participate in the armed resistance in other Latin American countries. He traveled from Mexico to Chile by bus, ship, and hitchhiking. In several interviews and writings, Bolaño recalls the day of the coup as a tragicomic event. He volunteered to help a communist cell (even though he did not identify as a communist) and was ordered to keep an eye on a street. He soon forgot the password they gave him and marvelled at their outrageous plan to bomb an iron bridge. According to his own account, shortly after the coup, Bolaño was accused of being a foreign terrorist (by then he had adopted the Mexican dialect of Spanish) and ended up imprisoned, incommunicado, and hungry for eight or nine days in Southern Chile, another episode that recurrs in his works. As portrayed in his short story "Detectives," from *Llamadas telefónicas*, two prison guards who had been his classmates in high school recognized Bolaño and saved him. After this traumatic experience, he decided to return to Mexico and would not visit Chile again for twenty-five years. In his interview with Stolzmann, Bolaño elaborates on what the coup meant for him and his generation:

> The Coup represents perhaps the end of the revolutionary utopia in Latin America. Henceforth, the impression one has is that everything falls into a black hole of despair and pain. Probably, well before the coup everything had become twisted for ever: Cuban political culture, the blindness of Latin American leftist parties, the almost infinite clumsiness displayed by everyone made the real possibility of a revolution impossible.[3]

In another famous adventure, Bolaño allegedly spent some time in El Salvador at the age of twenty, where he met several future commanders of the Frente Farabundo Martí para la Liberación Nacional guerrilla movement (Farabundo Martí National Liberation Front; FMLN), who would later kill the poet Roque Dalton while he was sleeping. Bolaño returned to Mexico in January of 1974.

In 1975, after his return from Chile, Bolaño became a founding member, along with his friends Mario Santiago and Bruno Montané (renamed Ulises Lima and Felipe Müller in *Los detectives salvajes*) of infrarrealismo (infrarealism), a marginal poetic movement that inspired many of the episodes in *Los detectives salvajes*. This bohemian group of provocateurs boycotted literary events by Octavio Paz, Carlos Monsiváis, and other iconic figures of the Mexican cultural establishment. As a result, Bolaño developed a reputation as a "literary *enfant terrible*." During this time in Mexico City, he also befriended the Mexican poet Efraín Huerta, one of the poets that the infrarealists admired the most. Following his infrarealist principles, he never sought or obtained a college position or a grant. However, the Chilean apparently abandoned them when—according to his editor, Jorge Herralde—he applied for a grant from the John Simon Guggenheim Memorial Foundation while living in Spain. Bolaño was seeking support for a year in order to complete *Los detectives salvajes.*

Bolaño's mother moved to Barcelona in the mid-1970s, but his father stayed in Mexico, forming a new family. In 1977, allegedly as a reaction to a failed romance with a young woman named Lisa Johnson, Bolaño traveled to France and North Africa, and then settled in Catalonia, Spain. There, he married the Catalan Carolina López, eight years his junior, and had different odd jobs—including dishwasher, campsite guard, garbage collector, and stevedore—typically writing at night. For some time, he made a modest living by winning prizes in regional literary competitions throughout Spain. This is reflected in the short story "Sensini" (perhaps one of his best, along with "El Ojo Silva" ("Mauricio ['The Eye'] Silva"), included in the collection *Llamadas telefónicas*, where the protagonist also submits the same story under different titles to different competitions.

In 1981, he moved to the touristic, coastal Catalan town of Blanes, Girona, where he enjoyed his beloved Mediterranean Sea and the privacy he needed for his writing. He had two children with Carolina López: Lautaro, born in 1990 and named after the Mapuche leader who fought the Spanish conquerors, and Alexandra. It was in Spain where he wrote most of his published narratives. His stays in Chile, Mexico, and Spain undoubtedly helped him recreate these three Spanish dialects in his narratives, an important aspect of his writing that is difficult to translate into English.

In his 1975 "Manifiesto infrarrealista" ("Infrarealist Manifesto"), Mario Santiago Papasquiaro's first lines were:

WHAT DO WE PROPOSE?

NOT MAKING ART A PROFESSION

SHOWING THAT EVERYTHING IS ART AND THAT EVERYONE CAN DO IT.[4]

Yet, as Rubén Medina points out, "Bolaño assumes writing as his profession since the mid-1990s, he enters a powerful editorial market and during the last five years of his life, he reaches a great worldwide recognition for his writing, particularly for his narrative."[5] Indeed, by 1993 Bolaño had become tired of having menial jobs and had decided, against the tenets of infrarealism, to make a living exclusively as a professional writer. Until that moment, he had been a virtually unknown author, who had won a few poetry awards in Mexico and the Ámbito Literario de Narrativa (Literary Field of Narrative) award in Spain in 1984;[6] he had only published a few poetry collections and a co-authored novel. Living in poverty, having separated from his wife, diagnosed with liver disease, and with his residence permit about to expire, Bolaño avowedly struggled to survive during those years. In the meantime, publishers routinely rejected the manuscripts of his novels until 1995, when Seix Barral decided to publish *Nazi Literature in the Americas*. More importantly, he met Jorge Herralde, founder and director of Anagrama publishing house, who decided to publish *Estrella distante* and a total of nine books in seven years.

On July 1, 2003, his partner took him to a hospital in Barcelona. After feverishly devoting his entire life to literature and at the top of his literary prestige, Bolaño died of liver failure at the age of fifty. At the time, he was third on a list to receive a liver transplant. His ashes were dropped into the Mediterranean Sea. By the time of his death, he was proofreading his massive novel *2666*, which he had planned to publish as five separate novels in order to increase his children's inheritance. Thankfully, the publisher, in consultation with Carolina López, Bolaño's wife, decided to publish the text in a single volume of more than one thousand pages.

In Mónica Maristain's 2014 *Bolaño: A Biography in Conversations*, Bolaño's friends describe him as a charming, personable, and generous man, especially with young writers. They also confirm Bolaño's love of literary discussions and of speaking on the phone with his friends. We also learn from one of the interviewees in Maristain's book that, besides shoplifting books from bookstores when he was a youngster, he would also steal them from his friends. And once again dispelling the myth of Bolaño's tortured artist or rebellious Beatnik image, several of the interviewees recall Bolaño's life as rather normal: he drank only tea, ironed his clothes, and frequently ate at Kentucky Fried Chicken.

In recent years, Carolina López and some of Bolaño's friends, such as Javier Cercas, have been trying to belie certain myths and misunderstandings about his life and writing. In Cercas's words,

> Be that as it may, the way things are now it is possible that sooner or later some of his less insightful or more scatterbrained readers may be disappointed to know that the outlaw writer into whom they have tried to turn Bolaño was, in his real life, a restrained and prudent man, someone who—by way of example—politically did not go beyond being a social democrat or a leftist liberal—which is, I suppose, the most prudent and moderate that one can be politically—but that is no longer a problem of Bolaño or his opus, but only of flighty people or those who feed their flightiness.[7]

Likewise, recently published interviews also appear to contradict assumed truths about Bolaño's habits. For instance, regarding his frenetic rhythm of writing and publishing (it is often said that he could spend forty-eight hours writing without rest), in an interview with Stolzmann he stated: "In an optimal state I work a couple of hours in the morning. Another couple of hours in the afternoon. And at night, if I'm not too tired, I can work two more hours again. The rest of the time I'm with my children or reading. Sometimes I watch television."[8]

Bolaño was, therefore, quite a normal man, but an extraordinary writer. Hopefully, this brief summary will not add new myths or exaggerations to his biographical accounts.

Notes

1. "Dejé la heroína y volví a mi pueblo y empecé con el tratamiento de metadona que me suministraban en el ambulatorio" (241).

2. "No me siento chileno, sin duda, pero soy chileno. Y saberse chileno es, al menos en mi caso, un acto de humildad" (Stolzmann 368).

3. "El Golpe representa tal vez el fin de la utopía revolucionaria en América Latina. A partir de entonces, la impresión que se tiene es que todo cae en un agujero lleno de desesperación y dolor. Probablemente mucho antes del Golpe todo se había torcido para siempre: la política cultural cubana, la ceguera de los partidos de izquierda latinoamericanos, la casi infinita torpeza desplegada por todos, hacía imposible la posibilidad real de la revolución" (366).

4. "¿QUÉ PROPONEMOS? / NO HACER UN OFICIO DEL ARTE / MOSTRAR QUE TODO ES ARTE Y QUE TODO MUNDO PUEDE HACERLO" (Medina 389).

5. "Bolaño asume la escritura como profesión desde mediados de los 90, entra a un poderoso mercado editorial y durante los últimos cinco años de su vida alcanza un gran reconocimiento mundial por su escritura, particularmente por su narrativa" (44).

6. In the early 1990s, he won several minor awards: the Premio de Narrativa Ciudad Alcalá de Henares (City of Alcalá de Henares Award for Narrative) in 1992; the Premio de Novela Corta Félix Urabayen (Félix Urabayen Novella Award) for *La senda de los elefantes* (later published under the title *Monsieur Pain*) in 1993; and two poetry awards: Premio Rafael Morales (Rafael Morales Award) in 1992 and Premio Literario Ciudad de Irún (City of Irún Literary Award) and Premio Literarios Kutxa Ciudad de San Sebastián for *Los perros románticos* in 1994.

7. "Sea como sea, tal y como están las cosas es posible que tarde o temprano a algunos de sus lectores menos perspicaces o más atolondrados les decepcione saber que el escritor forajido en que han querido convertir a Bolaño fue en su vida real un hombre morigerado y prudente, alguien que—pongo por caso—políticamente no pasaba de ser un socialdemócrata o un liberal de izquierdas—que es, supongo, lo más prudente y morigerado que políticamente se puede ser—, pero eso ya no es problema de Bolaño ni de su obra, sino sólo de los atolondrados y de quienes alimentan su atolondramiento" (n.p.).

8. "En un estado óptimo trabajo por las mañanas un par de horas. Otro par de horas por la tarde. Y por la noche, si no estoy muy cansado, puedo volver a trabajar dos horas más. El resto del tiempo estoy con mis hijos o leo. A veces veo la televisión" (Stolzmann 374).

Works Cited

Cercas, Javier. "Print the legend!" *El País*. Ediciones El País S.L., 14 Apr. 2007. Web. 5 Jun. 2015.

Bolaño, Roberto. "Mauricio ('The Eye') Silva." *Last Evenings on Earth*. Trans. Chris Andrews. New York: New Directions, 2006. 106–20.

_____. "El Ojo Silva." *Cuentos. Llamadas telefónicas. Putas asesinas. El gaucho insufrible*. Barcelona: Anagrama, 2010. 215–28.

_____. "Petición de una beca Guggenheim." *Para Roberto Bolaño*. Ed. Jorge Herralde. Santiago: Catalonia, 2005. 77–84.

_____. "Sensini." *Cuentos. Llamadas telefónicas. Putas asesinas. El gaucho insufrible*. Barcelona: Anagrama, 2010. 13–29.

_____. "Sensini." *Last Evenings on Earth*. Trans. Chris Andrews. New York: New Directions, 2006. 1–18.

Maristain, Monica. *Bolaño: A Biography in Conversations*. Trans. Kit Maude. Brooklyn: Melville House, 2012.

Medina, Rubén. *Perros habitados por las voces del desierto: Poesía infrarrealista entre dos siglos*. Mexico City: Aldus Biblioteca José Sordo, 2014.

Stolzmann, Uwe. "Entrevista a Roberto Bolaño." *Roberto Bolaño, estrella cercana. Ensayos sobre su obra*. Ed. Augusta López Bernasocchi & José Manuel López De Abiada. Madrid: Verbum, 2012. 364–77.

CRITICAL
CONTEXTS

"Latin America Is Sown with the Bones of These Forgotten Youths:" Revolution, Dictatorship, and Roberto Bolaño

Juliet Lynd

When Roberto Bolaño accepted the Rómulo Gallegos Prize for *Los detectives salvajes* (*The Savage Detectives*, 1998), he declared: "for the most part, everything I've written is a love letter or a farewell letter to my own generation."[1] Understanding Bolaño's work in historical context requires knowledge of the author's generation and his reference to it here. Bolaño and his contemporaries are scarred by battles, ideological and physical, between leftist utopian revolutionary movements in Latin America throughout the twentieth century and their brutal repression by right-wing military regimes that assumed power in the 1970s and 1980s. Bolaño came of age as a poet in Chile and Mexico amidst this traumatic history. In Spain in the 1990s, when his fiction began to attract attention from international publishers, newly re-democratized Latin American nations (and Spain, too, after its own civil war and dictatorship) struggled to reconcile this violent past. Bolaño, however, found new ways of confronting twentieth-century history through literature, rendering familiar narratives strange and implicating the reader in redefining the very historical context under scrutiny in his writing.

Declaring his work a "love letter or a farewell letter," Bolaño elaborates on the political context that connects national histories in a shared experience of struggle:

> my own generation, those of us who were born in the 1950s and who in a certain moment chose military service, though in this case it would be more accurate to say militancy, and we gave what little we had—the great deal that we had, which was our youth—to a cause that we thought was the most generous cause in the world and in a certain way it was, but in reality it wasn't. . . . [W]e fought our hardest, but we had corrupt leaders, cowardly leaders with a

propaganda apparatus that was worse than a leper colony . . . [W]e fought for and put all our generosity into an ideal that had been dead for more than fifty years, and some of us knew it, . . . but we did it anyway, because we were stupid and generous, as young people are, giving everything and asking for nothing in return, and now those young people are gone, because those who didn't die in Bolivia died in Argentina or Peru, and those who survived went on to die in Chile or Mexico, and those who weren't killed there were killed later in Nicaragua, Colombia, or El Salvador. All of Latin America is sown with the bones of these forgotten youths. (*Last Interview* 41–42)

Bolaño's description deserves to be unpacked to reveal the complex, violent history he engages throughout his work.

First, "those of us born in the 1950s" came of age during the final bursts of revolutionary activity in the late 1960s and early 70s. This generation not only did not see their utopian dreams realized, they were brutally punished by right-wing military regimes that persecuted anyone associated with leftist political thought. These dictatorships, often coordinating intelligence through the CIA, installed a "security" apparatus employing torture, executions, disappearances, and exile. Bolaño's use of "military service" ("milicia") and "militancy" ("militancia") distinguishes between serving the armed forces of the state—an apparatus of persecution— and serving a political party or sometimes a guerilla army. He aligns himself with leftist militants fighting for social justice in opposition to the armed forces defending the status quo of inequality and persecution.

Yet Bolaño problematizes leftist utopianism: a cause "we thought was the most generous in the world, but in reality it wasn't." It was a collective dream, a desire for a truly egalitarian society even if that meant having less for oneself, generous because so many were willing to put their lives on the line for it. But Bolaño distances himself from this noble cause, bitterly accusing leftist leaders of corruption, cowardice, propaganda, and repression; the ideal was worthy, but, he insists, the dream had already died in postrevolutionary realities.[2] Bolaño, distinguishing revolutionary dreams from realities on the ground, points out that young people were killed by the military dictatorships that wiped out revolutionary hopes. This history is reiterated throughout Latin America, but he specifically cites Chile (1973) and Mexico (1968), followed by the bloody civil wars of Central America in the 1980s, violent flashpoints in Cold War battles. With the dramatic image of Latin America as one enormous graveyard "sown with the bones of these forgotten youths," Bolaño insists that this violence defines the entire region. His writing is an effort to remember those young idealists, to march against the tide of forgetfulness that would wash away the past. He does so with a critical gaze that condemns dogmatism and violence on all sides of the political spectrum.

In his fiction, Bolaño masterfully interweaves the particulars of national histories, blending fiction and reality by blurring distinctions between his own autobiography and the experiences of his fictional alter ego, Arturo Belano, in Chile, Mexico, and Spain.[3] Both Bolaño's biography and Belano's experiences take the reader through the tumultuous history that marks the author's entire oeuvre, as Bolaño transforms relationships between literature and politics. This essay chronicles crucial flashpoints in Chile and Mexico, concluding with Bolaño's relationship to Europe and Latin America and the tension between the marginal poets populating his fiction, his own celebrated status in the international publishing industry, and his commitment to revitalizing the political relevance of the literary text.

Bolaño in Chile and "the Other September 11"

Bolaño was born in Santiago in 1953. His family moved frequently, but he spent much of his childhood in small provincial cities. His mother was a schoolteacher, his father a truck driver and amateur boxer, marking his family as working class.[4] Bolaño, nerdy and bookish, did not like school. In 1968, the family moved to Mexico City, and there the adolescent Bolaño discovered his passion for poetry and revolution. Convinced that his generation would revolutionize poetry and change the world, he dropped out of high school to spend his time reading and writing. In August 1973, he set out for Chile by bus to take part in the socialist revolution underway there. He was headed toward what would become one of the most significant chapters in Latin American history, culminating symbolically on the day of the military coup, which, after the terrorist attacks of September 11, 2001, in the US, became known as "the other September 11."

Chile, at that moment, was an experiment in socialism that the entire world was watching. In 1970, Salvador Allende, medical doctor turned politician, became the first Marxist Socialist to be elected President. Allende's "Chilean path to socialism" via the ballot box offered a route distinct from armed guerilla movements arising in Latin America, particularly after the 1959 Cuban Revolution.[5] However, he won with barely a third of the vote (36.2 percent), revealing a citizenry divided almost equally between Allende's center-left coalition (the UP, as the Unidad Popular, 'Popular Unity,' was known), the centrist Christian Democrats (28.7 percent), and the conservative party (34.9 percent). Facing a divided nation and a hostile Washington, Allende barely obtained the Congressional approval needed to assume office, but the UP pressed ahead with their agenda.

Chile's short-lived experiment in democratic socialism was turbulent. Popular Unity was hardly a unanimous front, some within it favoring radical approaches to economic redistribution, others demanding moderate compromises. Nonetheless, with the enthusiastic support of union workers, peasants, and leftist intellectuals and artists, Allende nationalized the health care system and copper mining industry (a process initiated by his centrist predecessor); increased spending on education and public housing; created a successful program guaranteeing a half-liter of milk a day to Chilean children; and radicalized land redistribution programs begun in the 1960s. Peasants worked the land; workers took over factories; unemployment dropped and wages rose. This project inspired the young Bolaño, who identified with radical elements of the UP who believed in arming the people to defend socialism.[6]

The opposition, however, was powerful. US president Richard Nixon, backing the economic interests of US companies and the Chilean elite and afraid of another Latin American nation (after

Cuba) joining forces with the Soviet Union, famously ordered his operatives to "make the economy scream." That they did, promoting a strike of truck drivers that brought distribution to a halt and hoarding products to maximize food shortages. With an increasingly polarized nation and regular rallies filling the streets with both Allende's supporters and opponents, the centrist Christian Democrats joined the opposition, eventually calling for military intervention.[7]

In his storied trip, Bolaño had arrived in Chile just weeks before the coup. On the morning of September 11, 1973, the armed forces betrayed the constitution and attacked their own government. Allende, aware of the situation, delivered his last radio address, promising Chilean workers that eventually they would prevail. Mid-morning, fighter jets swooped over Santiago and bombed the presidential palace. Allende died of a gunshot wound to the head and a military junta seized control, initiating the sixteen-year, notoriously brutal regime of General Augusto Pinochet.[8] During those years, over three thousand citizens disappeared (detained by security forces with no public record of their whereabouts, all presumed dead). Over thirty thousand were tortured and released; hundreds of thousands more went into exile.[9] Bolaño reports having joined a militia to oppose the regime. He was arrested in Concepción, but a prison guard recognized him from school, and he was released unharmed. He then left for Mexico with no intention of returning.[10]

This story is repeated in nearly every biographical sketch of the author, including his own; various iterations are represented in Bolaño's work through his fictional alter ego, Arturo Belano. It appears most extensively in *Los detectives salvajes* and the short story "Carnet de Baile" ("Dance Card" 2001). In *Estrella distante* (*Distant Star*, 1996), the unnamed narrator does not travel to or from Mexico, but is an aspiring poet in Chile in the early 1970s, detained near Concepción and released without mention of torture or abuse (in the novel, the violence of the period erupts instead with the character of a fictional fascist poet who murders female poets and writes victorious verses in the sky). Other characters— such as "El Ojo Silva," the Argentine mentor of the character "B" in

"Sensini," Amalfitano (*2666* [2004], *Los sinsabores del verdadero policía* [*The Woes of the True Policeman* 2011]), and the many exiles who take turns narrating the middle section of *Detectives*— reiterate the theme of exile.[11] Bolaño's fiction is populated with characters struggling to redefine themselves after the horror of state-sponsored terrorism. This aligns his work squarely with what is now known as postdictatorship literature: narratives that explore the consequences of dictatorship for individuals and the collective, either through *testimonio* or fictional accounts that mirror historical truths.[12] Bolaño's fiction, though, has generated an unusual level of enthusiasm and debate; his distinctive handling of the topic takes familiar tropes of postdictatorship literature and shifts our gaze to new perspectives and stories.[13]

The symbolic importance of Chile's history cannot be overstated: John Beverley identifies September 11, 1973, as the symbolic end of the Boom, the literary generation preceding Bolaño's, marked by aesthetic innovation and the utopian conviction that literature would help shape an egalitarian future. Idelber Avelar takes up this interpretation of transitional moments—symbolic and real—to insist that the 1973 coup marks an historic rupture that defines the present in Latin America. Avelar posits postdictatorship novels as allegories of mourning of those killed by the regimes, but also a collective mourning of loss of faith in revolutionary narratives: postdictatorship literature is marked less by processes of re-democratization in the 1980s and 90s and more by a fundamental shift "from the authority of the state to that of the market," brought about by dismantling socialist experiments and imposing a neoliberal economic model based on privatization and unregulated capitalism. Although the market success of Bolaño's literature makes him suspicious to some, his texts are consistently, deeply critical of these unresolved legacies.

In fact, Bolaño's "Chilean novels"—*Estrella distante* and *Nocturno en Chile* (*By Night in Chile* 2001)—are not only about life under dictatorship; they also critique the cultural amnesia involved in the complicated, compromised process of the return to democracy. In Chile, as in other nations, re-democratization has involved a tense negotiation between those demanding democratic accountability and those who would prefer to forget the violence upon which the current system is founded ("the bones of these forgotten youth"). In *Estrella*, the exiled narrator finds himself involved in the private investigation of a notorious freelance human rights abuser for the regime. The identification of the infamous criminal is unsettling precisely because justice has been outsourced, and there is no accountability for the crimes of the dictatorship. In *Nocturno*, the Opus Dei priest who once gave lessons in Marxism to Pinochet to help the dictator better know his enemy, offers the reader his death-bed confession, but shirks responsibility for having turned a blind eye to injustice throughout his life. Yet Bolaño's oeuvre as a whole casts a net much broader than the particular history of his country of origin. The story of Bolaño is incomplete without the story of his coming of age in Mexico City in the 1970s.

Infrarealism and the Tlatelolco Massacre, or the *Poètes Maudits* Take on Official Culture

The Bolaño family arrived in Mexico City in 1968, a year when students throughout the world were protesting injustice. In Mexico, students and workers took to the streets to demand greater transparency in government and to oppose Mexico's hosting of the 1968 Olympics amidst poverty and authoritarian rule. Mexico's ruling party, the PRI (Partido Revolucionario Institucional [Institutional Revolutionary Party]), had come to power after the Mexican Revolution (1910–1920) and frozen the processes of change that earlier upheaval had demanded. On October 3, protesters marched to the Plaza de Tlatelolco, also known as the "Plaza of the Three Cultures" (indigenous ruins, a Spanish colonial church, and modern apartment buildings), but they were cornered; soldiers opened fire, killing dozens, possibly hundreds. The official press minimized the violence, but the massacre initiated the extra-legal repression of leftist opposition that would last through the 1970s.[14] Mexico's 1968 is comparable to Chile's 1973, as both resonate symbolically throughout Latin American history and in Bolaño's work. Bolaño was not directly involved with student protests, but as Maristain attests, they would have been impossible to ignore. Moreover, the actions of the state redefined literary and cultural production in Mexico.

Bolaño's family lived near Tlatelolco Plaza at the time, and a Uruguayan citizen who famously hid out in the women's restroom of the university during the 1968 military occupation was a friend of Bolaño's mother. In *Detectives*, the real-life Alcira Soust Scaffo becomes Auxilio Lacouture, whose character inspired the spinoff novel *Amuleto* (*Amulet* 1999). In both texts, her story jars the reader with the irony of a bathroom stall as an effective hiding place, evidence of Bolaño's dark humor and determination to represent extraordinary historical moments through banal experiences. In *Detectives*, Lacouture tells the story of Arturo Belano's return to Chile, which accomplishes several things: it connects Mexico 1968 with Chile 1973; it offers the reader bizarre *testimonios* from the era, defamiliarizing what has become a familiar history; and it connects absurd acts of resistance with the literary gesture of writing despite all odds. Auxilio recalls how Arturo was different when he returned from Chile and started hanging out with a younger crowd, he and his friends speaking in "*gíglico*," the invented language of Julio Cortázar's *Rayuela* (*Hopscotch* 1963).[15] Despite their lack of shared language, she loved the young writers as she loved the poets of the Spanish Civil War exiled in Mexico City, the memory of whom kept her company in that restroom in 1968. She concludes the chapter with memories of her own story of resistance; her story as much as Belano's becomes the stuff of cultural memory because it keeps alive not the ideology of resistance, but the ethical stance sustained by the memory of other writers who had done the same. At the end of *Amuleto*, Lacouture has a vision of a "multitude" of young people, "united only by their generosity and their courage" (Bolaño, *Amuleto* 151–52) marching into an unexpected abyss—another tribute to Bolaño's generation, the image of young people singing in unison, unable or unwilling to see the dead end that awaits them. Their song, Lacouture tells us, "is our amulet" (154); their optimism saves us from evil.

In this context, Bolaño and his friend and fellow poet Mario Santiago Papasquiaro founded infrarealism. Monserrat Mandariaga

Caro explains how the administration of President Luis Echeverría (1970–1976) invested heavily in sponsoring cultural events in an attempt to make up for (or distract from) the violence of the previous administration. The young Bolaño and his friends found this loathsome, and they resented writers who were complicit with it, especially Nobel Laureate Octavio Paz (1914–1998). Reeling from the brutality of Chile and Mexico, the infrarealists sought to re-conceptualize cultural life, writing poems, but also disrupting official literary events, heckling poets (including Paz), and taking poetry to the streets.

In 1976, Bolaño composed the Infrarealist Manifesto, a poetic declaration of an ethical stance toward poetry. The infras demanded "poetic action" and insisted that poetry be integrated with life on the street, far from the salons of officialdom. They located themselves within a long line of politically committed avant-garde movements beginning with the Dadaists and surrealists of the early twentieth century, but at the post-1960s juncture marked by violence, horror, and disillusion: "We are preceded by A THOUSAND AVANT-GARDES HACKED APART IN THE SIXTIES."[16] The infrarealist poets "dreamed of utopia and woke up screaming"[17] as they confronted a reality others ignored from the safety of the salon:

> These are tough times for poetry, some say while sipping tea, listening to music in their apartments, talking (listening) to the old masters. These are tough times for mankind, we say, returning to our barricades after a long day of shit and tear gas, discovering / creating music even in our apartments, staring hard at the cemeteries-in-expansion, while the old masters desperately sip their tea or get drunk from pure rage or inertia.[18]

The manifesto concludes with an echo of André Breton's 1922 call: "Leave it all behind, again. Take to the street."[19] Indeed, the document is filled with references to the long history of avant-garde poetry and efforts to speak poetry to power. Bolaño's work is deeply informed by the context of truncated revolutions—political and literary—and immersed in aesthetic responses to historical problems.

The politics of avant-garde poetry in the face of repression is a constant theme throughout Bolaño's work, but *Detectives* most explicitly and extensively explores the topic, intertwining the infrarealist movement (in the novel *visceral realism*), Bolaño's time in Mexico, and dozens of characters from throughout the world. The main characters—Arturo Belano and Ulises Lima (literary double of Bolaño's dear friend Mario Santiago)—go on a quest to find the "mother of Mexican poetry," who has disappeared in the Sonoran desert and whose connection to the earlier avant-garde estridentista movement of post-revolutionary Mexico City (illusorily) promises to reinvigorate the "visceral realism" espoused by the protagonists. Myriad voices tell an unnamed interlocutor (and the reader) of their encounters with Lima and Belano and indirectly document efforts to survive after the failed revolutions of the twentieth century, from the Spanish Civil War to the Chilean coup. The novel is open-ended and does not resolve the tension between literature and politics; rather, it invites the reader to rethink the world through poetry and— arguably—to carry on the torch.

Los detectives salvajes, written in Spain two decades after the author's youthful commitment to poetry, is a novel about poets, not a manifesto. The tone of the narrative reflects the distance of time and space, and what emerges is a new conception of the relationship between art and life, literature and social change. The historical context of the radical youth culture of the 1970s and the repression of revolution is not the only historical context necessary to understanding Bolaño: one must also consider the politics of literature at the turn of the twenty-first century.

Writing Latin America from Europe

In 1977, Bolaño left it all behind, again, and set out for Europe, working odd jobs and writing prolifically. He eventually married, had two children, and lived a quiet, modest life in the town of Blanes, on the Mediterranean coast of Spain, near Barcelona. Like the character "B" in "Sensini," Bolaño entered his fiction in provincial literary contests, with limited success, until the publication of *Literatura nazi en América* (*Nazi Literature in America*, 1996) with Seix

Barral, quickly followed by an ongoing contract with Anagrama and other lucrative deals with giant multinational publishers. In the final years of his life, Bolaño became an international phenomenon; top presses continue to churn out his work posthumously.

The distinction between Bolaño the marginal poet heckling Octavio Paz and demanding that poets take to the streets, and Bolaño the capitalist success story of the publishing industry is unsettling to many. While his infrarealist-companion-turned-US-academic Rubén Medina insists that infrarealism is an ethical posture that Bolaño unerringly maintained, others, like Jean Franco, lament what they see as Bolaño's abandonment of politics for the sake of publishing success. Is Bolaño merely appealing to a sense of nostalgia for the youthful idealism of a bygone era or does his work offer new ways to think of relationships between poetry and life, literature and society?

In Europe, Bolaño settled into another continent at odds with its violent past of fascism and genocide; the young poet arrived in Spain just as the nation was emerging from the long rightwing dictatorship of Francisco Franco (1939–1975), the result of a bloody civil war (1936–1939) that defeated the center-left and revolutionary efforts to build an egalitarian Spain during the Second Republic (1931–1936). Exiles from European conflicts—anarchists, communists, and republicans from the Spanish Civil War; Jews fleeing the Nazis; and Nazis fleeing war crimes trials—populate Latin America, as well as Bolaño's fiction. The posthumous *2666* offers another take on the central importance of Chile, Mexico, and Europe to the author's concerns: literary critics, professors (including Chilean exile Amalfitano), and detectives alike converge in the Sonoran desert to confront the brutality of World War II as well as the ongoing, unresolved torture, rape, and murder of women along the US-Mexico border. Fascism and genocide, seen obliquely through individuals' experiences, are constants throughout Bolaño's work, and he connects "the bones of these forgotten youth" of his generation to violence grounded in hatred perpetuated throughout modernity: misogyny, racism, and anti-Semitism are woven into the history of the ideological conflicts of the twentieth century.

By the turn of the twenty-first century—thanks to decades of avant-garde artists, intellectuals, and writers who, like Bolaño, push the boundaries of what literature is and can be— what literature does and can do is very much in flux. Perhaps it always has been: there has always been literature supporting the status quo and literature of resistance. Bolaño's early poetry clearly belongs to the latter camp, but once his novels have been packaged for publication in international markets, how challenging can they be? The international publishing giants who retain the rights to Bolaño's work appear to commodify nostalgia for idealism and rebellion.[20] Yet the consumer appeal may very well be for a renewed commitment to that idealism and new forms through which to continue the struggle for a better world. We should not mistake Bolaño's "love letter" to his generation as nostalgia for his youth: disillusioned with revolution from his first encounters with the concept, he insists that literature is about keeping up the fight against all odds. To do otherwise is to accept defeat and forget the sacrifices of those who gave their lives to the most generous of causes: revolutionaries fighting for a better future for all and writers pushing the boundaries of art and life to eschew hierarchies and forge new paths.

Bolaño is defined by his own historical context—a broad context that spans oceans and continents, wars and literary movements—yet he also intervenes in that history. Initiating a new line in a long literary genealogy of politically committed writers, Bolaño's work confronts history and questions all authority, not as adolescent rebellion, but as ethical imperative. Ultimately—because of his consistently open-ended literary forms, his constant twisting of official narratives, his ability to challenge our complacency in the face of history—the relationship between Bolaño's literature and the possibilities of changing the world lie with the reader.

Notes

1. The acceptance speech, known as the "Caracas Address," is included in *Entre paréntesis* (*Between Parenthesis* 2004).

2. Bolaño himself was (briefly) a militant in a Trotskyite party in the 1970s. Leon Trotsky was the leader of the Russian Revolution but

he was ousted by Joseph Stalin. He was exiled to Mexico and later assassinated by Stalinists. Trotsky's essays defending the importance of art and literature are compiled in *Art and Revolution*. Trotsky opposed censorship and any limitation on artists and writers. On the question of Bolaño's affiliation with Trotskyites in Mexico, he said he was a "contrarian": "I did not like the priestly, clerical unanimity of the Communists. I've always been a Leftist and I wasn't going to turn right just because I didn't like the communist clergymen, so I became a Trotskyite. The problem is, once among the Trotskyites, I didn't like their clerical unanimity either, so I ended up being an anarchist. I was the only anarchist I knew and thank God, because otherwise I would have stopped being an anarchist. Unanimity pisses me off immensely. Whenever I realize that the whole world agrees on something, whenever I see that the whole world is cursing something in chorus, something rises to the surface of my skin that makes me reject it. They're probably infantile traumas. I don't see it as something that makes me proud" (*The Last Interview and Other Conversations* 76). Bolaño carries the torch of Trotsky's rejection of imposing propagandistic demands on literature.

3. In some stories, the character "B" shares characteristics with the author; in the final chapter of *Nazi Literature in America* the narrator is named Bolaño; in the spinoff novel *Estrella distante*, the character is unnamed. Many have explored the games the author plays with his literary doubles.

4. Mónica Maristain notes, "When Roberto Bolaño's social background is discussed, his working-class family is rarely mentioned. In Latin America, working class isn't the same thing as poor: they're very different concepts" (12). Bolaño's family lived a modest, but comfortable life. Bolaño never finished school and worked odd jobs until his writing could support him.

5. In 1959, Fidel Castro and Ernesto "Che" Guevara led a small group to topple the US-backed Cuban dictatorship of Fulgencio Batista. The revolutionary government raised the standard of living of the poor through public services and inspired leftists throughout the region. Castro's strategic alliance with the Soviet Union, however, drew Cuba into the Cold War and alarmed Washington, concerned about the spread of communism in a region the US had long dominated economically and politically.

6. See his statements in *The Last Interview* (77).

7. There is ample bibliography on the UP project and opposition to it, including the role of the CIA in destabilizing the government and economy and US support of the military junta. For a readable overview, see the first chapter of Constable and Valenzuela.

8. Whether Allende committed suicide or was murdered is controversial. His body was exhumed in 2014; an autopsy determined suicide. However, those results are questioned, and his death has become a symbol of truncated hopes for revolutionary change.

9. Numbers are minimum estimates, based on government reports (1991 Rettig Report on disappearance and death and the 2004 Valech Report on torture and political imprisonment); human rights groups put totals much higher. On exile, see Wright and Oñate. Between 1973 and 1988, some 200,000 people (nearly 2 percent of Chile's population) were forced out of the country, either officially exiled or seeking asylum. Still more left to find work when the dictatorship cut social spending, forced lower wages, and stripped workers of legal protections.

10. Bolaño did return, but not until 1998. In 1997, *Llamadas telefónicas* won the Santiago Municipal Prize, and the women's magazine *Paula* invited him to the jury for a short story competition. See *Between Parentheses* for his essays related to his return. Bolaño's relationship to other Chilean writers was fraught: he is celebrated and embraced by many for his incisive critiques of postdictatorship culture, but he generated numerous controversies by publically criticizing many esteemed writers, from Pablo Neruda (claiming the 1971 Nobel Prize winner wrote only a handful of good poems) to Isabel Allende (dismissing her as an "escribidora," an untranslatable epithet accusing her of a sort of sub-literary scribbling).

11. "Sensini" appears in *Llamadas telefónicas* and "Carnet de baile" and "El Ojo Silva" in *Putas asesinas*. In English, all appear in *Last Evenings on Earth* (2006).

12. Idelber Avelar's *The Untimely Present* is the seminal work on this genre, published just before Bolaño rose to prominence.

13. In a 2009 *New York Times* story, Larry Rhoter questioned the veracity of Bolaño's reported experience in Chile, provoking a scandal with rebuttals in *El Mercurio* and elsewhere. Whether or not he invented the story or parts of it, it offers many truths as a plausible narrative. A deceptively simple story, it tells of idealism (the young Roberto/

Arturo's commitment to revolution), horror (extralegal detention), compassion *and* corruption (prison guards' maneuvering to release their friend), and disillusionment (Roberto/Arturo's departure from Chile). The controversy surrounding this piece has hallmarks of the polemics surrounding the testimonial genre, but the story remains compelling. Moreover, discussing the veracity of the anecdote ought to serve as a reminder that fiction can contain powerful and compelling truths.

14. "Dirty War" (*guerra sucia*) is the term used throughout Latin America to refer to state-sponsored terrorism against leftists, gaining currency in Mexico only in the twenty-first century, so deeply was history officially repressed. For a testimonial presentation of the student movement and the Tlatelolco massacre, including the press' complicity with the government's version of the story, see Elena Poniatowska's *Noche de Tlatelolco* (*Massacre in Mexico* 1971).

15. Bolaño is often compared to Cortázar (1914–1984), Argentine novelist whose radically experimental *Rayuela* is a canonical work of the Boom.

16. Translations of the manifesto are mine. "Nos anteceden MIL VANGUARDIAS DESCUARTIZADAS EN LOS SESENTA" (7). The manifesto contains references to numerous avant-garde movements and figures, from French surrealist poet André Bretón to the Infras' contemporaries in Peru, Hora Zero. Bolaño's later fiction takes on the giants of avant-garde literary history, including Neruda (1904–1973) in "Carnet de baile," Paz (1914–1998) in *Detectives*, and César Vallejo (1892–1938) in *Monsieur Pain* (1984). He humanizes them and deconstructs their legacies, preferring the anti-hierarchical anti-poetry of Nicanor Parra (b. 1914) and the ironies and creative gestures of the everyday over the ivory-tower greatness of a few lionized individuals.

17. "Soñábamos con utopía y nos despertamos gritando" (11).

18. "Son tiempos duros para la poesía, dicen algunos, tomando té, escuchando música en sus departamentos, hablando (escuchando) a los viejos maestros. Son tiempos duros para el hombre, decimos nosotros, volviendo a las barricadas después de una jornada llena de mierda y gases lacrimógenos, descubriendo / creando música **hasta** en los departamentos, mirando largamente los cementerios-que-se-expanden, donde toman desesperadamente una taza de té

o se emborrachan de pura rabia o inercia los viejos maestros" (7; emphasis in the original).

19. "Déjenlo todo nuevamente. Láncense a los caminos" (11).

20. See Pollack's critique, but also Castellanos Moya's defense of the explosive messages contained with Bolaño's books, whatever the packaging.

Works Cited

Avelar, Idelber. *The Untimely Present: Postdictatorial Fiction and the Task of Mourning*. Durham: Duke UP, 1999.

Bolaño, Roberto. *Amuleto*. Barcelona: Anagrama, 1999.

_____. *Between Parenthesis: Essays, Articles and Speeches, 1998–2003* (2004). Ed. Ignacio Echevarría. Trans. Natasha Wimmer. New York: New Directions, 2011. 28–37.

_____. "Déjenlo todo nuevamente. Primer Manifiesto del Movimiento Infrarrealista." *Correspondencia Infra* (Oct./Nov. 1977): 5–11. Web. 4 May 2015.

_____. *Roberto Bolaño: The Last Interview & Other Conversations*. Trans. Sybil Perez. Brooklyn, NY: Melville House, 2009.

Castellanos Moya, Horacio. "Bolaño Inc." *Guernica: A Magazine of Art and Politics*. 2009. Web. 10 Aug. 2013.

Constable, Patricia & Arturo Valenzuela. *A Nation of Enemies: Chile Under Pinochet*. New York: Norton, 1991.

Franco, Jean. "Questions for Bolaño." *Journal of Latin American Popular Culture* 18.2–3. (2009): 207–17.

Mandarriaga Caro, Montserrat. *Bolaño Infra: 1975–1977*. Santiago: RIL Editores, 2010. Kindle.

Maristain, Monica. *Bolaño: A Biography in Conversations*. Trans. Kit Maude. Brooklyn, NY: Melville House, 2012.

Pollock, Sarah. "Latin America Translated (Again): Roberto Bolaño's *The Savage Detectives* in the United States." *Comparative Literature* 61.3 (Summer 2009): 346–65.

Poniatowska, Elena. *Massacre in Mexico*. 1971. Trans. Helen Lane. Colombia: Missouri UP, 1991.

Pérez Santiago, Omar. "Incoherencias de Larry Rohter en NYT sobre Bolaño." *Letras5*. Chilean Cultural Service, 2009. Web. 8 Sept. 2015.

Rohter, Larry. "A Chilean Writer's Fictions Might Include His Own Colorful Past." *The New York Times*. 27 Jan. 2009. Web. 16 Aug. 2013.

Trotsky, Leon. *Art and Revolution: Writings on Literature, Politics, and Culture*. 1970. Ed. Paul N. Siegel. Vancouver: Pathfinder, 2009.

Wright, Thomas & Rody Oñáte. *Flight from Chile: Voices of Exile*. Trans. Irene Hodgson. Albuquerque: New Mexico UP, 1998.

The Part About the Critics: The World Reception of Roberto Bolaño

Nicholas Birns

From Blanes to Caracas and Beyond

In the mid-1990s, Roberto Bolaño was little known even in the Spanish-speaking world. He was in his mid-forties, living on the Catalonian coast, eking out a living by winning writing contests in small seaside towns. Though he published two little-noticed works in the 1980s, he only had his first real success, *The Skating Rink*, at forty; and it was not until 1996, at forty-three, that he made a real impact on the literary culture with *Distant Star* and *Nazi Literature in the Americas*, both of which epitomized his talent for crystallizing the droll aftermath of historical atrocity. When his name was first heard in the English-speaking world circa 2003, some even confused him with Enrique Bolaños, the then-president of Nicaragua. Yet by 2010, seven years after his death, he was unquestionably one of the three or four names representing contemporary literature as a whole. This astonishing development was first pushed along within the Spanish-speaking world. *The Savage Detectives* (1998) won the 1999 Rómulo Gallegos Prize, catapulting Bolaño to the top sphere of writers from Spain and Latin America. When Bolaño went to Caracas to receive the prize, he gave a speech that, in its charm, self-deprecation, and complex sense of irony and sacrifice, multiplied the already considerable prestige of the prize he had won. The speech was notable for how he linked himself to Miguel de Cervantes: the author of *Don Quixote*, who had fought at the Battle of Lepanto, inserted a famous debate in his novel about which was superior, valor in poetry or in arms. Bolaño adapted this to the circumstances of recent revolutionary discontent in Latin America, criticizing the 1970s left, of which he had been a part, for its delusions and incipient totalitarianism, but defending the valor and honor of those who had put themselves forward in the cause. This combination of hard-edged political realism, lyrical aspiration, literary wit, and a simultaneous sense of humility and gravity struck a chord with those who listened to and read the Caracas speech. For Bolaño, winning the Premio Rómulo Gallegos was not a sufficient condition to gain world acclaim, but it was certainly a necessary one.

The Premio Rómulo Gallegos is an unusual literary prize in that it is awarded only every two years (originally every five), therefore tending—even though individual books are honored, not entire careers, as with the Nobel Prize—to honor writers who merit significant attention. The Pulitzer and Man Booker prizes in the English-speaking world often reward a best book of the year; the Rómulo Gallegos heralds, instead, a recognition of being canonical, especially as it is itself named after a distinguished Venezuelan novelist and statesman. Yet not all the prizewinners have been translated into English or have met acclaim in the English-speaking world. Some, like Fernando del Paso and Ángeles Mastretta of Mexico and Ricardo Piglia of Argentina, have garnered substantial academic acclaim in the US, but are not broadly disseminated; others, like Isaac Rosa Camacho of Spain, William Ospina of Colombia, or Mempo Giardinelli of Argentina, are only thinly known beyond the Spanish-speaking public sphere. But Bolaño very quickly made clear he was a Gallegos prizewinner in the tradition of its earliest recipients, Gabriel García Márquez, Carlos Fuentes, and Mario Vargas Llosa.

Bolaño's first champion in the English-speaking world was a British publisher, Christopher MacLehose, of the small, independent publisher Harvill Press in London, who brought out *By Night in Chile* in 2001. MacLehose praised Bolaño to an American publisher, Barbara Epler of New Directions, who had previously read the first translated publication of Bolaño's, the dark-toned and brief account of erotic moiling entitled "Phone Calls," which had come out in the literary magazine *Grand Street* in 1999. Epler, impressed not only with the brio, but also with the variety of Bolaño's styles led her to acquire both *By Night in Chile* and what is in many ways its companion novel, *Distant Star*, which appeared in 2003. But New Directions did not get to bring out all of Bolaño's oeuvre in English. After Bolaño's death in 2003, his widow, Carolina López, approached the larger and deeper-pocketed American publishing house Farrar, Straus, and Giroux and worked out management for that company to publish *The Savage Detectives*, the book that had first spurred Bolaño to world renown.

This unlikely rise from marginal to mainstream was, though, only part of how and why Bolaño became famous. The other part was the failure, outside the Spanish-speaking world, of the much-heralded Crack and McOndo writers, centered around Mexico and Chile respectively. As Wilfrido H. Corral and Sarah Pollack have pointed out, these writers positioned themselves to be theological successors to the Boom writers led by García Márquez. Whereas the older writers were, in general, leftwing, sometimes magical realist, committed to long, verbose novels, and emphasized the distinctiveness of Latin America, the young writers wrote briefer narratives set in the contemporary world and emphasizing the high and popular culture Latin America shared with the rest of the Western world. Yet favorites of the new generation, such as the Mexican Jorge Volpi and the Chilean Alberto Fuguet, although translated and published in North America, did poorly and found that their generational narratives did not resonate with a US reading public. There was a gap waiting to be filled by Bolaño, who contrasted with the Boom writers in a way that the above formula stipulated as desirable—he did not revere them and had a far more ironic sense of both literary and political possibility—as well as having more gravitas. Importantly, as opposed to writers born in the 1960s or 1970s, such as Fuguet, Héctor Aba Faciolince, Patricio Pron, or Alejandro Zambra, who related to the era of dictatorship in the 1970s mainly through the experience of their parents, Bolaño was just old enough to have been a young adult when the Pinochet regime overthrew the elected government of Chilean president Salvador Allende in 1973. Whether or not Bolaño was telling the truth when he spoke of his own political imprisonment in the days following the coup, he was certainly old enough and had the background to make that story plausible. Thus when he treated left-wing romanticization of the political struggle with irony, he did so only from a vantage point that was still leftist, but through the prism of personal experience.

As the portrayal of the visceral realists in *The Savage Detectives* indicates, even if this movement of the 1970s avant-garde was "something essentially cheap and meaningless" it was still "a love letter" to a certain transgressive daring that *The Savage Detectives* made ironic and transmitted. That book's moving rapprochement in Parque Hundido between the survivor of the visceral realists, Ulises Lima, a representative of Bolaño's generation, and Octavio Paz, seen by the visceral realists in their salad days as the epitome of all that is establishmentarian and repressive, Bolaño was a post-Boomer who had more to offer than *just* coming after the Boom. He seemed a weightier and more highbrow figure than Fuguet or even Volpi. Yet he was not simply these writers trussed up and made less obvious: Bolaño had a history with leftist politics and literary insurgency the younger writers did not, and his generational status made him more than a young man in a hurry or part of a new cohort, oedipally overthrowing their predecessors. If, as Harold Bloom has theorized, every writer is haunted by an anterior influence, which they try to creatively overcome, Bolaño's slightly askance vantage point gave his work the advantage of subtlety and intricacy in the struggle for recognition.

This is not to say that this mode of reception—Bolaño as an apt riposte to or corrective of the Boom writers—prevailed among all his worldwide audience. In 2011, the well-known translator Zhao Deming's rendering of Bolaño's *2666* was released in China. Although the book did very well, the reception was different in tenor than in the US. In China, the publication of *2666* followed by a few months a republication of Gabriel García Márquez's *One Hundred Years of Solitude*, which had previously been published in the 1980s. In China, Bolaño did not so much usurp García Márquez's place on a figurative marquee, but joined the Colombian author in consolidation the emergence of Latin America as a region in the eyes of the Chinese readers. Bolaño's own interest in China, as evidenced by the list of classic Chinese poets discussed by Joaquín Vásquez Amaral and Arturo Belano in *The Savage Detectives*, also made him viable in China and differentiated his stance from his quondam *bête noire* Paz's interest in India, establishing grounds for a mutual cultural recognition of China and Latin America. In other words, whereas in the West, Bolaño's work repelled stereotypes of Latin American fiction, in China, Bolaño's work helped consolidate a discernible image of Latin America that had not previously existed. On one level, this may have misrepresented or elided subtleties. On another level, though, Chinese readers may have discerned commonalities between Bolaño and his regional counterparts that Western readers, more micro-attuned to issues of taste and cultural capital, may have missed. The post-Communism, so key to Bolaño's ascendency in the West, necessarily would have resonated differently in China, as would the Chilean writer's portraits of family life and economic conditions. This very divergence, though, epitomized what a meteoric rise to world status Bolaño's work has undergone.

Andrews-Bolaño and Wimmer-Bolano

There were also divisions within how Bolaño was received in the United States. New Directions is an independent publisher founded by James Laughlin. It was long associated with modernism, having brought out Ezra Pound and William Carlos Williams, while these experimental poets were still at the height of their production, and also specialized in challenging writers in translation (Jorge Luis Borges) and countercultural dissenters (Lawrence Ferlinghetti). This beatnik-modernist-global triad was ideal for Bolaño. But New Directions was always a skeletal operation and only infrequently experienced great cultural success with its writers. By contrast, Farrar, Straus, and Giroux was a mainstream publishing house that, in the mid-twentieth century, under Robert Giroux and its principal publisher, Roger Straus, fashioned a distinctively highbrow image while remaining commercially successful. FSG, the acronym by which the company was popularly known, published Nobel Prize winners, like Nadine Gordimer, Aleksandr Solzhenitsyn, and Isaac Bashevis Singer, as well as prestigious poets, such as Robert Lowell, John Berryman, and Elizabeth Bishop. Straus's great protégé and discovery was Susan Sontag, who not only wrote books for the company, but also recommended and often blurred many of its more promising authorial recruits. Though both New Directions and

Farrar, Straus, and Giroux possessed cultural capital, as described by Pierre Bourdieu, the cultural capital of New Directions was raffish and more bohemian, while that of Farrar, Straus, and Giroux was more elegant and sophisticated. It is not thus a contrast between a commercial and a noncommercial publisher, as neither firm was going to publish spy fiction, romance novels, or mass bestsellers. But within the highbrow continuum, FSG had a far greater association with the institutions of the US literary world and also simply possessed far more financial resources. Its writers also often published short stories in *The New Yorker*, as did Bolaño after his work was under contract with FSG. The books it published were, for instance, nearly always reviewed in the *New York Times Book Review*, which was not always true of New Directions.

There was also a difference in the profile of the two translators. Chris Andrews was born only nine years after Bolaño, and, as an Australian, is a southern hemisphere figure who shares some of the same sense of being on the periphery and loved in a claustrophobic national literary world as did the Chilean he translated. Andrews is also a practicing poet and a theorist of translation and has written an academic book on Bolaño, something rarely the case with literary translators. Wimmer, on the other hand, is an American and, born in 1973, twenty years after the Chilean writer, is a generation younger than Bolaño. She got her start in the publishing business working for FSG, and this immersion in the institutions of American arts, letters, and, particularly, media (Wimmer frequently did media interviews, in effect substituting for the absent author) presents a notable contrast to Andrews's offshore and academic status. The profiles of the two translators seem to fit those of the companies for whom they worked. And thus one saw emerge in translation what might be called two different Bolaños. This is unusual: at other times, a writer might deliberately work in a highbrow and lowbrow mode simultaneously, as Graham Greene did in dividing his oeuvre between "novels" and "entertainments," or have different phases of their career marked by different levels of difficulty, genre, and constituencies, as occurred in the work of Doris Lessing, when she began to write science fiction. But Wimmer and Andrews were translating Bolaño books of the same era—all of his fiction was written within the last fifteen years of his life, and most of it in the last ten—and with the same style and point-of-view.

What then is the difference between Andrews-Bolaño and Wimmer-Bolaño? Why, for instance, is *Nazi Literature of the Americas* a New Directions/Andrews book, whereas *The Third Reich* is a FSG/Wimmer book? It could be argued that *Nazi Literature* was one of Bolaño's first published books, whereas *The Third Reich* was found by the estate posthumously and published at a time when the estate was giving FSG, rather than New Directions, most, though not all, of the remaining material. Yet, again, the material answer is not enough. Both books are about counterfactual rewritings of the Second World War, and, inferentially, the unrecognized resilience of Nazism in a world that has claimed to vanquish it. But *Nazi Literature* is a series of biographical sketches of fictional literary careers, a fake reference book, whereas *The Third* Reich tells a story, even though—aside from the interest of the war game, whose spectral reenactment the novel chronicles—its plot is skeletal and melodramatic. Even though there is a sense in which Wimmer-Bolaño is simply that Bolaño more successful and ambitions than Andrews-Bolaño, in another sense, Andrews-Bolaño might be said to have more highbrow cultural capital, attract the real connoisseurs rather than the ephemeral dilettantes. In addition, *Nazi Literature* is a series of fictional biographies of literary personages, whereas *The Third Reich* deals with conflict simulation games and a war gamer culture of the 1980s that was a precursor to contemporary digital gaming culture. Despite both being concerned with fictionalized Nazis, *Nazi Literature* was archival and encyclopedic and gnomic, whereas *The Third Reich* was hip and pop and marketable. Thus it was a given that the first was a New Directions book and the second an FSG book.

From New Directions and Andrews to Wimmer and FSG, we see two different literary worlds: one of precarious, if dignified, experimentation, the other of elegant, highbrow aesthetic complexity. Bolaño's status as FSG's prestige author was cemented by what amounted to a deathbed benediction by Sontag. The interesting aspect is that, even after Bolaño's ascension to the FSG empyrean, the New Directions aspects of him continued. Indeed, some critics, such as Roberto González Echevarría and Alberto Manguel, see the shorter Bolaño as the best Bolaño, and González Echevarría has acclaimed *By Night in Chile* as Bolaño's masterpiece. FSG got the large books and the books like *The Third Reich* with potentially large implications. New Directions got the shorter novels, the ones pertaining to Chile (while the two big FSG books are also the two big "Mexican" books), and the ones more akin to *récits* than to blockbuster or genre fictions. The FSG Bolaño, though cultured and ambitious, is empathically nonacademic. *Between Parentheses*, Bolaño's book of collected critical essays, speeches and interviews, is a charming and capacious book, of much interest to the general reader. But the very idea of Bolaño as critic was more in line with the quasi-academic tone of New Directions than the FSG model, which posited difficulty, but wanted that difficulty to be creative rather than analytic and, above all, aimed at the general reader. New Directions also published Bolaño's short story collections *Last Evenings on Earth* and *The Return*. This implied a preference on the part of FSG (since they had the pick of the litter presumably) for longer rather than shorter forms.

What of the third Bolaño, the Laura Healy/Bolaño—the poetry? (All of the poetry is published by New Directions, even though FSG is a famous publisher of prestige poetry and its director at the time of its publication of Bolaño, Jonathan Galassi, is a prominent translator of Italian poetry). Bolaño's poetry, for that of a contemporary Latin American poet, has received an extraordinary amount of reviews, but most of those are in periodicals that reviewed his fiction; in magazines or contexts primarily devoted to poetry, it has not been discussed much. Even though Bolaño's first and arguably still most intense literary energies were in poetry, a mode for him always associated with his facetious, caustic youth, it is clear the world wants fiction from him, and finds the poetry, on its own, not just in the wrong genre, but too negative and denuded, too close to anti-poetry. The *New York Times* critic Dwight Garner, for instance, labeled most of the poems in *The Unknown University* "merely larval," incomplete, unaccomplished, more journal entries than burnished, lacquered art. This was the critic's honest judgment; yet it also reflected North American assumptions of what a poem was, very different than a Chilean of Bolaño's inclinations, whose poetic idol would necessarily have been the consummate anti-poet, Nicanor Parra. Though prominent magazines, such as *Paris Review* and *BOMB*, published Bolaño's poetry, and the most prestigious poetry magazine in the US, *Poetry* magazine of Chicago, published perhaps Bolaño's signature poem, "Ernesto Cardenal and I," in December 2008, it did not develop a popular following independent of his fiction, or one more oriented towards the poetry than the fiction worlds. This is striking, again given Bolaño's own insistence on the centrality of poetry to his oeuvre and the privileged role given to poetry—even of the larval and unaccomplished sort—in *The Savage Detectives*.

Why Bolaño?

That a writer receives acclaim does not mean he or she is great; nor do great writers always efficiently receive, immediately, the acclaim they deserve. The shoals of literature are littered with enthusiasms of the moment that have not made it into the canon and also of figures now acclaimed as geniuses who were marginal at best during their lifetime. Though Bolaño's success was centered in the very last years of his life and immediately after his death, many other writers have had to wait until long after they passed away for such approbation.

Chris Andrews, a leading Bolaño critic as well as one of his three English–language translators, has given seven possible reasons why Bolaño might have been unusually successful. One of the more intriguing is that Bolaño might, for a literary writer, have an unusual appeal to male readers and that he is "a writer who speaks to men" (Andrews 24). It is usually assumed that most readers of fiction are female; for an author to have a sizable male readership, it expands their reach considerably. Andrews suggests that the size and ambition of Bolaño's books recommends them to men. Another theory might be that the outsider element in Bolaño's work, the way his protagonists are often estranged or marginal in their society, and the heavy crime element in his fiction makes Bolaño's profile more akin to writers such as Jack Kerouac or Charles Bukowski— writers traditionally much more popular with men than women. Bolaño is also influenced by the US hardboiled detective tradition, traditionally a male-themed and oriented genre. In other words, saying Bolaño appeals to men is a way of saying his appeal goes beyond conventional literary quarters, even while it met maximum acclaim within them.

Another contributor to Bolaño's particular appeal to men might be his concentration of themes relating to World War II. Bolaño's exploration of the hidden corners, culpabilities, and legacies of the war and the Nazi era linked him on the one hand to a highbrow miscellanarian, such as W. G. Sebald (also first published by New Directions, then picked up by a larger company), as well as to popular thriller-writers, such as Alan Furst. But Bolaño's emphasis on the war also put Latin America in a broader context, reminding the reader that Latin America is not just a surreal world on its own, like a science-fiction locale, but a part of the world, and the Western world at that, whose recent fate is linked to the crises and perturbations of that world itself. Whereas the Boom writers might have seen Latin America as a catastrophic special case, a laggard whose uneven development with the rest of the world at once supplied it with outrageously distinct stories, yet explained its cultural pathologies, Bolaño links issues in the political life of Mexico and Chile with the effect and aftermath of global totalitarianisms of both right and left. One also may hypothesize that 9/11 and the reaction to it put Bolaño's work in a context, as the Chilean writer at once made apparent that we were in a new age of political crisis, where the old nostrums could not suffice, yet refused to buy into official rhetoric of propaganda and self-justification. Additionally, after 9/11, Americans began to feel they did not know enough about the world, and there was a decided movement in favor of reading more writers in translation, instead of remaining in the English-only cocoon that the availability of the Internet—which offered the ability to read work from all over the world, but in your own language—had, if anything, tightened. Moreover, there had been no fresh news from Latin America for twenty years, and the Crack and McOndo movements had consciously failed to make news in the US. Given these facts, in June 1985, the Spanish novelist Juan Goytisolo had complained in the *New York Times* that Spanish-speaking writers were becoming "captives of our classics," that the Boom writers had so dominated the world impression of what literature in Spanish was that alternatives were being suppressed. Bolaño's breakthrough nearly twenty years later was, finally, the end of this captivity.

Andrews, following Pierre Bourdieu, speaks of "allodoxy," a willingness of people to believe something is good just because others say it is, which to Bolaño skeptics might have been one of the reasons for his success. Andrews, though, defines "allodoxy" as implying that there is a better, more deserving writer out there, a writer passed over in favor of the underserving one. Few would say this is true of Bolaño, for his success only served to highlight Latin American writing, including writers older and less commercially viable, such as César Aira, as well as younger, more marketable authors, such as Rodrigo Fresán, Juan Gabriel Vásquez, and Alejandro Zambra—writers for whom Bolaño was a role model. The rock musician Patti Smith, one of Bolaño's high-profile US champions, has also reviewed Aira for the *New York Times*. Even if Bolaño's initial success occluded other Latin American writers, since then, Bolaño contemporaries, such as Daniel Sada, Juan José Saer, and Mario Bellatin have been published in the US. If any writers would have been in the position to complain of allodoxy, it would have been them; but Bolaño's rise helped, rather than hindered, their own. If the twenty-first century consensus in the US about Latin America privileged certain countries (Chile, Mexico, Argentina—two of the three of which were associated with Bolaño) and entirely left out countries of significant literary achievement, such as Uruguay, it was also wide enough in scope that writers of many backgrounds, modes, and affiliations could plausibly give credit to Bolaño for helping them break through.

The question, then, with respect to "allodoxy" is not that Bolaño stole the legitimate success of another writer, but that Bolaño was welcomed into the world in a certain way, by certain means, and for certain reasons to which these particular emphases may not pertain in the Chilean writer's long-term respective histories. By 2100 or even 2050, Bolaño may be as passé as García Márquez is now, but he will always be in the canon—even perhaps in that remote distant star of a year, 2666.

2666 as Self-Reception

2666, Bolaño's last-written and posthumously published novel, is both the major object of Bolaño's contemporary reception and itself an agent of it. Indeed, the final form of the book is itself an act of reception. In discussions with his editor, Jorge Herralde, before his death, Bolaño had suggested publishing the five parts of the novel as five separate volumes, allegedly to maximize profits for his family after his death. After Bolaño had passed away, however, his widow, Carolina López, in consultation with Herralde, decided to publish it as one big book. This standard account leaves unsaid that, in the contemporary publishing economy, one big book has a far better chance of making a huge splash than a series of five books, at least in a high literary and not a genre context, and that the heirs' switch of literary agency, from the distinguished Spanish language representation of Carmen Balcells, agent for many of the Boom authors, to the notorious Andrew Wylie, nicknamed "the Jackal," for his ability to wring extortionate profits out of willing publishing companies, played a role here. Indeed, three years before its US translation, in 2005, Larry Rohter wrote a long article for the *New York Times* about *2666* that would surely not have been published if what was being anticipated was just the first novel of a quintet.

But what if the Bolaño estate had followed the author's instructions and done five books? *The Savage Detectives* would have remained the central, canonical work, with the five 2666 series volumes occupying a more ambiguous place, like Beethoven's string quartets. Indeed a 2666 series would be seen far more as an epitome of late style in the sense of Edward Said's use of the term, rather than being seen, as in the unified *2666* novel, as the quintessential epicenter of the writer's art. Bolaño's posthumous reputation would have developed less spectacularly, but with more stamina and staying power. As it was, Bolaño got huge publicity, and *2666* was established as one of the most heralded novels of the twenty-first century. But a process that could have taken ten years was abbreviated, leaving the Bolaño estate with a far thinner bill of fare—poetry and what amounted to a series of first drafts of later books—to offer fans whose appetites were whetted by the bonanza of *2666*.

The British novelist Anthony Powell said, with regards to his own sequence of twelve books, A Dance to the Music of Time, that in Britain, people preferred a series of novels, in the United States readers preferred having it all in one big book. One could compare Powell's twelve-e-book sequence, published over twenty-four years, with such American "monsters" as John Steinbeck's *East of Eden*, Thomas Pynchon's *Gravity's Rainbow,* David Foster Wallace's *Infinite Jest*, and the recent fiction of Jonathan Franzen. That the Bolaño estate made *2666* into one big book inevitably made 2666 into Bolaño's masterwork and also into an American-size big book that could get American-style publicity and win American prizes, rather than the more deferred gratification of a multi-book sequence, like those by the Europeans Stieg Larsson, Karl Ove Knausgaard, and Elena Ferrante. Of course, the difference is that, unlike these authors, Bolaño had already established himself with his pre-*2666* work. Had the Bolaño estate stopped releasing material after the publication of *2666*, or waited a bit to do so, the public would have had more time to absorb Bolaño's masterpiece. As it was, many more posthumous books were released, some clearly dry runs for later books, until the Bolaño industry, by 2015, had reached a rate of diminishing returns. By then, even a great admirer of Bolaño, the distinguished novelist Horacio Castellanos Moya, commented that the subject of Bolaño had been "squeezed dry." There was a danger of Bolaño becoming more a fleetingly trendy author than a long-term classic.

On the other hand, by including the note at the beginning of *2666*, Bolaño's heirs provided knowledge of this process and of the choices they had made, thus equipping the reader with the ability to construct imaginary alternate versions of what *2666* might have been and map their own road through the text. Bolaño's interest in diaries, oral histories, scraps of memoir—intimate, spontaneous disposable forms—galvanizes plurality. The contingent nature of the posthumous Bolaño material occasions this plurality, the interpretive plurality necessary for his books to survive, and thrive, in academia. Indeed, within the novel itself, by having the character Óscar Amalfitano prefer long novels to short ones, and yet by having Amalfitano himself be a rather problematic figure in the book, Bolaño frames a debate that readers of the work might well continue.

The novels of Benn von Archimboldi are themselves part of the story in *2666*, and the opening section, "The Part About the Critics," concerns the various scholars—Jean-Claude Pelletier, Piero Morini, Manuel Espinoza, Liz Norton (who herself bears the last name of an American publisher, one intermediate in cultural capital between New Directions and FSG)—in their attempts to puzzle out the meanings of a heralded, but reclusive author—enact the same manner of reception as will inevitably accrue to Bolaño's book. The crucial difference is, necessarily, that Archimboldi, though elderly and self-immuring, is alive, but Bolaño is reclusive only because he is dead. The critics of each are left with the weakened position of being mere decipherers of riddles and scrutinizers of hidden portents.

In some sense, Bolaño *is* Archimboldi, because of the esoteric aura about his work and because he epitomizes both the highbrow and the disruptive. Indeed, that Archimboldi's name is taken from Giuseppe Arcimboldo, the seventeenth-century Italian-born Hapsburg court painter whose seemingly frivolous paintings of fruit-and-vegetable-composite heads have been judged by critics to be aesthetic masterpieces, is at least murkily pertinent to Bolaño's own picture of the ephemeral and the portentous, the prankish and the all-determining. Yet Bolaño is also *not* Archimboldi: not withholding, not authoritarian in his sense of his own meaning, and certainly having nothing in his own past that pertains to either Nazism or violence towards women. For the more modest and self-satirizing side of Bolaño, we have to look for Arturo Belano, one of the co-protagonists of *The Savage Detectives*. Bolaño stated that Arturo Belano, despite not appearing in the book, was the true narrator of *2666*. They almost sound-alike (with the "n" in Belano not needing the tilde, therefore easier to spell for non-Spanish-speakers, perhaps, along with "Bolaño" and "Belano" sounding closer alike when pronounced by English speakers, allegorizing Bolaño's own popularity in translation) is, despite the "Arturo" perhaps alluding to the knightly quest of King Arthur, not an authorial self-mystification. Indeed, Belano is often more a cog in the narrative machine or a passive observer than a hero-protagonist. If Archimboldi is the author as reservoir of occult significance, Belano is the devil-may-care everyman, who provides open space for the reader to react in a manner less insistent than the Archimboldians Morini, Norton, Espinoza, and Pelletier.

In March 2009, Bolaño's *2666* won the US National Book Critics Circle Award—an award voted on by hundreds of members of the organization, all working book critics. That a Spanish-language novel won this US award was unprecedented and testifies to how thoroughly Bolaño had made himself part of the Anglophone literary conversation. Yet, tragically, he was not there to see it.

Works Cited

Andrews, Chris. *Roberto Bolaño's Fiction: An Expanding Universe*. New York: Columbia UP, 2014.

Castellanos Moya, Horacio. "Bolaño Inc." *Guernica*. Guernica, 1 Nov. 2009. Web. 9 Sept. 2015.

Corral, Will H., *Bolaño traducido: nueva literatura mundial*. Madrid: Ediciones Escalera, 2011.

Garner, Dwight. "At Play in the Field of Verse." *New York Times*. 10 July 2013: C1.

Pollock, Sarah. "Latin America Translated (Again): Roberto Bolaño's *The Savage Detectives* in the United States." *Comparative Literature* 61.3 (2009): 346–65.

Poetic Realism and the Neoliberal Transition in Roberto Bolaño's *Los Detectives Salvajes*

David Lau

One of the great strengths of Roberto Bolaño's writings is their political character, which cuts across the poetry and the multiverse of his prose fiction. What Marxist critic Fredric Jameson might regard as a demystifying historical literalism (or "visceral realism") pervades Bolaño's account of the social conditions in the wake of dictatorships and the defeat of the left in 1970s Latin America. This is the context for the literary adventures of *Los detectives salvajes* (*The Savage Detectives,* 1998), Bolaño's formal feat of a long novel, executed in endless variations on colloquial utterance. Told across two decades (1975–1996) by a veritable sea of speakers located on a few different continents, the story's restless and urban voices offer explanations and first-person narrative accounts of our central, but absent or voiceless protagonists: Ulises Lima and Arturo Belano, fictional versions of the poet Mario Santiago Papasquiaro and the author Roberto Bolaño. These decades provide crucial instruction in the impersonal structure of the economic transition to neoliberal capitalism and the associated drift of politics to the right. From a Marxist perspective (derived from Georg Lukács's *The Historical Novel*), the novel presents a dialectical process at the heart of the passage through two different historical periods in late twentieth-century Mexico.

In both the long diary that bookends the novel and the deposition-like entries that form the labyrinth of the novel's central section, we learn the stories, hearsay, and gossip about the visceral realist poets on the margins of Mexican literature. Their lives wind and twist away from the Mexico City of 1975, the year in which the novel begins; the book's timeline ends some twenty years later, having spanned the locust years of neoliberalism and structural adjustment. A kind of last avant-garde, the visceral realists both extend and retain traces of distinctively Mexican revolutionary literature, art, and politics (emanating from the 1910 revolution), as all three of these twentieth-century developments are partly subsumed into the postwar Mexican state. The visceral realists also notably connect to several Mexican post-revolution-era avant-gardists, who formed the long-defunct stridentists of the 1920s. The uncovering of this buried history sets up a sharp contrast with a contemporary poetic culture (beginning in the mid-1970s) overseen by a politically rightward-drifting Octavio Paz and his many adherents and devotees, the novel's much-derided "peasant poets." Bolaño's examination of literary history canvases an obscure convolution of the Mexican literary left under the twin forces of political repression during the 1970s-era dirty wars and the coming-of-state economic insolvency during the Third World's debt crisis of the 80s. The action of the novel (principally condensed into its long prelude and spirited envoi) takes place against the background of the emergence of the extra-legal, state-criminal nexus in Mexico, a country even now beset by the twin problems of economic stagnation and extra-legal state violence.

Poetic Realism

Literary history is full of opinionated, hairsplitting disputes, reversals, and abrupt changes of aesthetic direction. Political developments in the twentieth century (for example, the emergence of the Soviet Union, with its anti-imperialist outlook, the communist-Trotskyist split, Stalinization, etc.) lent an unprecedented heat and range to the character of possible divisions among writers. The organizing dispute of *Los detectives salvajes* is Mexican poet Octavio Paz's change of political direction that began in the mid-part of the 1970s. Bolaño's novel initiates us immediately into the scene of young and even younger Mexico City poets, their hostility toward onetime-communist Paz, one of the twentieth century's indispensible poets and guides to Spanish-language literature. The year 1976 marked the first publication for Paz's new journal *Vuelta* (a key term in his origins-obsessed poetics), an editorial labor that repudiated his own complicated revolutionary past, as he increasingly criticized any movement with socialist aspirations while accompanying with support the foreign policy of the United States. This change occurred at the time of a new aggressive phase of US imperial strategy, the beginnings of the so-called second Cold War (1979–1989).

What were the terms of the visceral realists' polemic with Paz? The novel never clearly sketches them out in an overt fashion, but they nonetheless seem involved with the institutionalization of poetry, the narrowing of the avant-garde's cultural revolution into a mere literary pursuit with state funding, awards, fellowships, and publications sponsored by the Mexican government under president Luis Echeverría. Indeed, the visceral realists at one point plot to kidnap the grand figure of Mexican letters. (Lima and Paz encounter each other late in the novel many years after the kidnapping plans, which never materialized [472–481].) Their opposition to Paz lies in the practical mode of life the grouping of poets lead, at least as we encounter them in the novel's opening passage, "Mexicans Lost in Mexico." The literary scene in and around Mexico's prestigious National Autonomous University of Mexico (UNAM) furthered the reification of the avant-garde then taking place in Paz's criticism. The results of writing, painting, and filmmaking, would be seen as episodes in a history of literature, art, or cinema, shorn of their lived political effectuality in a struggle for a different future.

Who were these young poets? Good guesses abound, resulting in a new world of literature on Bolaño's work. The most "consistent" narrator and participating poet, Juan García Madero (based possibly on Juan Esteban Harrington), gives us a sense of the poetry scene in his Werther-like diary entries. We first encounter him as a student and participant in Julio César Álamo's poetry workshop (possibly based on the UNAM workshop of Juan Bañuelos); he swells and teems with encyclopedic knowledge of ancient poetic form, which puts Álamo on the defensive: "'A rispetto, professor, is a kind of lyrical verse, romantic to be precise, similar to the strambotto, with six or eight lines, the first four in the form of a serventesio and the following composed in rhyming couplets'" (Bolaño, *Detectives* 4). Álamo cuts García Madero off. The visceral realists (Belano and Lima) arrive and the situation escalates: "It was clearly a hostile visit, hostile but somehow propagandistic and proselytizing too. . . . The visceral realists questioned Álamo's critical system and responded by calling them cut-rate surrealists and fake Marxists" (5). In the culminating thickness of the workshop, criticism and correction has broken down. Challenged by Álamo to read a poem, Lima obliges: "finally I heard his voice, reading the best poem I'd ever heard" (6). Read aloud, the poem is jarring, charged with its unrepeatable circumstance of literary abundance—the poetic forging of a new way of life. Juan Rulfo, Salvador Novo, Enrique Lihn, and equally Trotsky and Cuba hang in a stalled-out, post-liberation atmosphere, along with sex and marijuana in endless supply. Suffused with defeat, the novel also depicts advancing feminist and sexual liberation, with most of the quasi-pornographic action centered on the Font house, the culturally elite family at the center of García Madero's diary. (He falls in love with María Font, one of the two poet sisters.) Paz, increasingly the critic and state-sponsored lecturer, seems distant from this circle of marginal poets and their bohemian ways.

The novel's character Paz symbolizes, at the level of official literature, elites adrift in the 1970s' widening class separation; Paz is disconnected from the vital social energies of the late avant-garde, itself an immediate practice of life involved as much in the creation of literature as in the defense of radical subterranean currents of literature's past—and too involved in the creation of human bonds and the defense of friends from ruthless exploitation, which will be the ethical-political motif of Lupe's escape from a violent pimp in the final passage of the novel. In 1970s Mexico (and, by extension, Latin America), such a truly class-conscious proletarian avant-garde develops because of the growth of avenues for literary pursuit and the growing strength of the educational opportunities sponsored by tax revenue and state spending.

Day after day in García Madero's diary, he and the other visceral realists move through the same assortment of *pulquerías*, bars, and pizza spots as workers, barmaids, and the marginally employed. There, in the humble confines of a bar table, literature seems to draw its strength from the impossibilities of the everyday. They remain faithful to the ideal of a social revolution, now written out of the future by the dramatic transformation of a Paz in the beginnings of his new ideological battle during the run-up to the economic transformations and the Mexican debt crisis of the early 1980s. García Madero's diary, too, stands in sharp contrast to the total absence of any quotations from the visceral realists' poems. The novel asserts, through this absence, that poetry is not a value for critics, editors, and publishers, but is instead part of the electricity of social entanglements between the "children of the mire." Literary culture cannot be separated from the experiential horizon of its time. Love and sex, stoned composition, event-related poetry recitation form the novel's concrete utopia of alternative social values.

Moments of Danger

Close to the middle of the expansive central section of the novel, Ulises Lima secures passage to revolutionary Managua as part of a Mexican literary delegation's visit to Sandanista-controlled Nicaragua. Hugo Montero, employed by Álamo (who appears more powerfully ensconced in official literature), is our storyteller in 1982: "There was a free spot, and I said to myself, why don't I get my buddy Ulises Lima into the Nicaragua group? . . . Of course, I had no idea that I was signing my own death warrant" (Bolaño, *Detectives* 309). Like many others across Mexico in the early 1980s, he will lose his job. (He's telling us all this from a bar in Mexico City). When Álamo is surprised and unhappy to see Lima ("that idiot") on the plane, Montero gets his first whiff of what he's in for, in addition of course to a crucial solidarity mission. Looking back on the tail end of his former employment, the testimony here is searching, sincere: "sometimes, when I'm in a certain mood, when I wake up with a hangover and it's one of those apocalyptic Mexico City mornings, I think that I did the wrong thing, that I could have invited someone else, in a word, that I fucked up, most of the time I'm not sorry" (310). The foreboding aside, the basic plot point is Lima's disappearance from the hotel in Managua. He will not be found by trip's end, despite recourse to police investigation and concern from all corners of the delegation. Lima's disappearance is deeply unsettling in the novel. Saturated with endangerment, the passage speaks to part of the novel's method of representing the past. "To articulate the past historically," Walter Benjamin writes, "means to seize hold of a memory as it flashes up at a moment of danger" (255). This sentiment of the historical materialist will test several times the limits of the characters in *Los detectives salvajes* (*The Savage Detectives*, 1998).

Ironically, no one from the solidarity mission can imagine why Lima might be gone. He entered into the social currents of a Managua in transformation, with masses participating in defense of government initiatives in land reform and education; a whole story for Lima appears as a suggestion, entirely off stage and unreported. Unwedded to the delegation's institutional parameters, Lima wards off his own subsumption into their careerist machinations. The framing institutional presence of the university, augmented by publishing networks and access to salaries and support, has now co-opted a once antagonistic modernism, displacing and scrambling the relative freedom of former generations of the Mexican literary avant-garde. Lima is dedicated to recovering the spirited antagonism. The novel portrays, in passing, the still-ascending possibility of socialist revolution in Central America in the early 1980s. Something of a hesitation is sketched in this midpoint passage, which follows from a humorously extended takedown of the radical credentials of Lima and Belano ("This was the closest those deadbeats got to politics" [Bolaño, *Detectives* 303]), including an account from Trotsky's great-granddaughter, Mexican poet and essayist Veronica Volkow (305–06).

The literal dimension of *Los detectives salvajes* is historically freighted stuff. The novel contains both sweep of a period epic and the anthropological level of detailed gossip swarming with subsistence criminality. The central section of the novel is a series of almost literal one-offs in monologue form; a sea of characters floats before us, where the disconnected lives of Belano and Lima never quite intersect. The interviews seem the raw material for a great journalistic survey never to emerge. One way to approach this work then is in its *form* as a postmodern historical novel, freely mixing voiced subjectivities in an odd weave of time periods; we advance toward the present moment of composition (the mid-1990s) only

---

being threaded continually back through the turning of the year from 1975 to 1976.

Georg Lukács ascribed to the historicity of the novels of Walter Scott the ability to register historical change (Perry Anderson: "a tragic contest between declining and ascending forms of social life" [24]) among marginal social types. Revolutionary ascent in Nicaragua provides a useful counterpoint to its eclipse in Mexico during this period. In a conversation between visceral realist poets Xochitl García and husband Jacinto Requeña regarding Ulises Lima's disappearance, Xochitl appeals to Jacinto to call Lima's mother and report the situation to her. Xochitl is angered by his refusal: "And I said: how can you call yourself a Marxist, Jacinto, how can you call yourself a poet, when you say things like that? Do you plan to make a revolution with clichés?" (Bolaño, *Detectives* 302). Jacinto's rejoinder is condensed in free indirect style (a kind of direct speech within direct speech):

> And Jacinto responded that frankly there was no way he was planning to make a revolution anymore, but that if some night he happened to be in the mood, then making with clichés and the lyrics of sappy love songs wouldn't be such a bad idea . . . and who's to say, he said that Ulises did get lost in Nicaragua, he might not have gotten lost at all, he might have decided to stay of his own free will, since after all, Nicaragua must be like what we dreamed about in 1975, the country where we all wanted to live. (Bolaño, *Detectives* 302)

Historically, the novel begins with the Mexican state-capitalist polity, where the legacy of industrial development and class struggle make for an uneven landscape of political and poetic closures after the 1968 revolt and massacre at Tlatelolco. The openness of poetic possibility suggests that the political horizon for epic transformations is not fully gone. The novel's backdrop is Mexico's transition from a developmental state, with a certain measurable post-revolutionary sovereignty, to a neoliberal state set of apparatuses ever more dependent on international creditors (and their "conditions") and the United States. The novel's persistent lingering in this mid-1970s moment holds open the promise of those not-yet depoliticized years. The historical transition (economic liberalization and depoliticization) the novel measures is consonant with Perry Anderson's critical account of the postmodern historical novel. It corresponds with this period of transformation and transition in Mexico, with developments in social services and education capsizing into funding crises for state institutions writ large—the catastrophic reversals of the first measures of progress. Whereas 1960s and 70s-era novels for Anderson looked backward to the early twentieth century, Bolaño's book stages a survey of the entire century, with the mid-70s as its crucial inflection point.

The novel's reference to historical events and political struggles crucially underscores the economic dynamics of the late 1970s and early 80s. Perhaps no short entry of the central section of the book is more poignant in this regard than a visit the institutionalized Joaquín ("Quim") Font is paid by Álvaro Damián, father of a dead young poet and financial sponsor of the Laura Damián Prize for poets, created in her honor. Quim's daughter, the visceral realist Angélica had won the prize some years earlier. The time is April 1980. He has come with bad news: "The prize is finished, he said. What prize? I said. The Laura Damián Prize for young poets, he said…. And why is that, Álvaro, I said, why is that? Because I've run out of money, he said, I've lost everything" (Bolaño, *Detectives* 280). Twenty days go by and an unspecified Font daughter visits Quim with even worse news: "And she said: Álvaro Damián shot himself in the head. And I said: how could Álvarito do such a terrible thing? And she said: business was going very bad for him, he was ruined, he'd already lost practically everything he had…. and that's when I knew beyond a doubt that everything was about to go from bad to worse" (281). Following the turmoil of the interest rate hikes in October 1979 (the season of what David Harvey and others call the "Volcker shock," named for FED chairman Paul Volcker's sudden rate rise), a long period of bankruptcies and contracting credit conditions saw Mexico's economy enter a depression-like crisis. The dialectic of economic structure within political history has been smuggled, like some of Lima's especially strong Veracruz marijuana, into the novel. Instead of the mere costumes of history, we see the events of the crisis flash forth in ongoing moments of risk.

Plural Past

In such moments, everything is opened back up again, including the legacy of 1968 and the Mexican leftist youth, as a certain fullness is restored to the past. (Auxilio Lacouture, the heroine of Bolaño's 1968 novella *Amuleto* [*Amulet,* 1999], will make an appearance in a kind of condensed version of that later novella.) Published some thirty years hence, the mass of voices that structure the novel could be said to retain some of the unrealized political hopes and dynamics of that post-1968 period, principally with its concentration on the poetic avant-garde taking shape in the landscape of leftist defeat during the 1970s, fighting out some late skirmishes with Paz and the company's deepening embourgeoisement. Looking back on this period of his life in an interview, Bolaño claimed,

> The truth for me—and I want to be very sincere—is that the idea of revolution had already been devalued by the time I was twenty years old. At that age, I was a Trotskyite and what I saw in the Soviet Union was a counterrevolution. I never felt I had the support of the movement of history. To the contrary, I felt quite crushed. I think that's noticeable in the characters in *The Savage Detectives.* (*Last Interview* 46–47)

But 1968 is not the only legacy of the past that the novel holds open in its search for a less hollowed-out form of revolution. In the long tequila-drinking bout that works like the central vertebrae of the novel, always returned to in some measured way, Lima, Belano, García Madero, and Lupe find themselves holding court with Amadeo Salvatierra, a forgotten avant-gardist, who, like the mysterious Cesárea Tinajero, formed a fictional part of the real stridentist movement in the 1920s, a poetic era dominated by the *Contemporáneos*, especially in subsequent historical accounts of Mexican literature. (Paz published a monograph in 1978 on one of the central figures, Xavier Villaurrutia.) The focus on the neglected and even forgotten stridentists allows for a return to the post-revolutionary 1920s in Mexico and political aesthetics possible after the defeat of Villa's and Zapata's popular armies. In the long aftermath of the revolution, the stridentists represent an undiminished avant-garde, extending out of both the prewar and the interwar years of revolution and cultural transformation. Indeed, Amadeo's story of Cesárea's life encompasses her work for a post-revolutionary general, her staunch feminism as well as her practical break with the group over their male chauvinism. As the tequila drinking continues, "vivas" and toasts take over: "The one who always inspired us was Flores Magón. . . . And they: *viva* Flores Magón, Amadeo" (Bolaño, *Detectives* 276). Magón, the social movement leader, writer, newspaper editor, and revolutionary precursor to the 1910 upheavals, here stands in for, even symbolizes, the buried, subterranean currents of epic transformations in the early twentieth century; here Flores Magón appears as the deepest influence for subsequent avant-gardes. Stalled out with revolution drifting ever further into the past in 1975–1976, Amadeo stumbles, half rambles into a gorgeous image of the remnants of the avant-garde and their intergenerational contact in the present historical situation as "a warship lost at the mouth of the river of history" (278).

When Cesárea Tinajero reemerges at the end of the novel, that warship seems to find its way out of the river mouth, albeit for brief moment of danger. As the gang of Lima, Belano, García Madero, and Lupe search for clues to her whereabouts, we begin to stitch together an image of Cesárea. Often attached to bullfighters in newspaper accounts, and alive with revolutionary potential, Cesárea produced startlingly little in terms of poetic output. A poem-ideogram, a simple two-dimensional diagram of a boat on a more and more turbulent surface of the sea, is all that survives. This image condenses postmodern experience in Latin America, conditioning the very possibilities of the Latin American historical novel. Bolaño's own novel is a late variation on the form. Perry Anderson writes:

> the collective take-off of these forms dates from the early 1970s and what they transcribe, essentially, is an is an experience of defeat:

history as what, for all its heroics, lyricism and colour, went wrong in the continent – the discarding of democracies, the crushing of guerrillas, the spread of military tyrannies, the disappearances and tortures, of that period. . . . The distorted, fantastical shapes of an alternative past, according to this reading, would stem from the thwarted hopes of the present, as so many reflections, admonitions or consolations. (28)

Following from the analysis of Anderson and Lukács, this postmodern historical novel opens up windows on alternatives in the past, ones that resonate in the present moment of the novel's composition— 1990s Mexico, familiar to readers of *2666*—as well as the current develops in the second decade of the twenty-first century. When we do finally encounter Cesárea, alive all these years later in Sonora, Lupe's pimp Alberto and the police are in hot pursuit of the visceral realists. A violent end seems inevitable for the outmatched poets. The figures of Alberto and the cops preserve in their emergence the extra-legal authoritarianism and quasi-state violence of a state-capitalist polity in decline. Cesárea will sacrifice herself to save her young friends in the novel's concluding fight to the death. The onset of the 1980s economic calamity—under whose signs and values Mexican society still struggles, even in the present—has not quite come to pass. Though immediately safe, the group will never be the same again, as Lima and Belano will enter into a period of wandering for many years. We can infer that they fled a Mexico increasingly transformed by forces of foreign capital and violent coercion. These ascendant dynamics of the counterrevolution today command the heights of the neoliberal Mexican polity. But the present is always multiply predicated, a discrepant unity called totality. If the present impasse of Mexican politics is to be found in the past of *Los detectives salvajes*, so too is an absent future in which the lived poetry of popular rebellion, in a manner not unlike Walter Benjamin's Angel of History, "make[s] whole what has been smashed" (257) in the recent neoliberal period.

Works Cited

Anderson, Perry. "From Progress to Catastrophe." *London Review of Books* 33.15 (2011): 24–28.

Benjamin, Walter. *Illuminations*. Trans. Harry Zohn. New York: Schocken Books, 1968. 255–57.

Bolaño, Roberto. *Amulet*. Trans. Chris Andrews. New York: New Directions, 2006.

_____. *Los detectives salvajes*. Barcelona: Editorial Anagrama, 1998.

_____. *The Savage Detectives*. Trans. Nathasa Wimmer. New York: Farrar, Straus & Giroux, 2007.

_____. *Roberto Bolano: the Last Interview & Other Conversations*. Trans. Sybil Perez. Brooklyn, NY: Melville House, 2009. 46–47.

_____. *The Unknown University*. Trans. Laura Healy. New York: New Directions, 2013.

Harvey, David. *Spaces of Global Capitalism*. London & New York: Verso, 2006. 17–25.

Jameson, Fredric. *The Antinomies of Realism*. London & New York: Verso, 2013. 1–11. 259–313.

Lukács, Georg. *The Historical Novel*. Trans. Hannah Mitchell & Stanley Mitchell. Lincoln: U of Nebraska P, 1983. 19–88.

Paz, Octavio. *Children of the Mire*. Trans. Rachel Phillips. Cambridge and London: Harvard UP, 1991.

Poniatowska, Elena. *Massacre in Mexico*. Trans. Helen R. Lane. New York: Viking Press, 1975.

Hauntology of the Revolution in Neoliberal Times: Roberto Bolaño's *Amuleto* and Elena Poniatowska's *Paseo de la Reforma*

Salvador Oropesa

Critics have noticed that the last scene of *Amores perros* (2000), where the former guerrilla fighter El Chivo (Emilio Echevarría) walks toward the horizon, represents the symbolic ending of revolutionary Mexico. They have also pointed out that this film is part of the new Mexican cinema, which is completely immersed in a global economy and market (Sánchez Prado 173). These premises are necessary to understanding my hypothesis that Mexican literature and cinema of the late 1990s and beginning of the new century address the ghostly end of revolutionary utopias and the attempt to grasp the consequences of Mexico's immersion into neoliberalism (Harvey 39–63; José Agustín 100). The two novellas analyzed in this chapter represent the moment in which the paradigm changed, allowing capitalism to become the dominant economic model, without a viable alternative. The innocuous uprising of the Ejército Zapatista de Liberación Nacional (Zapatista Army of National Liberation, EZLN) in 1994 tested the strength of Mexican capitalism, but failed to shake it. Along these lines, the assassinations of Luis Donaldo Colosio and Cardinal Juan Jesús Posadas Ocampo of Guadalajara in 1993, as well as that of José Francisco Ruiz Massieu in 1994 are clear symptoms of how deep and traumatic the paradigmatic change was.

Bolaño and Poniatowska novelize the impossibility of the revolution through two incompetent and flawed female characters, Amaya and Auxilio. The presence of weak women in protagonist roles helps the novellas succeed in representing the triumph of neoliberalism. The message is that neoliberalism thrives in an underdeveloped civil society in which the progressive weakening of patriarchy is not accompanied by a strengthening of women's agency. In this context, redemption can only come from high culture and art because they contain the seeds of criticism and self-consciousness that can unmask the normality and invisibility of ideology. This is an attempt to reconstruct master narratives from the ruins of postmodernism and poststructuralism in order to expose the radical historicity of texts. Radical historicity is a term coined by Juan Carlos Rodríguez (*El escritor* 72, 405) that blurs the distinction between history and literary criticism. It emphasizes the internal logic of the text and claims that the role of the critic is to analyze the ideological unconscious of the text, that is, to find where it betrays itself and shows its contradictions and differences, in the Derridean sense of term. It is not that the text is generated within a historical context, but that it is historical; it is one more artifact of the cultural production of society.

The texts selected here are of an urban nature. They agonize about modernity and the anxieties it produces. The two artistic antecedents to represent the challenges of modernity from the point of view of the city are the novel of nineteenth-century realism and postclassical Hollywood cinema, both of which responded to this task by resorting to a conservative-liberal dynamic (Bordwell 1–18; Labanyi 1–28). The form is mostly progressive: we hold in our hands beautiful books that are impeccably written and perfectly edited by top publishing houses; they are also rich in interesting characters, and most of them are based on real people. The techniques are also flawless, featuring an unreliable eccentric homodiegetic and intradiegetic narrator in *Amuleto* (Solotorevsky calls Auxilio homodiegetic, autodiegetic, and unreliable, 253) and an ambiguous, but sympathetic, extradiegetic third-person narrator in *Paseo*. Both novellas depict different, but complementary, perspectives of governmental repression as well as scenes of Mexico City's rich cultural life.

The content is ideologically ambiguous. *Perros*, our litmus test, portrays the lumpenproletariat in a bleak form, and the professional class as immoral and frivolous. *Paseo* moves between the Mexican elite and *los de abajo*, the lowest social classes, including indigents, without any room for the middle class. *Amuleto*, in turn, moves mostly in the realm of culture, with young, mostly unpublished poets hoping to be assimilated by the literary establishment). There is no reference to creating a new poetic language, reforming the letters, or developing new metaphors or genres. *Amuleto* represents the middle class. León Felipe and Pedro Garfias have middle class houses, as does Arturo Belano's family. The most interesting character, in this regard, is Elena, a philosopher, lame in one foot, and owner of a Volkswagen and a beautiful house full of books in Coyoacán. She is in love with an Italian journalist who is in Mexico waiting for his visa to interview Fidel Castro. Elena introduces Auxilio to a world of consumption unknown to her. They go to an expensive restaurant on Insurgentes Avenue then to a Spanish tapas bar in the cosmopolitan Zona Rosa, where they have Rioja wine and all kinds of cheese, and finally to coffee houses where they order cappuccinos. The novel repeatedly stresses Auxilio's lack of a stable job and how her inability to consume is linked to her incapacity to produce literature. She can clean the houses of old Spanish poets, sleep with young Mexican poets, type theses or the research of professors or listen to Arturo's stories, but she is not a citizen of the lettered city because she is not a consumer. In this context, citizenship is defined by the ability of each person to consume goods. García Canclini describes the modern consumer as a critical agent who shapes society in the "private realm of commodity consumption and the mass media." (15)

In *Paseo de la Reforma* (2007), Poniatowska developed the idea of presenting the main artery of Mexico City as a microcosm of the social and cultural tensions of the nation. This avenue links the indigenous and vice-royal Zócalo with the liberal, utopian Chapultepec Park. Poniatowska, following the model of nineteenth-century realist writers, guides the reader to the districts that surround the Paseo and beyond: Centro, Zócalo, Bellas Artes, Alameda, San Rafael, Delegación Cuauhtémoc, Polanco, Roma, Delegación Coyoacán, Colonia Dolores, Colonia del Valle, Las Américas, Las Lomas, and Venustiano Carranza. She historicizes these places to offset the fact that gentrification and ghettoization usually hide history.

Poniatowska, in *Paseo de la Reforma*, and Roberto Bolaño, in *Amuleto*, coincide in defining three intellectual groups in the Reforma axis: the university, the avant-garde and the Spanish exile. Both novels develop an intellectual mapping that provides legitimacy to certain areas of the city. Poniatowska introduces us to the philosopher José Gaos lecturing at the House of the Mascarones (where UNAM [Universidad Nacional Autónoma de México]'s Philosophy Department was located at that time) (*Paseo* 44) or the *tertulia* held by Gaos and León Felipe at Café Paris on Hidalgo Street, by La Alameda. Bolaño will introduce us to the poets of Bucareli.

In consonance with the disturbing negative image of the working class found in *Perros*, the lack of middle class or petite bourgeoisie in *Paseo* reveals a cultural absence: the idea that they do not have anything to offer to Mexican culture and that there is no room for them in a Mexican economy in which the only two social classes are those in the extremes. *Paseo de la Reforma* represents a different problem, which is also related to the anxiety of modernity: excessive consumerism. Following the indistinguishable model of realism, excessive consumerism and adultery are represented together. This is a staple of late nineteenth-century literature. For instance, *Lo prohibido* by Benito Pérez Galdós and *La febre d'or* by Narcis Oller are both classic models that depict a couple of adulterers who travel to Paris and spend fabulous sums in luxurious items and hotels, putting the protagonists at the brink of ruin (Oropesa 117–37). As is typical of a modern novel, the trip in *Paseo de la Reforma* has two parts: one in New York and the second, in Paris. These two cities are meccas of consumerism that shake Asby's finances and stability: "Amaya left and Ashby thought she was a bottomless pit. He learned very soon she would spend five times what was expected. She chose the Plaza Hotel and did her shopping at Saks Fifth Avenue and Tiffany's" (Poniatowska, *Paseo* 130, my translation)[1] Ashby depletes, in this trip, a big part of his fortune, which brings unhappiness to the protagonists. Amaya's proneness to limitless spending is as damaging as Auxilio's lack of purchasing power. While both texts advocate the need to control consumerism, they are not entirely against it. In fact, nice restaurants, diners, cafes, and well-catered literary soirées are portrayed in a sympathetic way. Yet the confusion between citizenship and consumerism haunts the novels. Thus, Amaya is always asking Ashby to buy goods for the political demonstrations in which she is involved. He, in turn, is always buying food, transporting student leaders, renting the sound equipment, or providing the fabric needed to paint slogans; he has to furnish the entire revolutionary kit. Without his money, the activists cannot exercise their constitutional right to express their opinion.

In order to develop my hypothesis further, I have to explain briefly what I mean by 'revolutionary Mexico.' While it is a standard explanation, it also includes some revisionist elements. This endeavor is challenging, as there are conflicting ways of defining the concept, all of them overshadowed by the 1910 Revolution, the revolution *par excellence*. Clearly, the bourgeois Mexican Revolution of 1910 is not the antecedent of Latin American socialist revolutionary movements, beginning with the Cuban Revolution and followed by milestones such as the 1970 election of Salvador Allende as president of Chile and the 1979 Sandinista overthrow of dictator Anastasio Somoza in Nicaragua, just to provide some relevant examples of different processes. The revolution institutionalized a democracy of consensus that governed the country for seventy years, from the 1930s to the end of the century. It moved the country from *caudillismo* to a technocratic government that alternated nominal Marxism and conservatism with a vertical state structure that covered most of the political spectrum, business, and unions.

In the Mexican texts analyzed here, we find melancholy, nostalgia of socialism and the revolution that never came and will never come. We also find the reality of the ugly socialism of the Luis Echeverría presidency (1970–1976). In recent history, the last significant moment of real socialism was Echeverría's *tercermundismo*, which completed the Mexican Revolution by creating the statehoods of Baja California Sur and Quintana Roo, and by nationalizing the mining and electric industries. In this context, I understand the 1910 Revolution as an attempt by the liberal state to Mexicanize Mexico, to complete the task of creating the nation state Mexico that was unsuccessfully attempted by the Reforma and the Porfiriato. Echeverría's nationalist socialism completed the statehood process and put a significant portion of farmland in Sinaloa and Sonora in private hands. Paradoxically, these processes opened the door for contemporary neoliberalism, as it turned the Mexican nation into a complete market when it finalized the privatization of Mexican agriculture and capitalized industries needed for the modernization of the country. Later, within the context of the Cold War, the government led a dirty war against Marxist and communist guerrillas.

The only socialism and capitalism allowed in Mexico were those created and controlled by the governing Partido Revolucionario Institucional (Institutional Revolutionary Party, PRI), which Mario Vargas Llosa considers the perfect dictatorship. When this model died under the governments of Carlos Salinas de Gortari (1988–1994) and Vicente Fox (2000–2006), the signing of NAFTA in 1994 left not only the specter of Marxism, as Jacques Derrida (99) theorized, in Mexico, but also with the specter of capitalism, as theorized by Juan Carlos Rodríguez: "the ghost that travels across Europe and the world is neoliberal capitalism" (*De qué hablamos* 5, my translation); "Capitalism has permeated our unconscious and our skin, and we speak of human condition, human nature, human being, and ontological human being" (8, my translation).[2] Rodríguez shrewdly rewrites the beginning of *The Communist Manifesto*: capitalism rules, but in contemporary Mexico, it lives under the form of drug-trafficking, *maquiladoras* (sweat shops), pollution, the femicides in Juárez, mass graves, income inequality, and one of the most deficient educational systems in the global Organization for Economic Cooperation and Development. (OCDE)

This pessimism haunts the texts by Bolaño and Poniatowska. The two protagonists who are outside the world of consumption are Auxilio and Ashby, who became irrelevant after rejecting his inheritance. He is disowned by his family. Likewise, Auxilio does not publish, and her motherhood of Mexican letters is sterile. The assassination of Amaya Chacel by Mexican *federales* in Poniatowska's text, and the marginality of the Uruguayan poet

Auxilio Lacouture in Bolaño's novella embody the last gasps of the revolution. These are the last women of the socialist revolutions: a contrary rich woman, loosely based on Elena Garro (Poniatowska, *Cabritas* 109–32) and an exiled non-poet poet, the stereotype of the hippy Latin American intellectual, the artist without an oeuvre, like the *jipitecas* studied by José Agustín.

José Agustín realized—at the same time these novellas were written and published—that the real 1968 revolution was not the one in Tlatelolco, but the hedonistic change of mores in Mexico. His depiction of post-1968 Mexico is sobering. It explains, in Mexican terms, what Juan Carlos Rodríguez and Derrida theorized about the triumph of capitalism and the ghosts it produced:

> The system closed ranks against student rebellions and counterculture. Therefore, the hope for a better world for the individual, society and nature did not die of natural causes, but were instead crushed by an intense, dirty, and unequal war. Dominant forces, political and financial, programmed a cultural counter-revolution by demonizing drugs; mystifying drug-trafficking by labeling it the international villain; sensationalism about AIDS, the identification of communism with terrorism, and of terrorism with the manifestation of the Devil. Everything was over. There was no point in rebelling; we had to play the game with all its consequences and inconceivable rules, the so-called market economy or neoliberalism, and accept the manipulation of rights the decrease of freedoms and the increase in repression and intimidation, and the unstoppable advance of moral and material misery. (Agustín 100, my translation)[3]

These words by José Agustín transpire in the texts analyzed here. They can be linked to the death of Amaya Chacel, who is just another police file among the thousands of missing activists from Mexican revolutionary movements. Bolaño's masterpiece, *2666* (2004), addresses the problem of the femicides of mostly young women in Ciudad Juárez (Santa Teresa in the novel), connecting this crime against humanity with the zero degree of monstrous capitalism: Nazism and the Holocaust. The success of this novel resides in its making invisible ideology visible, reminding readers of what they do not want to know: the fact that at the root of our economic system is human exploitation (Fourez 22, 43).

Poniatowska's *testimonios* about the Tlatelolco massacre and the 1985 earthquake also unmask the hypocrisy of the new economic and political system. Unlike *Amores perros*, Bolaño and Poniatowska do not condemn the Mexican lumpenproletariat. Instead, they partially redeem Mexican society through a positive representation of underprivileged groups by making Amaya and Auxilio interact with three formidable forces of Mexican culture: the Spanish exile, already assimilated to Mexican life after having lived thirty years in the country in an environment that they had carved for themselves; the university, especially the UNAM, which endured the invasion by the *granaderos* and the overthrow of its leadership; and the avant-garde.

Sebastiaan Faber, following the research of Guilberto Guevara Niebla, indicates that the Spanish Republicans working at UNAM transformed the university from a conservative institution to a PRI seedbed (23). The first step was to free the university from reactionary forces (mostly Catholic professors opposed to the revolution); the second one was to make it an instrument of the PRI. The Spanish exile, which helped to free UNAM from reactionary forces and to institutionalize it, is celebrated by Poniatowska and deconstructed by Bolaño. Spaniards are given due credit, as the texts acknowledge that they have fulfilled their educational mission.

Following this pattern of cultural traditions, María Luisa Fisher makes a smart observation that Bolaño is interested in literary genealogies, in how each generation rescues forgotten figures or disregards other writers through readings and misreadings (4). Following this line of thought, Auxilio recalls José Gaos in *Amuleto*:

> Don Pedro Garfias, by contrast, used to give me philosophy books. Right now, I remember one by José Gaos, which I tried to read but I didn't like. José Gaos was also a Spaniard and he also died in Mexico. Poor José Gaos. I should have made more of an effort. When did he die? I think it was in 1968, like León Felipe, or rather 1969, so he might even have died of sadness. (12)[4]

The narrator follows the same pattern in *Paseo de la Reforma*:

> In the wonderful Mascarones Building, José Gaos used to give lectures.The philosopher had arrived from Spain because of the Civil War. His voice carried in a hall packed with young people who barely breathed to avoid missing any of his words. Ashby was marveled. Gaos' stature extended to his listeners. They would grow when listening to him. He was a tall, bald, stooped over man, who looked over the rims of his glasses sitting behind his desk. (44, my translation,).[5]

Both quotations complement each other. Poniatowska recreates the zenith of Gaos's career in Mexico, when he was one of the top intellectuals and the father of contemporary Mexican philosophy (Soler 15–22). She represents Gaos as she has done with other artists and intellectuals, such as Tina Modotti, Remedios Varo, Kati Horna, and Leonora Carrington: in his environment, linking the artist and the intellectual to the intellectual map of Mexico City, re-historicizing the city, and rescuing it from the forgetfulness of urbanization and gentrification. Gaos brought both the university and high culture at large to the historical center. In Bolaño, we find the inability of Gaos's philosophy (because of his idealism and existentialism) to connect with a post-1968 culture akin to the one described in José Agustín's book. By the mid-seventies, the decadent existentialism depicted in the novellas was over (Agustín 21), and Mexico was ready to give way to La Onda (Agustín 82–85). In this sense, according to Martín Camps, the first part of *The Savage Detectives*, "Mexicans Lost in Mexico," could be a *novela de la onda* because of its use of colloquial language and the representation of the concrete jungle that is Mexico City (107).

In his literary biography of Mexico City, Vicente Quirarte notes that since the 1930s, writers moved to San Juan de Letrán (Eje Central y Victoria), Juárez Avenue (south side of the Alameda) and Paseo de la Reforma (524). The first two were under the influence of Bellas Artes, which became a cultural center of the city. This is why Bucareli is the meeting place where the poetic groups of *Amuleto* gather and Café Quito, its center.

I have already pointed out that Bolaño's avant-garde poetry does not represent a break with the poetic movements of the first quarter of the twentieth century; his is, instead, a revival of their poetic language and their *épater le bourgeois* motto. In this context, Alberto Medina has accurately explained:

> The infra-realists are very conscious of the fact that the avant-garde in the 1970s was quite different from that of the 1910s and 1920s. Displacement and risk now meant, paradoxically, not only to break with genealogies, but to return to them. (548)

The 1970s avant-garde echoes a nostalgia for the estridentistas, the contemporáneos, all the other great Latin American poetic movements and the Generación del 27 in Spain. This is a departure from the most basic definition of avant-garde, which is to break with previous literary movements and make of the continuous rupture a poetic (Paz 195).

Spanish exiles nurtured intellectual life in Mexico and simultaneously structured it, trapping it in the poetic language of Spanish-language avant-gardes. Mexican culture, therefore, could not escape the prison house of the hermeneutics and phenomenology of Heidegger, Hispanic philology, and existentialism via José Gaos and his collection of Orteguian humanisms, which were inappropriate epistemological tools to create a revolutionary language. The novellas do not question the merits of these important cultural movements; instead, they just state the fact that by the mid-1970s, they were exhausted.

The advent of neoliberalism coincided with the inability of intellectuals, poets, and philosophers to create a revolutionary language. Eventually, pop culture, rock and roll, and urban tribes renewed culture, but these changes resulted in a more commodified culture within capitalist and individual parameters, even if at times it could sound subversive (at the time, it was certainly subversive for the government). In this sense, both novellas could be read as exercises in reflective nostalgia, as theorized by Boym: "reflective nostalgia is more about individual and cultural memory . . . cherishes shattered fragments of memory and temporalizes space . . . can be ironic and humorous" (49). Like all nostalgias, it attempts to reconstruct a lost past, making us revisit it and learn from it. Gaos, León Felipe and Garfias, Casa de los Mascarones, the poets of Bucareli are all pieces of a broken puzzle. The novels resort to the nostalgia of the time when intellectuals and artists believed in utopias. At the same time, these novels opt for the spectralization of culture. The iconic figures in *Paseo* and *Amuleto* are ghostly. I will return to this topic when I analyze the denouements of the novels. According to popular beliefs, ghosts are supposed to be dead people who refuse to die because when they were alive, their cause was just. For this reason, it may be worthy for future generations to revisit them. In the author's views, Gaos and Garfias did not deserve to lose the Spanish Civil War, and the landless peasants of Morelos or Guerrero had rights to their land. These are the main reasons the specters of the losers of history inhabit the novellas.

In *Amuleto*, we learn that as soon as Auxilio arrives in Mexico City, she meets the Spanish poets Pedro Garfias and León Felipe, two key social poets. Yet there is not a single reference to their poetry or to the fact that they are considered engaged poets. They are only represented in their domesticity, and as men who needed help with housecleaning and grocery shopping. Although when we first meet the alter ego of Roberto Bolaño, Arturo Belano, he is celebrating Salvador Allende's victory in his native country of Chile's presidential elections, there is no reference to his revolutionary ideals. We understand that Belano goes to Chile to help the Allende government, but returns with his tail between his legs after the president's assassination. Nothing is said about what happened in Chile during his brief stay. Auxilio meets an Italian journalist waiting in Mexico City for the final permit to interview Fidel Castro. But Castro is just a celebrity to be interviewed; he is not introduced as a communist leader, a figure of hope, or a threat to society. He is neither a hero nor a villain. There is not an Oriana Fallaci moment in the novel, in spite of the Italian origin of the journalist. Arturo Belano often visits Cafetería Quito in Bucareli Street (Café La Habana in real life), a Cuban café of the 1950s that sells revolutionary nostalgia. According to legend, Fidel Castro and

Che Guevara planned the first stages of the Cuban Revolution in this café:

> Tell us about Che Guevara, she would say. He was normal. That was all. As it happened, a number of those failed journalists had known Che Guevara and Fidel during their stay in Mexico, and no one was surprised to hear Lilian say that the Che was normal, although perhaps they did not know that Lilian had actually *slept* with him. (Bolaño, *Amulet* 123)[6]

Che and Fidel Castro, like Pedro Garfias and León Felipe before them, are presented in their domesticity as private characters. The only concern about Che is how good a lover he was. Castro and Che are just pieces of the neoliberal wax museum of the revolution. In this sense, *Amuleto* and *Paseo de la Reforma*, with the fantasy of Elena Garro becoming a revolutionary leader and dying for the cause, are part of the merchandising of this museum. *Paseo* presents the Elena Garro as she would have liked to be, instead of the instigator of conspiracy theories she was (Poniatowska, *Las siete cabritas*).

The three texts, including *Amores*, finish with characters moving out of the city to an unknown place. They are fascinated and terrified by modernity and express an uneasy relationship with it. The future is contingent, unknown, and condemned to a perpetual state of crisis. In the film *El infierno* (2010), the character Benny (Damián Alcázar), upon returning to his village after twenty years in the United States, questions his godfather about the situation of the town and the country. He cannot believe it when he is told that life is even worse than when he left in 1990: endemic poverty is still as prevalent as it was when he emigrated, and by 2010, the entire local economy is based on drug-trafficking. As a result, the situation of violence is overwhelming.

The denouements of both works are telling because they give us the authors' final word regarding the triumph of neoliberalism. Ashby learns that Amaya never painted; like Auxilio, she was the quintessential non-artist artist. She was an activist; according to Ashby, the last one of them. The novel has an existentialist ending: Ashby learns that nothing redeems Amaya; since she was neither an artist nor a good activist, Ashby has a bleak future. Once she is gone, there is nothing left. He cannot be redeemed; he has failed as a member of the elite, as a family member, and as a revolutionary activist. This differs from the ending of *Amores perros*, in which El Chivo wants to return to domesticity, to his daughter Maru, after his last hit, shaved and dressed up, recovering the remnants of his bourgeoisie life:

> Ashby's doubts died out in the downtown hubbub and its streets among swarming people walking around and stray dogs . . . Walking is good . . . The desire to save souls, including her own, faded away with Amaya. He did not even want to save his own soul. He now knew it, the Ashby who could barely walk . . . would be accompanied forever by the forest of prodigies, the road to Cuernavaca assaulted by tigers, the town of Santiago in the shadow of the Tepozteco mountains, the oil wells reddening the night, the mimeographed fliers, the demonstrations, the meetings, the streets, La Carimonstrua and El Gansito hugging, and up there, Amaya and the long flight of birds in the sky.[7] (179–80, my translation)

Ashby wanders alone in the city, conscious that he is going to spend the rest of his life surrounded by ghosts, the specters of socialist struggles, the indigents, and the overwhelming fact that he is powerless to change the status quo. The ending of *Amuleto* is also revealing:

> I saw them . . . They were probably ghosts . . . They were walking toward the abyss . . . They were singing . . . the prettiest children of Latin America . . . So the ghost children marched down the valley and fell into the abyss . . . And although the song that I heard was about war, about the heroic deeds of a whole generation of young Latin Americans led to sacrifice, I knew that above and beyond all, it was about courage and mirrors, desire and pleasure. And that song is our amulet. (181–84)[8]

Moira Álvarez provides the standard explanation: these are the young Mexicans sacrificed in the Plaza de Tlatelolco (434). Celina Manzoni sees in the young men all Latin American youth sacrificed in successive revolutionary movements and believes that the image comes from a painting of Remedios Varo (31). Jean Franco concentrates on the "hippy sensibility" of Auxilio (210) and the fact that the dying youth lack "a common goal" (216). My reading emphasizes their ghostly appearance, the fact that they march defeated, but do not deserve to be the losers of history. Two of the last words in the plot are "desire and pleasure." This may be the reason Marxism and communism failed: they did not give a chance to the individual, to their desires, or to their need for pleasure.

Notes

1. "Amaya se fue y Ashby se hizo a la idea de que era un pozo sin fondo, supo muy pronto que allá gastaría cinco veces más de lo previsto. Escogió el Hotel Plaza e hizo sus compras en Saks Fifth Avenue y en Tiffany's" (130).

2. "El fantasma que de hecho recorre Europa—y el mundo—es la realidad del capitalismo neoliberal" (5). "El capitalismo se ha permeabilizado con ello en nuestro inconsciente y en nuestra piel: y hablamos así de la condición humana, de la naturaleza humana, del ser ontológico" (8).

3. "El sistema había cerrado filas contra las rebeliones estudiantiles y la contracultura, así es que las esperanzas de un mundo mejor en el individuo, en la sociedad y la naturaleza no murieron por causas naturales sino que fueron aplastadas de una guerra intensa, sucia y desigual. Los grupos dominantes, políticos y financieros, programaron una contrarrevolución cultural a través de la satanización de las drogas, la mitificación del narcotráfico como villano internacional, el amarillismo sobre el sida, la identificación del comunismo como terrorismo y del terrorismo como manifestación del demonio. Ya todo se había consumado. No tenía caso rebelarse, había que entrarle al juego con todo y sus inconcebibles reglas, la llamada economía de mercado o neoliberalismo, y aceptar la manipulación de los derechos, la disminución de las libertades, el aumento de la represión y la intimidación, y el avance incontenible de la miseria moral y material" (100).

4. "Don Pedro Garfias, en cambio, me regalaba libros, libros de filosofía. Ahora mismo recuerdo uno de José Gaos, que intenté leer pero que no me gustó. José Gaos también era español y también

murió en México. Pobre José Gaos, tendría que haberme esforzado más. ¿Cuándo murió Gaos? Creo que en 1968, como León Felipe, o no, en 1969, y entonces hasta es posible que muriera de tristeza" (20).

5. "En el maravilloso Edificio de Mascarones, José Gaos daba conferencias. El filósofo había llegado de España a raíz de la guerra civil. Hacía oír su voz ante una sala a reventar llena de jóvenes que apenas si respiraban para no perderse una sola de sus palabras. Ashby se asombró. La talla de Gaos se extendía a sus oyentes. Crecían al escucharlo. José Gaos era un hombre alto, calvo, encorvado, que miraba por encima de sus anteojos sentado tras el escritorio" (44).

6. "Si alguien le decía, por ejemplo, háblanos del Che Guevara, ella decía: normal. Eso era todo. En el café Quito, por otra parte, más de uno de los viejos periodistas fracasados había conocido al Che y a Fidel, que lo frecuentaron durante su estancia en México, y a nadie le parecía raro que Lilian dijera normal, aunque ellos tal vez no sabían que Lilian se había acostado con el Che" (104).

7. "Las dudas de Ashby acabaron por perderse en el barullo del centro y sus calles pululantes de gente que camina y de perros que van también de aquí para allá. . . . Es bueno caminar. Con Amaya se esfumaron los deseos de salvar almas, inclusive la suya propia. Ahora lo sabía, al Ashby que avanzaba trabajosamente . . . lo acompañarían, hasta el fin, el bosque de prodigios, la carretera a Cuernavaca en la que de repente saltaban los tigres, el pueblo de Santiago casi a la sombra de las montañas tepoztecas, los pozos petroleros enrojeciendo la noche, los volantes mimeografiados, las marchas, los mítines, las calles, la Carimonstrua y el Gansito abrazados y, arriba, Amaya y el vuelo largo de las aves del cielo" (180–81).

8. "Los vi . . . Probablemente eran fantasmas . . . Caminaban hacia el abismo. . . Estaban cantando . . . Los niños más lindos de Latinoamérica . . . Así pues los muchachos fantasmas cruzaron el valle y se despeñaron en el abismo . . . Y aunque el canto que escuché hablaba de la guerra, de las hazañas heroicas de una generación entera de jóvenes latinoamericanos sacrificados, yo supe que por encima de todo hablaba del valor y de los espejos, del deseo y del placer.
Y ese canto es nuestro amuleto" (151–54).

Works Cited

Agustín, José. *La contracultura en México. La historia y el significado de los rebeldes sin causa, los jipitecas, los punks y las bandas*. Mexico City: Grijalbo, 1996.

Álvarez, Moira. "La voz de Auxilio en *Amuleto* de Roberto Bolaño." *Revista de crítica latinoamericana* 38.75 (2012): 419–40.

Amores perros. Dir. Alejandro González Iñárritu. Perf. Emilio Echevarría and Gael García Bernal. Mexico: Filmax, 2000. Film.

Bolaño, Roberto. *Amulet*. Trans. Chris Andrews. New York: New Directions, 2006.

_____. *Amuleto*. 1999. Barcelona: Anagrama, 2011.

Bordwell, David. *The Way Hollywood Tells It. Story and Style in Modern Movies*. Berkeley: U of California P, 2006.

Boym, Svletana. *The Future of Nostalgia*. New York: Basic Books, 2001.

Camps, Martín. "'Con la cabeza en el abismo': Roberto Bolaño's *The Savage Detectives* and *2666*, Literary Guerilla, and the Maquiladora of Death." *Roberto Bolaño, a Less Distant Star. Critical Essays*. Ed. Ignacio López-Calvo. New York: Palgrave, 2015. 105–27.

García Canclini, Néstor. *Consumers and Citizens: Globalization and Multicultural Conflicts*. Minneapolis: U Minnesota P, 2001. Cultural Studies of the Americas Ser.

Derrida, Jacques. *Specters of Marx. The State of the Debt, the Work of Mourning, and the New International*. Trans. Peggy Kamuf. New York: Routledge, 1994.

Faber, Sebastiaan. *Exile and Cultural Hegemony: Spanish Intellectuals in Mexico, 1939–75*. Nashville: Vanderbilt UP, 2002.

Fischer, María Luisa. "Los territorios de la poesía en Roberto Bolaño." *Ciberletras* 30 (2013): n.p. Web.

Fourez, Cathy. "Entre transfiguración y transgresión: el escenario especial de Santa Teresa en la novela de Roberto Bolaño, *2666*." *Debate feminista* 33 (2006): 21–45.

Franco, Jean. "Questions for Bolaño." *Journal of Latin American Cultural Studies* 18.2–3 (2009): 207–17.

García Canclini, Néstor. *Consumers and Citizens. Globalization and Multicultural Conflict*. Trans. George Yúdice. Minneapolis: U of Minnesota P, 2001.

Guevara Niebla, Gilberto. "La cultura mexicana moderna y el exilio español." *Cincuenta años de exilio español en México*. Tlaxcala, Mexico: U Autónoma de Tlaxcala, 1991. 173–81.

Harvey, David. "The Construction of Consent."*A Brief History of Neoliberalism*. Oxford: Oxford UP, 2005. 39–63.

Labanyi, Jo. *Gender and Modernization in the Spanish Realist Novel*. Oxford: Oxford UP, 2000. 165–208.

Manzoni, Celina. "Reescritura como desplazamiento en *Amuleto* de Roberto Bolaño." *Hispamérica* 32.94 (2003): 25–32.

Medina, Alberto. "Arts of Homelessness: Roberto Bolaño or the Commodification of Exile." *Novel. A Forum on Fiction* 42.3 (2009): 546–54. Web.

OCDE. *México en PISA 2012. Resumen Ejecutivo*. Mexico City: Secretaría de Educación Pública, 2013. Web.

Oropesa, Salvador. *Literatura y comercio en España: las tiendas (1868–1952)* . Málaga: Universidad de Málaga, 2014.

Paz, Octavio. *Los hijos del limo. Del romanticismo a la vanguardia*. Barcelona: Seix Barral, 1981.

Poniatowska, Elena. "Elena Garro: la partícula revoltosa." *Las siete cabritas*. Mexico City: Era, 2003. 109–32.

_____. *Paseo de la Reforma*. 1996. Barcelona: Lumen, 1999.

Quirarte, Vicente. *Elogio de la calle. Biografía literaria de la Ciudad de México, 1850–1992*. Mexico City: Cal y arena, 2001.

Rodríguez, Juan Carlos. *De qué hablamos cuando hablamos de marxismo (Teoría, literatura y realidad histórica)*. Madrid: Akal, 2013.

_____. *El escritor que compró su propio libro. Para leer* El Quijote. Barcelona: Debate, 2003.

Sánchez Prado, Ignacio. *Screening Neoliberalism. Transforming Mexican Cinema 1988–2012*. Nashville: Vanderbilt UP, 2014.

Soler, Ricaurte. "Algunos conceptos de José Gaos aportativos a la historiografía de las ideas en América". *Cincuenta años de exilio español en México*. Tlaxcala: U Autónoma de Tlaxcala, 1991. 15–22.

Solotorevsky, Myrna. "Pseudo-Real Referents and their Function in *Santa María de las flores negras* by Hernán Letel and *Amuleto* by Roberto Bolaño." *Partial Answers: Journal of Literature and the History of Ideas* 4.2 (2006): 249–56. Web.

CRITICAL READINGS

Looking into the Fragmented Mirror: Bolaño's *Los sinsabores del verdadero policía*

Ignacio López-Vicuña

Roberto Bolaño turned rewriting into an art form. He published a number of texts in variant or expanded versions. His characters and storylines echo each other across different works and appear to exist in parallel worlds. Prominent examples are the elaboration of the final episode of *La literatura nazi en América* (*Nazi Literature in the Americas*, 1996) into the novella *Estrella distante* (*Distant Star*, 1996); the brief section on Auxilio Lacouture in *Los detectives salvajes* (*The Savage Detectives*, 1998) that will expand into the short novel *Amuleto* (*Amulet*, 1999); and the novel *Amberes* (*Antwerp*, 2002,), also published, with minimal variations, as the long poem "Gente que se aleja" ("People Walking Away"), included in *La universidad desconocida* (*The Unknown University*, 2007). Bolaño made an artistic decision to publish rewritten versions of his works based on a creative understanding of rereading and rewriting, as the homage to Borges's Pierre Menard in the preface to *Estrella distante* suggests. There, the author mentions how he discussed "the reuse of numerous paragraphs with . . . the increasingly animated ghost of Pierre Menard" (1).[1] Bolaño, like Borges, considered writing a form of active re-reading. The existence of slightly different versions of his characters and stories creates both a sense of unity and the need for the reader to be attentive to the dissonances and repetitions, engaging actively with Bolaño's texts much in the way a reader of poetry must engage the multiple voices and conflicting versions in the text of a poem.

With the publication of posthumous works, such as *Los sinsabores del verdadero policía* (*Woes of the True Policeman*, 2011), reading the parallel storylines in Bolaño's universe becomes more challenging. The book is presented as a novel, yet it is also a fragmentary work that contains material later included in slightly modified or, in some cases, nearly identical form in Bolaño's mature novels. According to Bolaño's widow, Carolina López, "this is a project that was begun in the 1980s and continued to be a work in progress up until the year 2003" (*Woes* 249).[2] Juan Antonio Masoliver Ródenas, in his prologue to the book, describes it as a novel: a unitary, if provisional and evolving, work *(Woes* ix–xiv*)*. Other critics have asked "whether it might be more appropriate to define *Los sinsabores* as a novel or as a collection of materials used by the author as a workshop for experimenting with themes and characters" (Cecchinato 2, my translation). Ignacio Echevarría denies that the work is a novel, stating rather that it "consists of materials destined for a novel project that was ultimately parked" (Echevarría, n.p., my translation)[3] while, in his review of the book, Larry Rohter characterizes it as "a collection of outtakes, alternate versions and demos" (n.p.).

In spite of its uncertain status, *Los sinsabores del verdadero policía* is now part of Bolaño's narrative universe, its fragmentary surface reflecting alternative versions that can sometimes provide insight into underlying themes in Bolaño's oeuvre. While the book could be seen as a series of drafts for other novels, it also contains, as Echevarría acknowledges, "some of the best [pages] of Roberto Bolaño" (n.p.) This fragmentary work, "an unfinished novel, but not an incomplete one," according to Masoliver Ródenas (Woes x)[4], establishes a counterpoint, a rhizomatic divergence, in relation to the better-known works by Bolaño. We thus have characters that are and are not the same: for example, Pancho Monje appears to be an incarnation of Lalo Cura, and Joan Padilla echoes Ernesto San Epifanio. Other characters appear as themselves, with significant variations: Amalfitano and his daugher Rosa are nearly identical to their counterparts in *2666* but, while Amalfitano's homosexuality is only implied in *2666*, it is explicit in *Los sinsabores*. The writer J. M. G. Arcimboldi (without an h) is French in this work, while Benno von Archimboldi (with an h) is German in *2666*. Other characters bear a distant resemblance. For example, Amalfitano's new lover in Santa Teresa, Castillo, evokes Dean Guerra's son in *2666*. If the book can be seen as a draft or earlier version of *2666*, it may also be read as a novel that complements Bolaño's other works: a parallel world, an image in the mirror, a forking path in the Borgesian garden.

The novel highlights a number of themes that will become obsessions in Bolaño's fiction. In particular, through the relationship between Amalfitano and Padilla, *Los sinsabores* constitutes a reflection upon youth, maturity, and temporality, where writing becomes a vehicle to explore the border between life and mortality. The theme of illness, which is more implicit and submerged in Bolaño's later works, is on the surface here. Other themes include the rejection of literary and cultural institutions through the trope of barbarism and the development of a poetic narrative voice, a voice that has its origins in poetic monologue. I will explore these themes by focusing on the main narrative thread of the book, the relationship between Amalfitano and Padilla. It is not my intention to provide a comprehensive reading of *Los sinsabores*; rather, my purpose is to show that there are strong continuities in Bolaño's ethical and aesthetic preoccupations. Reading *Los sinsabores* does create, as López-Calvo observes, a sense of *déjà-vu* (52). As he notes, however, reading (a version of) the same passage in a different context, even when it might seem close to self-plagiarism, enriches and expands the passage's meanings and resonances. It is in this spirit that I attempt to trace resonances and reiterations of some of Bolaño's major themes in this novel.

Temporal Frameworks

López-Calvo has analyzed how the "melancholic skepticism and disappointment" that pervades Bolaño's body of work relates to a demythicizing gesture towards the heroic narratives of the Latin American Left. The disillusioned tone of his work may thus be understood as a form of self-reflection and critique that inaugurates an "anti-epic literature" (López-Calvo 35–36). The idea is pervasive in Bolaño that the revolution failed or was betrayed and that what we are left with are only love and courage, no longer the possibility of a radical, revolutionary change in society, although perhaps it remains possible to "fight in minor, local battles" (40).

In *Los sinsabores del verdadero policía*, the sense of disenchantment is closely related to Amalfitano's own life story and also becomes associated with a specific time frame. The first section of the novel is titled "The Fall of the Berlin Wall," which sets the narrative against the background of the collapse of the Eastern Bloc around 1989.[5] This date could be taken to indicate the end of the possibility of leftist revolution, the untimeliness of any hope for socialism at a time when the free market and neoliberalism have triumphed completely. The fall of the Berlin Wall, however, also stands in *Los sinsabores* for the crumbling of many certainties, including Amalfitano's certainty about political and ethical values. Amalfitano comes to examine his own evolving sexual orientation in this context. Coming to terms with his homosexuality at age fifty, as a widower and father of a teenage daughter, Amalfitano begins to examine his own life and ask to what extent he may have betrayed or remained faithful to the political ideals of his youth.

Although he continues to believe in the ideals of political revolution, Amalfitano also discovers in himself a profound sense of disenchantment with the politics of the Latin American Left. Unlike his counterpart in *2666*, who is losing his mind and sinking into paranoia, in this text, Amalfitano is engaged in a process of self-questioning and awakening. His melancholic disenchantment is thus perhaps related to the Spanish concept of *desengaño*, which implies disillusion, but also wisdom, awareness. This self-examination is prompted by his departure from the University of Barcelona after it is discovered that he had an affair with one of the male students, Joan Padilla. Forced to resign and to leave for northern Mexico, where he has found employment at the University of Santa Teresa (in the fictional city of Santa Teresa, widely regarded by readers of Bolaño as an avatar of Ciudad Juárez), Amalfitano prepares to start a new life in a place as remote as could be imagined from the cosmopolitan city of Barcelona. Once in Santa Teresa, Amalfitano struggles to justify himself, wondering how he will explain to his daughter Rosa his newfound love of young men. His reflections form a silent dialogue he imagines having with Rosa: "At the root of his argument was an attempt to console himself—and also, hypothetically, his daughter—by reasoning that if the Eastern Bloc could crumble, so, too, could his thus far unequivocal heterosexuality" (130).[6]

Although it is an open novel with multiple narrative lines, *Los sinsabores* begins and ends with Amalfitano and Padilla, with their relationship and their shared love for literature. In the final section, "Killers of Sonora," we meet Pancho Monje, the young policeman assigned to keep an eye on Amalfitano. The last few chapters, however, return to the correspondence between Padilla and Amalfitano. Padilla has discovered that he has contracted AIDS and struggles to finish his novel *El dios de los homosexuales*, while he develops a relationship with an enigmatic young woman named Elisa. The novel ends abruptly with what is perhaps Padilla's last letter, where he mentions that he is now living with Elisa, and announces: "Something's going to happen soon" (248).[7]

Amalfitano's relationship with Padilla captures the tension between the passionate intensity of youth and the disenchantment of maturity, which is a central theme in much of Bolaño's fiction. This tension opens up a sort of temporal disjunction, as Padilla comes to represent incompatible roles and desires for Amalfitano. His feelings for his former student constitute "A mixture of desire, paternal affection, and sadness, as if Padilla were the embodiment of an impossible trinity: lover, son, and ideal reflection of Amalfitano himself" (47).[8] The *impossible* coexistence of Platonic, parental, and erotic love creates a sense of mixed times, opening up a utopian space outside of historical time: "if only I'd met you sooner, but he didn't say it . . . so that Padilla couldn't say you idiot, sooner? when? in a time outside of time, thought Amalfitano as Padilla kissed him softly on the back, in an ideal time, when to be awake was to dream, in a country where men love men" (45).[9] Amalfitano's love for Padilla is also a desire to be a young man again—yet he can only love the intensity and fire of Padilla's youth by viewing it from the vantage point of maturity, as if from a distance. The homoerotic bond between Amalfitano and Padilla thus transcends the generational divide and creates a "time outside of time," a utopian space in which Amalfitano's lost youth becomes actualized through Padilla's freedom.

In his "Caracas Address," Bolaño speaks of the love he has for the young men and women of his generation, who sacrificed themselves for an ideal, an ideal that Bolaño, in the poem "A Stroll through Literature," calls "a fucking chimera" (*Tres* 156–57).[10] Bolaño says that "to a great extent everything that I've written is a love letter or a farewell letter to my own generation" (*Between Parentheses* 35).[11] As he celebrates the courage and generosity of those who fought for a better world, his words disrupt the temporal narrative commonly associated with idealism and disillusion. At first sight, it might appear that Bolaño is outlining a narrative where the idealism of youth gives way to the disenchantment of maturity. But if we read the passage closely, we might notice that the temporal dynamic is more complex: Bolaño is, in reality, saying that many of the young people already knew or sensed that the revolution was doomed, yet marched towards the abyss courageously (perhaps singing songs as in the haunting final image of his novel *Amulet*):

> It goes without saying that we fought our hardest, but we had corrupt leaders, cowardly leaders with a propaganda apparatus that was worse than a leper colony, we fought for parties that if they had won would have sent us straight to labor camps, we fought for and put all our generosity into an ideal that had been dead for more than fifty years, and some of us knew it, and how could we not when we'd read Trotsky or were Trotskyites, but we did we did it anyway, because we were stupid and generous, as young people are, giving everything and asking for nothing in return (*Between Parentheses* 35).[12]

The temporal line is broken when we read what Bolaño says about the young revolutionaries: "some of us knew it, and how could we not when we'd read Trotsky or were Trotskyites." Many already knew that the revolution had been betrayed, that it was doomed to failure, but they fought against fascism and for a better world, even if it was a futile effort. The passage does not set up a simple equation between idealism and youth on the one hand and disillusion and old age on the other. Rather, the struggle and rebellion of the young already incorporates a disillusioned knowledge, just as there is a rebellious knowledge in the disenchantment of maturity.

This passage throws some light on Bolaño's ethical concerns, in particular his notion that love and courage are all that remain and all that we can trust. Romanticism and disillusion go together, they are two sides of the same coin. The idea that the revolution has already been defeated is recurrent in Bolaño's writings. Thus, in the poem "Visit to the Convalescent" ("La visita al convaleciente") he writes, "It's 1976 and the Revolution has been defeated / but we've yet to find out. / We are 22, 23 years old" (*The Romantic Dogs*, 57).[13] The date 1976 is significant in the Bolañian universe, given that it is the year when the savage detectives find Cesárea Tinajero in the desert of northern Mexico in *Los detectives salvajes*. In *Los sinsabores*, it is 1989 that acquires symbolic overtones as the date of the fall of the Berlin Wall, marking perhaps the end of the revolutionary period. Repeatedly, Bolaño describes literature as a struggle in which the battle is already lost. Literature becomes a form of faithfulness to ethical ideals even in the face of defeat.

Illness, Queerness, and Barbarism

In a world where revolutionary ideals and socialist projects have crumbled, moral coordinates become uncertain. This does not mean that Bolaño's narratives succumb to despair or moral nihilism. Chris Andrews has demonstrated, for example, how there is a space for a "minimalist ethics" in Bolaño's narrative works (178). There is a sense in which Bolaño's turning to ethical considerations represents a turning away from politics, or at least implies a critique of the way traditional politics has been imagined. If this is so, however, it does not mean a turning away from the political, since questions of power, responsibility, and ethical choices continue to be present in his works.

The question of evil will become central in Bolaño's later works, particularly in *2666*. In *Los sinsabores*, however, evil is merely hinted at as a dark shadow in the background of life in Santa Teresa. The greatest negative forces are perhaps illness and mortality, represented by AIDS. Towards the end of the novel, Padilla's letters chronicle his inexorable approach towards death, even as his life and writing become more intense, as if burning with inspiration and the will to live life to the fullest. In his preface to the novel, Masoliver Ródenas summarizes one of its key themes: "we exist–we write, we read–so long as we're alive, and the only conclusion is death" (x).[14] What is common to *Los sinsabores* and other novels, such as *2666*, is the sense that we live, read, and write against the background of defeat and mortality.

Writing, then, becomes a form of defiance against mortality, a defiance represented in *Los sinsabores* by Padilla, who also represents rebellion more broadly. Padilla challenges established moral and cultural conventions, including sexual norms, and allows the novel to explore the aesthetic possibilities of queer sexuality as a form of dissidence. There is also a wild or savage element to Padilla, who embodies the untamed fire of youth. He is rebellious, anarchic, sometimes even violent (once he beats up a young skinhead and, on another occasion, one of his ex-lovers, in a fit of jealousy [25–27]). His sexual dissidence appears to be a mark of his existence at the margins of the socially acceptable. If the character of Padilla will become Ernesto San Epifanio in *Los detectives salvajes*, in this incarnation, he is more intense and closer to barbarism. It is only death, in the form of illness, which puts a stop to Padilla's burning intensity. At one point, Padilla asks Amalfitano if he thinks he looks like a "gay German." Amalfitano replies, "No . . . the gay Germans I know . . . are happy brutes [*bárbaros y felices*] like you, but they tend toward self-destruction and you seem to be made of stronger stuff [*material incombustible*]."[15] The novel, of course, shows that this happy barbarian is *not* incombustible, but rather is marked for death.

The erotic friendship between Padilla and Amalfitano comes to stand for the tension between the fire of youth and the melancholic self-reflection of maturity. This relationship between inspiration (fire, barbarism) and self-reflection manifests itself in a doubled perspective in Amalfitano's vantage point. The novel brings together the aggressive voice of the younger poet and the disenchanted gaze of the older professor in an attempt to incorporate the contradictory poetic modes that configure Bolaño's art. I am not arguing that Bolaño's characters are mere allegories for poetic modes or voices, but rather that the play of contradictory voices becomes an enduring trope in Bolaño's works: it is present in his poetry, fiction, and essays. The doubling of the self in discourse as it looks upon its own younger self with a sense of disenchanted melancholy, all the while embracing the younger self's anarchic fire, is at the heart of Bolaño's literary dynamics.

It is important to keep in mind that *Los sinsabores* is dedicated "To the memory of Manuel Puig y Philip K. Dick," which might be read as a desire to bring together the wild, delirious anarchism of Dick with Puig's deconstruction of political discourse from a queer perspective (in particular in *El beso de la mujer araña* [*Kiss of the Spider Woman*, 1976]). The dedication may also represent an attempt to inscribe the novel within a possible (or perhaps impossible, or entirely new) genealogy of Spanish-language literature. Bolaño's interest in a queer perspective (associated with Ernesto San Epifanio in *Los detectives salvajes* and *Amuleto*) is more prominent here, given the centrality of Padilla's character and the placement of the opening section on the "homosexual" classifications of poetry.

The opening section will appear in nearly identical form in *Los detectives salvajes* in the words of Ernesto San Epifanio (*Savage Detectives* 72–74). Here it is Amalfitano who evokes Padilla's words: "According to Padilla, remembered Amalfitano, all literature could be classified as heterosexual, homosexual, or bisexual. Novels, in general, were heterosexual. Poetry, on the other hand, was completely homosexual" (3).[16] Within poetry, categories, combinations, and modes of "homosexuality" proliferate: "Walt Whitman, for example, was a faggot poet. Pablo Neruda, a queer. . . . Borges was a philene, or in other words he might be a faggot one minute and simply asexual the next. Rubén Darío was a freak, in fact, the queen freak, the prototypical freak" (3).[17] Further down, Bolaño includes poets closer to his own literary genealogy or who at least strongly influenced him: "Nicanor Parra, fairy with a hint of faggot . . . Enrique Lihn, sissy" (5).[18]

This way of thinking about poets and poetry is not merely strange or ingenious: its amusing use of word play and odd/queer ways of categorizing poetry works to question the ways in which literary influence and genealogy are often understood. Through this "queering" of the canon, Bolaño both *repeats and parodies* the gesture of phallic competitiveness inherent in canon-formation and, at the same time, *questions and destabilizes* the metaphors commonly used to describe literary influence and filiation (fatherhood, inheritance, murdering the father). The introduction of queer desire and queer modes of understanding introduces a mad subversion of the categories, opening up a non-patriarchal temporality. Such an attempt to destabilize or rethink patriarchal literary genealogy is not unique to *Los sinsabores*, but establishes a dialogue with *Amuleto* (1999), where Auxilio pronounces herself the "mother" of all the young Mexican poets. As Padilla's gesture opens up the possibility of a queer genealogy, Auxilio's opens up the idea of motherhood as a trope for literary genealogy. Auxilio was, of course, not only the literary mother, but also the friend and, on occasion, the lover of the young poets.

Padilla takes to an extreme, and thus exposes, the inherent phallic masculinity involved in the system of literary genealogies. The greatest poets, he implies, are the queerest. Parodying the idea of phallic competitiveness ("who's got it bigger"), Padilla's version here becomes outrageous ("who can take it bigger"): "Faggots . . . seem to live as if a dick were permanently churning their insides, and when they look at themselves in the mirror . . . they see the Pimp of Death in their own sunken eyes" (5).[19] This is perhaps a form of incandescence, of ongoing literary inspiration akin to the incandescence of Archimboldi in *2666*, who is described as "a Germanic barbarian, an artist in a state of permanent incandescence" (839).[20]

The counterpart of this section in *Los detectives salvajes* says that the "faggots" (*maricones*) live as if they had "a stake" (*una estaca*) in their insides, which connotes a sense of being impaled or perhaps sacrificed, whereas the version in *Los sinsabores* says "a dick" (*una polla*), a much more (homo)sexual image. This description draws attention to phallic competitiveness, it repeats phallogocentrism in order to mock and expose it. In addition to other smaller changes (in *Los detectives*, many references are changed to

Mexican poets in order to compose a Mexican poetic landscape, whereas in *Los sinsabores*, there are several examples of Spanish poets), perhaps the most notable is how the section ends. In *Los sinsabores*, Amalfitano tells Padilla he forgot to mention "talking apes" (*simios parlantes*), which Padilla dispatches with the phrase "the faggot apes of Madagascar who refuse to talk so they don't have to work" (5),[21] whereas in *Los detectives salvajes* someone asks San Epifanio whether Cesárea Tinajero is a "faggot" (*maricona*) or a "queer" (*marica*). "Oh, Cesárea Tinajero is horror itself," replies San Epifanio (74).[22] Cesárea Tinajero's name interrupts, breaks, and challenges the already queered poetic cartography, questioning its ability to fix or contain her.

Padilla's queerness becomes a form of freedom, of defiance, of nomadism. As Amalfitano attempts to settle into his new life in Santa Teresa, Padilla continues living on the edge. As his illness progresses, he continues to travel, make love, read, and write with increased intensity. In his essay "Literature + Illness = Illness," Bolaño will come to articulate the view that literature, traveling, and life are one and the same. This idea is already formulated in *Los sinsabores*, where we are told of how Amalfitano's students in Santa Teresa come to understand literature: "They learned that a book was a labyrinth and a desert. That there was nothing more important than ceaseless reading and traveling, perhaps one and the same thing" (102).[23]

Padilla's letters tell of his adventures and of his strange relationship with Elisa, but little or no mention is made of any progress on his novel. Perhaps living and writing have become so entangled that Padilla cannot finish his novel as long as he is alive. It is possible to see the title of his novel, *The God of Homosexuals*, as an allegory of AIDS, but it may also be taken as a reference to a larger theme, since we find out from Padilla and Amalfitano that the "god of homosexuals" is "the god of beggars, the god who sleeps on the ground, in subway entrances, the god of insomniacs, the god of those who have always lost. . . . the god of poets, the god of the poor, the god of the Comte de Lautréamont and Rimbaud" (41).[24] The god, in other words, of the losers, of the cursed poets.

It is in this context that the novel mentions the Barbaric Writers, who will reappear in Bolaño's novel *Estrella distante*. The Barbaric Writers here represent writing outside of the officially recognized literary system, to the point of being close to criminality. Padilla even speculates that Arcimboldi's disappearance might somehow be related to these Barbaric Writers (111). In Bolaño's later novels, the Barbaric Writers will become a sign of evil, associated with the fascist poet Carlos Wieder (*Estrella distante*; Carlos Ramírez Hoffmann in *La literatura nazi en América*). Here, the proximity to Arcimboldi sheds light on the fact that both Padilla in *Los sinsabores* and Archimboldi in *2666* are described as barbarians, but in a positive way. Barbarism stands not for evil and fascism, but for life and literature on the edge, outside of the accepted literary canons and academic culture.

Bolaño thus enriches and complicates the range of meanings of "barbaric" and "barbarism." In a Latin American context, barbarism might appear at first to be a reference to the violent history of Latin American nations. In fact, in *Amuleto*, Auxilio Lacouture claims that "death is the staff of Latin America and Latin America cannot walk without its staff" (75).[25] But for Bolaño, barbarism becomes an aesthetic trope that connotes living and writing outside of established literary and cultural institutions: words like *savage* in "savage detectives," *visceral* in "visceral realism," *barbaric* in "Barbaric Writers," all connote living in the open ("a la intemperie").[26] The savage detectives are not necessarily violent, but they do live on the margins of the established cultural system. The poet-detective is an existential detective, a wandering fighter.

It is in this sense that Bolaño can later write in *2666* that Benno von Archimboldi is a "Germanic barbarian," as mentioned above. In Bolaño, the barbarian stands for anarchic existential vitalism. Amalfitano expresses this idea in *Los sinsabores*: "But we will always be on the outside. Far from Octavio Paz and Neruda" (85).[27] Integrity lies with the damned poets, the ones who never win, the ones who stay far away from the academia. Bolaño's characterization of the field of poetry here and in other works can also be seen as a thinly veiled allusion to political militancy.[28] In a book such as this, made up of resonances and mirrorings, it is possible to interpret Joan Padilla's name as an allusion. It mirrors the name of Cuban poet Heberto Padilla, whose book of poetry titled *Fuera del juego* (*Out of the Game*, 1968) triggered the "Padilla affair" and divided leftist intellectuals in their attitude towards revolutionary Cuba. Perhaps an echo of that other Padilla, this resemblance brings Bolaño's ethical/aesthetic commitment to be "out of the game," "away from Octavio Paz and Neruda," back to its political context as a critique of left-wing orthodoxy.

Poetry and Self-Mirroring

Los sinsabores provides some insight into how Bolaño experimented with an understanding of narrative as a form of poetry. Enrique Salas Durazo has studied *Amberes* as a work that "represents the hinge of the past and future of Bolaño's writing" (189), in the sense that it bridges between his early poetic compositions and his later narrative works. *Amberes* was written in the early 1980s, but not published until after Bolaño had acquired fame as a novelist. An earlier version of this work was included as "Gente que se aleja" in Bolaño's posthumous volume of poetry, *La universidad desconocida* (2007). As a text that has been published both as a poem and as a novel, it offers a glimpse into the zone of contact between both genres in Bolaño. Salas Durazo argues that the shifting points of view and multiplicity of voices that make *Amberes* a fragmented and difficult text point to its origins in poetry: a "doubleness of voice" that "strongly relates to Parra's *antipoesía*," in which the poetic voice is one and many at the same time (194).

Though clearly a much more narrative text and easily classified as a novel, *Los sinsabores del verdadero policía* also functions as a reflection on poetry and an exercise in narrative poetry. It incorporates elements of poetry that will become trademarks of Bolaño's literary style, such as discontinuous and fragmented stories, quasi-lyrical monologues, and multiple narrators and voices. This multiplicity of voices relates to the doubling of voice in poetry mentioned above, which gives this novel the texture of a fragmented mirror. The protagonism of Amalfitano in this text is unusual compared to Bolaño's polyphonic novels, but resembles *Amuleto*, a sort of narrative poetic monologue.

One important difference between Amalfitano here and in *2666* is that, in the latter work, Amalfitano's mind is descending into delusion and paranoia, so that the doubling of voice is closely related to mental illness. This is not the case in *Los sinsabores*, where Amalfitano's mind is tormented by self-doubt, triggered by his struggle to examine his own life in light of his recently acknowledged homosexuality. The long monologue that makes up chapter 5 (41–46), where Amalfitano reflects upon his life and wonders how he will be judged by others, recalls the extended monologue-poems of poets dear to Bolaño, such as Nicanor Parra's "The Soliloquy of the Individual" ("Soliloquio del Individuo") or, perhaps, even more so, Enrique Lihn's "The Old Man's Monologue with Death" ("Monólogo del viejo con la muerte") and "Written in Cuba" ("Escrito en Cuba").[29]

Amalfitano relates how he was expelled from the Communist Party in 1967, yet continued fighting for the American Revolution until he was arrested and tortured during the early days of the Pinochet regime (21). After his release, he fled to Buenos Aires, where, he says, "I . . . kept up my ties with leftist groups, that gallery of romantics (or modernists), gunmen, psychopaths, dogmatists, and fools, all brave notwithstanding, but what good is bravery? How long do we have to keep being brave?" (21).[30] Amalfitano's questions are not those of a delirious mind, but those of a subject caught in the tension between action and reflection, between conviction and disenchantment. These questions are less about specific political paths than they are about moral convictions and commitments.

What is at stake is faithfulness and love towards one's comrades, especially those who died fighting, as Bolaño makes clear in his "Caracas Address." What Amalfitano is asking is whether he is guilty of having survived, of having lost his political beliefs, of having become a different person, of having embraced another sexuality. Faithfulness is not related here to ideas, to orthodoxy, but to love for one's brothers in arms, those who "took to the hills because they never grew up and they believed in a dream and because they were Latin

American men, true macho men, and they died" (85).[31] Amalftiano's reflections stage the splitting of the voice, its detachment from itself even in the act of trying to examine and define its feelings, similarly to what occurs in the poetry of Enrique Lihn.[32]

Another dimension of this splitting or doubling of voice is that the very words used to indicate political commitment become entangled in a poetic play of meanings. As in the case of Padilla's name, which may evoke the Cuban poet Heberto Padilla, the name Rosa has connotations of its own.[33] Amalfitano recalls having translated Arcimboldi's novel *La rosa ilimitada*: "I who translated J.M.G. Arcimboldi's *The Endless Rose* for a Buenos Aires publishing house, listening as my beloved Edith speculated that our daughter's name was an homage to the title of Arcimboldi's novel and not, as I claimed, a tribute to Rosa Luxemburg" (21).[34] The slippage in meanings betrays an uncertainty of affiliation, questioning whether the name honors the writer Arcimboldi or the political activist and thinker Rosa Luxemburg. Political words become materialized as language in a process that aptly expresses the novel's political questioning and uncertainty. The word *rosa* opens up several resonances—it is even possible to hear an echo of Jorge Luis Borges's book of poetry *La rosa profunda* (*The Deep Rose*, 1975), a connotation that might be significant given the place of Borges's name in the Latin American literary imaginary and his association (in particular in the mid-1970s) with reactionary politics.

Marching Towards the Abyss

[W]hile we are looking for the antidote or the medicine to cure us, that is, the *new*, which can only be found by plunging deep into the Unknown, we have to go on exploring sex, books, and travel, although we know that they lead us to the abyss, which, as it happens, is the only place where the antidote can be found.

(Bolaño, "Literature + Illness = Illness," *The Insufferable Gaucho* 142)[35]

In *Los sinsabores*, Bolaño worked out a way to bring together the youthful fire of inspiration with the disenchanted and introspective attitude of maturity. It is as if he found here the vantage point that

---

would become central to his later production. "[T]rue poetry," we learn in this novel, "resides between the abyss and misfortune" (*Woes* 102).[36] In Bolaño's mature novels, the abyss takes different shapes: while it represents illness, mortality, and defeat in *Los sinsabores*, its scope widens to include the European violence of the Paris Commune in the episode about Rimbaud (in *Los sinsabores* and also mentioned in *Los detectives salvajes*, 158–60) and the French invasion of Mexico in 1861, with an element of sexual violence that persists in the murders of women in northern Mexico mentioned here and developed at length in *2666*. But, as Bolaño seems to remind us again and again, living and writing are always done in the face of this ever-widening abyss (even if what the abyss represents is not always the same), and the poet's integrity consists in facing the abyss while remaining true to bravery, love, and creativity.

In his essay on literature and illness, "Literatura + enfermedad = enfermedad," Bolaño finds in Baudelaire the idea that the new can only be found by plunging into the unknown: "Once we have burned our brains out, we can plunge / to Hell or Heaven–any abyss will do— / deep in the Unknown to find the *new*!" (Baudelaire 157). This struggle continues in spite of the knowledge that travel will only reveal to us that there is nothing new under the sun: "It is a bitter truth our travels teach! / Tiny and monotonous, the world / has shown–will always show us–what we are: / oases of fear in the wasteland of ennui!" (Baudelaire 155). Bolaño used this verse, translated as "an oasis of horror in a desert of boredom," as the epigraph for *2666*. The Baudelaire verse may be read as suggesting that boredom and horror are reverse images of each other. We do not see the horror of everyday life because we have become numb to it. Places like Santa Teresa (or its real world counterpart, Ciudad Juárez), constitute "oases of horror" that force us to see, to become aware. It is perhaps for this reason that Bolaño said in his interview with Mónica Maristain that he envisioned hell as "Ciudad Juárez, our curse and mirror" (*Last Interview* 114).[37]

While life adds horror upon horror, Bolaño writes, art attempts to oppose horror by searching for the new: "A losing battle from the start, like all the battles poets fight" (*The Insufferable*

Gaucho 141).[38] This search for the new, this attempt to escape the boredom and horror of everyday life, is nothing but a mirage in the desert, writes Bolaño (141). However, he finds that one way to face the abyss is to start again and cites Mallarmé's poem "Sea Breeze" as a possible response to Baudelaire: "Mallarmé wants to start all over again, even though he knows that the voyage and the voyagers are doomed" (142).[39]

"Starting over," of course, recalls the ideals of the artistic avant-garde and, in particular, Bolaño's own advice in his "First Infrarealist Manifesto," where he urges the young poets: "Leave everything, again. Take to the roads" (my translation).[40] Bolaño's mature works, from the vantage point of disenchantment, wish to capture and remain faithful to that counterpart of melancholia, that spark of youthful defiance expressed in nomadic exploration and the search for the new. Knowing that it is a lost battle, that the abyss will eventually swallow everything, that defeat is certain, the writer nevertheless strives to start anew, to find a new beginning. In *Los sinsabores,* through Padilla's last letters, just as in the final part of *2666* through Archimboldi's travels and feverish reading and writing, we get a glimpse of the counterpart of melancholia, the joyous barbaric incandescence that literature can offer. Literature cannot stop or redeem death, but it represents an act of affirmation and defiance in the face of mortality and horror.

Any reading of *Los sinsabores del verdadero policía* must remain incomplete, as the text is inherently fragmentary. I have attempted to read how the novel mirrors, expands, or provides alternative versions of prominent themes in Bolaño's work. Among these themes are the coexistence of idealism and melancholia, the trope of barbarism as anarchic rejection of the status quo, and literature as the voyage of life in the face of defeat and death. The ethical questions that lead to Amalfitano's self-examination have their origins in political disenchantment combined with a strong desire to remain faithful to political ideals in the face of defeat and disillusion. While this political background is present in many of Bolaño's novels, as the metaphor of the abyss grows in scope, the theme of literature as an affirmation of life in the face of death acquires a more polysemic, existential significance, and its political resonances become more implied and latent. In spite of Bolaño's melancholia, *Los sinsabores* also expresses a desire to capture the irreverence, rebelliousness, and inspiration that allow for a new beginning, the other side of melancholia that is always latent. As Bolaño writes in the essay cited above, paraphrasing Mallarmé: "a roll of the dice will never abolish chance. And yet every day the dice have to be rolled" (*The Insufferable Gaucho* 143).[41]

Notes

1. "con el fantasma cada día más vivo de Pierre Menard, la validez de muchos párrafos repetidos" (*Estrella* 11).

2. "se trata de un proyecto que se inició en la década de los ochenta y se mantuvo vigente hasta el año 2003" (*Los sinsabores* 321).

3. "se trata de materiales destinados a un proyecto de novela finalmente aparcado" (Echevarría, "Bolaño. Penúltimos sinsabores" n.p.)

4. "una novela inacabada, pero no una novela incompleta" (8).

5. We learn that Amalfitano was born in 1942 (195) and that he is around fifty years old, which sets the events of the narrative in the early to mid-1990s.

6. "En el fondo de su argumento, Amalfitano se consolaba y de paso consolaba hipotéticamente a su hija arguyendo que si el Bloque del Este se había derrumbado también podía hacerlo su hasta entonces inequívoca heterosexualidad" (182–83).

7. "Algo va a ocurrir en los próximos días" (320).

8. "Una mezcla de deseo, de afecto filial y de tristeza, como si Padilla encarnara una trinidad imposible: amante, hijo y reflejo ideal de sí mismo" (76).

9. "si te hubiera conocido antes, pero sólo lo pensaba . . . de tal manera que éste no pudiera decirle idiota, ¿antes?, ¿cuándo?, en un tiempo fuera del tiempo, pensaba Amalfitano mientras Padilla le besaba dulcemente la espalda, en un tiempo ideal, en donde estar despierto fuera estar soñando, el país donde los hombres amaban a los hombres" (73–74).

10. "Soñé que estaba soñando y que en los túneles de los sueños encontraba el sueño de Roque Dalton: el sueño de los valientes que

---

murieron por una quimera de mierda" ("I dreamt that I was dreaming and in the dream tunnels I found Roque Dalton's dream: the dream of the brave ones who died for a fucking chimera" [*Tres* 156–57]). "Quimera" could also be translated in this context as "pipe-dream."

11. "en gran medida todo lo que he escrito es una carta de amor o de despedida a mi propia generación" (*Entre paréntesis* 37).

12. "De más está decir que luchamos a brazo partido, pero tuvimos jefes corruptos, líderes cobardes, un aparato de propaganda que era peor que una leprosería, luchamos por partidos que de haber vencido nos habrían enviado de inmediato a un campo de trabajos forzados, luchamos y pusimos toda nuestra generosidad en un ideal que hacía más de cincuenta años que estaba muerto, y algunos lo sabíamos, y cómo no lo íbamos a saber si habíamos leído a Trotski o éramos trotskistas, pero igual lo hicimos, porque fuimos estúpidos y generosos, como son los jóvenes, que todo lo entregan y no piden nada a cambio" (*Entre paréntesis* 37–38).

13. "Es 1976 y la Revolución ha sido derrotada / pero aún no lo sabemos. / Tenemos 22, 23 años" (*The Romantic Dogs* 56).

14. "somos–escribimos, leemos–mientras vivimos y el único final es la muerte" (8).

15. "No . . . los alemanes homosexuales que conozco . . . son bárbaros y felices como tú, pero ellos van hacia la autodestrucción y tú pareces hecho de material incombustible" (77).

16. "Para Padilla, recordaba Amalfitano, existía literatura heterosexual, homosexual y bisexual. Las novelas, generalmente, eran heterosexuales. La poesía, en cambio, era absolutamente homosexual" (21).

17. "Walt Whitman, por ejemplo, era un poeta maricón. Pablo Neruda, un poeta marica. . . . Borges era fileno, es decir de improviso podía ser maricón y de improviso simplemente asexual. Rubén Darío era una loca, de hecho la reina y el paradigma de las locas" (21).

18. "Nicanor Parra, mariquita con algo de maricón . . . Enrique Lihn, mariquita" (23).

19. "Los maricones . . . pareciera que vivan permanentemente con una polla removiéndoles las entrañas y cuando se miran en un espejo . . . descubren, en sus ojos hundidos, la identidad del Chulo de la Muerte" (24).

20. "un *bárbaro germánico*, un artista en permanente incandescencia" (1051, italics in original).

21. "los monos maricones de Madagascar que no hablan para no trabajar" (24).

22. "Ah, Cesárea Tinajero es el horror" (85).

23. "Comprendieron que un libro era un laberinto y un desierto. Que lo más importante del mundo era leer y viajar, tal vez la misma cosa, sin detenerse nunca" (146).

24. "el dios de los mendigos, el dios que duerme en el suelo, en las puertas del metro, el dios de los insomnes, el dios de los que siempre han perdido . . . [el] dios de los poetas pobres, el dios del conde de Lautréamont y de Rimbaud" (67–68).

25. "[L]a muerte es el báculo de Latinoamérica y Latinoamérica no puede caminar sin su báculo" (*Amuleto* 68).

26. "A la intemperie" (in the open) is a phrase Bolaño uses several times, notably in the essays "A la intemperie" ("Out in the Cold") and "La poesía chilena y la intemperie" ("Chilean Poetry Under Inclement Skies") in *Entre paréntesis*.

27. "Pero nosotros siempre estaremos afuera. Lejos de Octavio Paz y Neruda" (126).

28. In an interview, Bolaño affirms: "En *La literatura nazi en América* yo cojo el mundo de la ultraderecha, pero muchas veces, en realidad, de lo que hablo ahí es de la izquierda." And also: "Cuando hablo de los escritores nazis de América, en realidad estoy hablando del mundo a veces heroico, y muchas más veces canalla, de la literatura en general" (Braithwaite 112).

29. In fact, Parra's "Soliloquio del Individuo" is one of the poems Amalfitano has his students in Santa Teresa study as one of the seminal poems of modern Latin American poetry (*Woes* 88).

30. "seguí manteniendo lazos con grupos de izquierda, una galería de románticos (o de modernistas), pistoleros, psicópatas, dogmáticos e imbéciles, todos sin embargo valientes, ¿pero de qué sirve la valentía? ¿hasta cuándo hemos de seguir siendo valientes?" (43).

31. "se echaron al monte porque nunca dejaron de ser niños y creyeron en un sueño y porque eran machos latinoamericanos de verdad y murieron" (125).

---

32. See in particular "Escrito en Cuba," where the poet questions/ examines himself in front of a mirror, with the Cuban Revolution as a crucial backdrop (Lihn 116–43). In Lihn's last poems, collected in *Diario de muerte* (1989), the first poem begins: "Nada tiene que ver el dolor con el dolor" ('Pain has nothing to do with pain'), dissociating the words that are used to speak about pain from the experience of pain in the very act of describing this experience in language (Lihn 319).

33. It might even be possible to see Elisa's name in the final section of the book as having a poetic resonance. Elisa appears to be a harbinger of death for Padilla, perhaps an angel of death. Padilla says at one point that "Elisa era la muerte" (319). *Elisa* is also the name of a test used to discover the presence of the HIV retrovirus, the Enzyme-linked immunosorbent assay (ELISA), commonly known in Spanish as "Test de Elisa."

34. "yo que traduje del francés *La rosa ilimitada* de J. M. G. Arcimboldi para una editorial de Buenos Aires mientras escuchaba cómo mi Edith adorada decía que acaso el nombre de nuestra hija era un homenaje al título de la novela de Arcimboldi y no, como yo le aseguraba, una forma de recordar a Rosa Luxemburgo" (43).

35. "[M]ientras buscamos el antídoto o la medicina para curarnos, lo *nuevo*, aquello que sólo se puede encontrar en lo ignoto, hay que seguir transitando por el sexo, los libros, y los viajes, aun a sabiendas de que nos llevan al abismo, que es, casualmente, el único sitio donde uno puede encontrar el antídoto" (*El gaucho insufrible* 156, italics in original).

36. "[L]a poesía verdadera vive entre el abismo y la desdicha" (146).

37. "Ciudad Juárez, que es nuestra maldición y nuestro espejo" (Braithwaite 69).

38. "Una batalla perdida de antemano, como casi todas las de los poetas" (*El gaucho insufrible* 155).

39. "Mallarmé quiere volver a empezar, aun a sabiendas de que el viaje y los viajeros están condenados" (155–56).

40. "Déjenlo todo, nuevamente. Láncense a los caminos" ("Déjenlo todo, nuevamente. Primer Manifiesto Infrarrealista" n.p.).

41. "un golpe de dados jamás abolirá el azar. Sin embargo, es necesario tirar los dados cada día" (*El gaucho insufrible* 157–58).

Works Cited

Andrews, Chris. *Roberto Bolaño's Fiction: An Expanding Universe*. New York: Columbia UP, 2014.

Baudelaire, Charles. *Les Fleurs du Mal*. Trans. Richard Howard. Boston: David R. Gordine, 1982.

Bolaño, Roberto. *2666*. Barcelona: Anagrama, 2004.

_____. *2666*. Trans. Natasha Wimmer. New York: Farrar, Straus & Giroux, 2008.

_____. *Amuleto*. Barcelona: Anagrama, 1999.

_____. *Amulet*. Trans. Chris Andrews. New York: New Directions, 2006.

_____. *Between Parentheses*. Trans. Natasha Wimmer. New York: New Directions, 2011.

_____. "Déjenlo todo, nuevamente. Primer Manifiesto Infrarrealista." *Archivo Bolaño*. 2 Jul 2015. Web.

_____. *Los detectives salvajes*. Barcelona: Anagrama, 1998.

_____. *Distant Star*. Trans. Chris Andrews. New York: New Directions, 2004.

_____. *Entre paréntesis*. Barcelona: Anagrama, 2004.

_____. *Estrella distante*. Barcelona: Anagrama, 1996.

_____. *The Insufferable Gaucho*. Trans. Chris Andrews. New York: New Directions, 2010.

_____. *El gaucho insufrible*. Barcelona: Anagrama, 2003.

_____. *Roberto Bolaño: The Last Interview & Other Conversations*. Brooklyn, New York: Melville House, 2009.

_____. *The Romantic Dogs*. Trans. Laura Healy. New York: New Directions, 2008.

_____. *The Savage Detectives*. Trans. Natasha Wimmer. New York: Farrar, Straus & Giroux, 2007.

_____. *Los sinsabores del verdadero policía*. Barcelona: Anagrama, 2011.

_____. *Tres*. Trans. Laura Healy. New York: New Directions, 2011.

_____. *Woes of the True Policeman*. Trans. Natasha Wimmer. New York: Farrar, Straus & Giroux, 2012.

Braithwaite, Andrés. *Bolaño por sí mismo. Entrevistas escogidas.* Santiago de Chile: Ediciones UDP, 2006.

Cecchinato, Erica. *"Los sinsabores del verdadero policía*: La intertextualidad salvaje de Roberto Bolaño." *Orillas: Rivista d'Ispanistica* 3 (2014). Padova University, 2 Jul 2015. Web.

Echevarría, Ignacio. "Bolaño. Penúltimos sinsabores de un novelista convertido en leyenda." *El Cultural.* El Cultural, 21 Jan. 2011. Web. 2 Jul 2015.

Lihn, Enrique. *Porque escribí: Antología poética.* Mexico City: Fondo de Cultura Económica, 1995.

López-Calvo, Ignacio. "Roberto Bolaño's Flower War: Memory, Melancholy, and Pierre Menard." *Roberto Bolaño, a Less Distant Star.* Ed. Ignacio López-Calvo. New York: Palgrave MacMillan, 2015. 35–64.

Masoliver Ródenas, J. A. Introduction. *Los sinsabores del verdadero policía.* By Roberto Bolaño. Barcelona: Anagrama, 2011.

Rohter, Larry. "Harvesting Fragments from a Chilean Master. *Woes of the True Policeman,* by Roberto Bolaño." *New York Times.* The New York Times Company, 19 Dec 2012. Web. 10 Sept. 2015.

Salas Durazo, Enrique. "Roberto Bolaño's Big Bang: Deciphering the Code of an Aspiring Writer in *Antwerp." Roberto Bolaño, a Less Distant Star.* Ed. Ignacio López-Calvo. New York: Palgrave MacMillan, 2015. 189–209.

Does It Matter That Roberto Bolaño's Francophiles Have Never Been to Paris?: Aesthetic Purity in the World Republic of Letters___

Brantley Nicholson

> Of course it was a French custom, a common habit at the hole-in-the-wall taverns off the Boulevard du Temple and around the Faubourg St. Denis, and Manuel and *mi general* Diego Carvajal got to talking about Paris and the bread and cheese that people ate in Paris, and the tequila that people drank in Paris and how you could hardly believe how well people drank, how well the Parisians around the Marché aux Puces could drink, as if in Paris, or so I thought everything happened around some street or place and never on a specific street or in a specific place, and this was because, as I later discovered, Manuel had never been to the City of Light, and neither had *mi general*, although both of them, I don't know why, professed a fondness or passion for that faraway and presumably intoxicating metropolis that struck me as worthy of better objects. (Amadeo Salvatierra, *The Savage Detectives* 334)

In *Los detectives salvajes* (*The Savage Detectives*, 1998), a montage novel whose narrative thread the reader slowly brings into focus after wading through a mass of characters and shifting geographies, there is a pronounced tension between two aesthetic orbits that undergird the work's otherwise centrifugal force. On one hand, Cesárea Tinajero, the long lost poet of the Sonora Dessert, acts as a spiritual guide whose literary production is consonant with a presumably pure Latin American voice. On the other, the world literary system, with its perceived center in Paris, as is noted in the quote above, anchors literary discourse as such. In his characteristic point-counterpoint style, Bolaño uses well-heeled literati that coalesce around an imagined Paris as a contrast to the peripatetic and down-and-out poet ruffians Ulises Lima and Arturo Belano. These characters sets—the "savage detectives," in search of a presumably pure poetry and inhabitants of the world republic of letters—stand as metaphors for contrasting aesthetic constellations: the former based on a fetishized marginalization and the latter on a power of consecration based on a knowledge of elsewhere. It is telling, as such, that a common theme in Bolaño's soirées is Paris, its grand boulevards, its rich cultural history, and its street corners imbued with literary lore. The only catch, one narrator remarks matter-of-factly, is that no one has actually ever been there.

Bolaño's emphasis on the dissonance between imagined and real cosmopolitan centers falls in line with what Mariano Siskind has recently defined as the traditional "deseo de mundo," or "desire for the world," among the Latin American literati. With Bolaño, we witness the realization of this desire, though the result is not the promised empowerment, but a deflating letdown. The "desire for the world" is only an affective cultural variable insofar as it does not give way to the *actual experience of the world*, under the terms of which the fantasy of cosmopolitanism cannot sustain the weight of material metropolitan experience. In this chapter, I argue that the trope of much of Bolaño's most ambitious and critically acclaimed works, *Los detectives salvajes* and *2666*, turns precisely on the interplay between a hypothetical pure aesthetics that glorifies the Latin American experience in and of itself and the disarticulation of this local idealism when it enters into world systems.

At its most bare, *Los detectives salvajes* is about the relationship between the publishing industry, literary icons, and the tensions between local and global literary communities. Not subtly critiquing the Boom and Gabriel García Márquez in particular, Bolaño's text follows the two founders of an avant-garde literary group named the *viscerrealistas*, an obvious jab at the Latin American, potboiler style of *realismo mágico*. Members of the *viscerrealistas* forge bonds when challenging literary figures that enjoy prominence on the local and international scene. Octavio Paz stands in as Mexican literature-for-export, and anyone that benefits from state money or wins literary prizes that are not locally administered receive a dressing down at some point in the work. Bolaño, who in the introduction to one of his first written novels (though published much later), *Amberes*

(*Antwerp*, 2002), discusses how he himself lived off local literary prizes in Spain early in his career, attempts to articulate the tension between a literature that focuses on a stripped down version of a local experience and the literary trends that are caught up in the markets of global prestige. An underlying "real," local experience, or a "real literature," implied by the name of the group to be a purely visceral, or entirely stripped down aesthetic, is treated as an enigmatic form that the head *viscerrealistas*, Belano and Lima, attempt to decipher throughout the work. There is a purity that we always almost reach in *Los detectives salvajes*, an allusion on Bolaño's part, perhaps, that acknowledges the impossibility for a large international audience to ever fully understand the complexities of Latin American literature.

For Belano and Lima, this enigma is embodied by Cesárea Tinajero, a long-forgotten literary icon that disappeared in the Sonora Dessert after publishing only a few issues of a literary magazine that the young group emulates. Beyond her name, which alludes to a Cesarean section from which a new form will be born, and a Spanish feminization of the word Cesar, Tinajero is a poetic figure who, in her impossibility to be reached, represents an experience that cannot be articulated literarily. Yet, this sort of enigmatic insiderness does not ever amount to anything of substance in the novel, and the world literary model ultimately wins out. The *viscerrealistas* disband after publishing only a few anthologies of poetry and the founders become lost in a labyrinth of global exile. When Lima, by sheer luck, is presented with the chance to confront Octavio Paz, he fails to produce a meaningful interaction. Lima stumbles upon Paz in a park, and despite his lengthy diatribes against him earlier in the text, he only impishly walks around him in circles. He physically encircles Paz in a way that parallels the group's relationship to Cesárea Tinajero and her pure local form that they encircle figuratively. With Paz standing in as both a version of literary Mexico for export and as a nationally protected icon, on the one hand, and Cesárea Tinajero representing a pure local literature, on the other, the *viscerrealistas* base their own aesthetic drive and epistemological currents on the clash between the two figures without ever successfully capturing or reproducing either. Bolaño alludes to both forms, the local and the global, in the extreme and highlights his own inability, as a writer, to fully rebel against the prestige of Paz or fully capture the voice of Tinajero. Caught somewhere between the two epistemologically and paralleling his alter ego, Belano, who is physically adrift and unmoored geographically, Bolaño sends two messages about what a successful local literature might resemble in times of globalism, while drawing attention to the fact that he, himself, can only encircle it. For Bolaño, the writer caught up in the machinery of world literature can at best allude to an artist entirely unconcerned with his (or her) reading public. And for Bolaño, he (or she) can only complain about its currents.[1]

If in *Los detectives salvajes*, Bolaño expresses his own misgivings about the ability of his generation to write a "pure" counter-current to the aesthetics of the Boom, in *2666*, he casts the entire framework of world literature in a harsh light. Bolaño takes the secular trinity of literary prestige—publishing houses, academics, and lay literati—and places them alongside a series of violent rapes and femicides in Santa Teresa, his fictionalized version of Ciudad Juárez. By the time Bolaño wrote *2666*, he had a firm understanding of the machinery of world literature and his place therein. With the reception of *Los detectives salvajes* reaching feverish levels, Bolaño knew that his work and image resonated with reading publics that were ready for a shift away from Boom literature. Bolaño's writing deserves the cachet that it has received, but his carefully cultivated image is arguably just as deliberate a construction. Bolaño makes a cameo in many of his works, and by the end of the nineties, it appears that the fiction that he had built up around himself had begun to bleed into the way that publishing houses tailored his image. The mystique surrounding him as an icon and commodity hinges on two, now all but debunked myths, for instance: one, that Bolaño was imprisoned in Chile under Pinochet, and two, that he contracted the hepatitis C through heroin use, which would eventually contribute to his death. While Larry Rohter of the *New York Times* has suggested that there is no evidence to support either of these points, Sarah Pollack has argued that the rise of Bolaño as a literary icon has as much to do with a continued cosmopolitan expectation of barbarian peripheral literature, even if the barbarians are now, in fact, all poets, as it does with the quality of Bolaño's body of work alone.[2] With a combination of literary critics eager to write him into the canon—according to the dust jacket for the English translation of *Los detectives salvajes*, critics for *El País* claim that the work is "the kind of novel that Borges would have written"—and academics keen to celebrate a literary icon that will facilitate the wide analysis of post-Boom literature, by the time that Bolaño won the Premio Rómulo Gallegos in 1999, he clearly understood how to manipulate the flows of literary prestige.[3] And in *2666*, more than anywhere else, Bolaño ironizes the very system that contributed to his fame. Bolaño's writing is not so much a sham, as perhaps Pollack implies, but with the rapid decontextualization of his work, following his quick ascension in the world republic of letters, Bolaño, like other writers surrounding him generationally, realizes that he must send mixed messages to his reading public. And in his final work, *2666*, taken by many critics to be his masterpiece, one of the central thematic concerns revolves around how to do just that.

Bolaño bookends the five-novel collection of *2666* with studies on the enigmatic and cultish literary star Benno von Archimboldi. While he writes parts of himself and his life into many scenes and characters in the novel, it is no stretch to argue that the cult of Archimboldi is set as a metaphor for Bolaño's own success. Bolaño begins and ends with ironic depictions of his fans and critics. The first novel, *La parte de los críticos* (*The Part About the Critics*), takes jabs at an academic audience that rushes to capitalize on his prestige with fast and loose readings of his work. Some rush to buy everything they can based simply on Archimboldi's last name (exotic, it is implied, for a German author). Others write at length treatises on Archimboldi's corpus, having only read one or two of his novels. And others forget that authors and artists are actual people, not just mythological personae.

A common trope in Bolaño's work is to advance themes and emotions through a multitude of characters, making use of what María Luisa Fischer has referred to as his employment of moral mirror characters that will help us gauge the actions and context of his work's central figures.[4] In *La parte de los críticos*, Bolaño refracts the image of Archimboldi of the cult artist, Edwin Johns. Johns fascinates one of the four critics that we follow throughout the section, not least because Johns cut off his painting hand while he was still reasonably young and developing as an artist, an act that simultaneously projected him onto the European artistic map and ended him in an asylum. The narrator establishes that Archimboldi's literary agent cares much less about the quality of his work than the profit he generates from it. Bolaño describes the relationship between Archimboldi and his agent, Schnell, as purely monetary when he writes: "Schnell had never seen Archimboldi; the money that his books and translations generated was deposited in a Swiss bank account." Later, the owner of Archimboldi's publishing house admits to him that she had never read his work: "When Archimboldi wanted to know why she kept publishing him if she didn't read him, which was really a rhetorical question since he knew the answer, the baroness replied (a) because she knew he was good, (b) because Bubis had told her to, (c) because few publishers actually read the books they published,"—we quickly learn that Johns, despite all of the mystique that surrounds him, acts not out of artistic impulse but out of economic interest (41, 863). We are as surprised as Morini, the critic obsessed with Johns, when we find out that his artistic actions resemble more a banker's concern with the bottom line than an artist yearning for meaning. Morini asks Johns point blank why he cut off his hand, when he visits him in his asylum, to which Johns responds by whispering in Morini's ear bluntly: "For money." He "believed in investments, the flow of capital, one has to play the game to win, that kind of thing" (132).

The scene plays a trick on both Bolaño's audience and Bolaño himself; Bolaño's work is filled with peripheral artists who go to drastic lengths to give metaphors for their social impotence. But beyond a prod at the cult surrounding Bolaño, the refraction of artistic importance between Archimboldi and Johns sets the basis for a theme that will run throughout the collection: that the relationship between aesthetics, institutions of prestige, and the flows of cultural capital is thorny and rarely clean cut. Once more, Bolaño uses interspersed metaphors of a common theme to allude to an underlying aesthetic purity that he cannot quite reach. But unlike the purity that Tinajero represents in *Los detectives salvajes*, we do not approach aesthetics from the perspective of the artist who strives for a perfect Latin American form, but from that of the critic who dedicates himself (and herself) to deciphering the transcendental truths conveyed by the artists and authors they follow.

The two most telling metaphors for purity and their relation to critical cultures come in the second and third novels of the collection, *La parte de Amalfitano* (*The Part About Amalfitano*) and *La parte de Fate* (*The Part About Fate*). *La parte de Amalfitano* explores at length a Chilean critic and Heidegger specialist who works in La Universidad de Santa Teresa. We meet him in the first novel, when three of the four critics around whom the section turns—Pelletier, a French academic based in Paris; Espinoza, a Spanish academic based in Madrid; and Norton, an English academic based in London—travel to Santa Teresa after hearing a rumor that Archimboldi has been living there. When the critics—whose presence at the United States-Mexico border clashes heavily with the landscape and lived experience of the inhabitants of Santa Teresa and whose work seems utterly trivial in the context of a series of unsolved femicides—ask Amalfitano, who moved to Santa Teresa after working in a university in Barcelona, what it was like being a European philosopher and literary critic in a small town in Mexico, Amalfitano responds that it is like being at a symphony, but only the people at the very front can see into the orchestra pit. The conductor has his back to the audience, even to the people in front. And while it is clear that cultural production is taking place and that everyone in the hall can hear the music, no one is allowed to observe the process. The orchestra, for Amalfitano, is less an invisible pit and more a natural, cultural void.

Bolaño bolsters Amalfitano's image with a corresponding metaphor based on a popular register, when the protagonist of the third novel, Fate, a journalist for a small Harlem based daily, *Black Dawn*, covers a boxing match in Santa Teresa. In opposition to Amalfitano's figure that sits in the back of a concert hall, Fate has ringside seats to a boxing match. The music in the boxing scene does not come from the ring, but from the upper tier of the arena, where all of the fans sing popular songs mixed with Norteño and Sonoran Jazz rhythms, which Fate describes as, "solemn and defiant, the battle hymn of a lost war sung in the dark" (308). When Fate looks to the arena's upper tier to observe the singing public, the glare of the floodlights used to light the ring blinds him. If in the high cultural register Amalfitano's hypothetical critic is not permitted to witness the inner workings of the cultural machine, then, in its popular equivalent, the infrastructure of the spectacle itself blinds the journalist that is there to describe the event for an international audience.

Paralleling the point-counterpoint style that Bolaño uses to weight his characters, the string of metaphors comments on the miscommunication between large subjective groups for whom culture acts as a mediator and the distortion that occurs when a cultural artefact enters into massive circulation. If *Los detectives salvajes* hinges on Bolaño's inability to depict a pure Latin American literary aesthetic for a large audience, *2666* presents the claim that, even if Bolaño were, in fact, capable of condensing Latin American aesthetics into a pure form, the agents that make up the political economy of cultural circulation would undoubtedly distort that purity. This impossibility of sight is redoubled and portrayed as a collective problem rather than just that of the Latin American artist. Pure form does not simply emanate from the Sonora Dessert, as it would in *Los detectives salvajes*, but is layered over the disjointed presence of high European aesthetics. Like the outsider looking in for Amalfitano and the insider looking out for Fate, the failure of the aesthetic gaze is reciprocal.

Bolaño uses two metaphorical currents to critique the agents of world literature in *2666*, both of which resonate on an aesthetic and violent level: the first consists of the presence of a singular, universal form in Santa Teresa, made most explicit through Amalfitano's obsession with a geometry book, *Testamento geográfico*, and the second of gatekeepers, whether they are epistemological gatekeepers, as in guardians of the canon, or actual doormen at nightclubs, as is the case in another instance. By the time we witness to what extent Amalfitano has come off the rails in Santa Teresa, the thematic connection between his obsession with a universally pure form based on a mathematical and innate order and the presence of the three European critics in Santa Teresa has dawned on us. Just as Pelletier, Espinosa, and Norton do not fully grasp the absurdity of their presence in Santa Teresa until they are actually there, Amalfitano does not question the utility of teaching Heidegger in the Sonora Dessert until he is in the act. The aesthetic and philosophical epistemology of the four critics clashes with the lived experience in Santa Teresa, and Amalfitano pushes this existential problem to its limit. Putting Pelletier, Espinosa, and Norton's high-academic undertakings in relief against a background of hundreds of rapes and murders, Amalfitano hangs the *Testamento geográfico* on a clothesline in his back yard, where he observes how it responds to nature, how it reacts to the breeze of the Sonora Dessert. Having already attempted to establish enigmatic links between European and Latin American philosophers through geometrical models, Amalfitano's contrast between form and terrain stands in for the world literary and philosophical agents in an incongruous space. And just as the critics all question their social function while in Santa Teresa, the breeze of the Sonora Dessert harries Amalfitano's geometry book.

Wind is a constant in *2666*, which contrasts with the rigidity of social and aesthetic institutions. It represents a natural freedom that universal inscriptions in the work, predominantly literary, cannot encumber. When Norton crosses the border between the United States and Mexico to catch a flight to London, for example, she is fixated by a bird sitting atop a fence that acts as a barrier between the two countries. Wind and nature are the constants in quickly shifting geography in the collection as well: in varying instances, wind blows messages into rocks over the course of millions of years in Mexico, it artfully blows through dresses in Harlem, and it rustles trees in the suburbs of Paris and Madrid. And, for Bolaño, the critics are wind catchers, in a sense. They seek to reduce and harness what is, according to the logic of the collection, free and natural. The scene at the border crossing alludes to the freedom of the bird that the guard cannot stop from entering and exiting the country, while in a more violent encounter, the critics witness the doormen at their hotel in Santa Teresa beat a taxi driver to a pulp over a turf war, which reminds them of an instance in which, without explanation, they, themselves, attack a Pakistani taxi driver, leaving him on the verge of death, in London months earlier. The theme of gatekeepers always appears with an undercurrent of violence, and the critics' presence and academic impotence at the United Sates border brings economic and literary globalization together in a fictionalized version of Ciudad Juárez, whose femicides are not at all figurative.

When Bolaño, in the fourth novel of the series, *La parte de los crímenes* (*The Part About the Crimes*), depicts hundreds of crimes with detail and background about the victims' lives, he draws a connection between the physical entropy of Amalfitano's geometry book, the tendency for the geography of northern Mexico to harry the sanity of academics and critics there to research and teach European philosophy and letters, and the *maquiladora* project's descent into extreme violence. He reduces the global publishing industry, the academic ivory tower, and economic globalization onto one plane and forces the reader to watch as things fall apart.

Reminiscent of *Los detectives salvajes*, Bolaño maintains that there is a form that can resist the political economies of prestige and for-profit literary institutions. Laying out lists of authors, tropes, and formal aesthetics that miss the mark, only to abstractly allude to a pure and underappreciated literary source is one of Bolaño's signature conceits. He fills a text with demons and then casually refers to an angel, one that is never in a position of authority and many times exhibits physical or social handicaps. By the time Bolaño writes *2666*, this set piece feels awkward. One of Bolaño's contemporaries, the Chilean writer Carlos Franz, reads this tendency as an irreverent take on one of the two clichés of twentieth-century Latin American literature. For Franz, there are two epicenters of tone that act as models for Latin American writers throughout the twentieth century: 1) a magical realism based in the Caribbean and 2) the intellectually brooding realism centered on the Río de la Plata. Bolaño obviously gives a caustic take on magical realism, but he also, according to Franz, shows us how badly the introverted Porteño intellectual fits in contemporary Latin American reality.[5]

Bolaño's irreverence undercuts his audiences at home and abroad, his publishing house and editors, his critics, and even his own trajectory as a literary star. One might argue that Bolaño's handicapped angels have established their own currency in the market of clichés, and his insistence on a symbolism of tragic impotence may only performatively resonate with younger generations of writers. And following his "star is born" reception on the global scale, Bolaño consciously represented and chronicled the anxiety of international projection experienced previously and in parallel by the Generation of '72.[6] The tipping point at which Bolaño apprehensively gains favor in the international economy of prestige raises questions about how he might disengage with such well-trodden aesthetic avenues, no longer writing as an outsider, but as an insider looking back on outsiderness.

It makes sense, then, that Bolaño's most ardent Francophiles can only sustain the fantasy of cultural cosmopolitanism if they have not left home. Imagined literary centers can open up avenues of imagination and help work through the occasionally overbearing burden of the local. However, we should take seriously the fact that Bolaño's final work turns precisely on a collective misunderstanding of cultish literary and artistic stars by scholars and literati from all over the world. Perhaps by the time Bolaño wrote *2666*, he had given up on the idea of an aesthetic purity lost somewhere in the Mexican hinterland, but he still reminds us that compared to the breeze that has blown messages into rocks and dunes in the Sonora Dessert over eons, Paris is a mere blink of the eye.

Notes

1. For an extensive study of the debate surrounding world literature, see bibliography.
2. For more, see María Helena Rueda's analysis of the marketing of violent literature in: "Dislocaciones y otras violencias en el circuito

transncional de la literatura latinoamericana." *Revista de Crítica Literaria Latinoamericana* 69 (2009): 69–91.

3. Two of the first articles that concentrated on a sociological reading of the image of Bolaño and the questionable tactics behind the marketing of his literature are the following: Larry Rohter's "A Chilean Writer's Fictions Might Include His Own Colorful Past" in the *New York Times* (27 Jan. 2009) and Sarah Pollack's "Latin America Translated (Again): Roberto Bolaño's the Savage Detectives in the United States." *Comparative Literature* 61 (2009): 346–65. While Pollack's necessary and important argument does not allow Bolaño's work to stand alone and fails to consider his own role in cultivating the image of the Latin American poet-ruffian, we can inarguably read Bolaño's success as a capitulation of the world literary system.

4. María Luisa Fischer describes the function of Bolaño's tendency to employ moral mirror characters when she writes, "Se indica así la manera en que la imaginación móvil del narrador interpreta los hechos, a través de procedimientos analógicos. Con ellos, las historias de vida encuentran una completitud que deberíamos llamar poética, en el sentido de ordenarse por contraste condenación, como unidades móviles en un espacio textual. Con ellos, las historias de vida encuentran una completitud que deberíamos llamar poética, en el sentido de ordenarse por contraste y condensación, como unidades móviles en un espacio textual" (157). This quote is taken from: Patriau, Paz Soldán & Gustavo Faverón. *Bolaño Salvaje*. Barcelona: Editorial Candaya, 2008.

5. This is a summary of a talk that Franz gave on trends in contemporary Latin American literature at the University of Cambridge on October 24, 2010. The event was entitled "Four Visions on Contemporary Latin American Literature" and also included Santiago Roncagliolo, Jordi Soler, and Juan Gabriel Vásquez.

6. For a study on "The Generation of '72," see Nicholson and McClennen in the bibliography.

Works Cited

Agustín Pastén, José. "De la institucionalización a la disolución de la literatura en *Los detectives salvajes*, de Roberto Bolaño." *Revista canadiense de estudios hispánicos* 33.2 (2009): 423–46.

Appiah, Kwame Anthony. *Cosmopolitanism*. London: Penguin, 2006.

Bolaño, Roberto. *2666*. Barcelona: Anagrama, 2004.

_____. *2666*. New York: Farrar, Strauss & Giroux, 2008.

_____. *Amberes*. Barcelona: Anagrama, 2002.

_____. *Amuleto*. Barcelona: Anagrama, 1999.

_____. *Los detectives salvajes*. Barcelona: Anagrama, 2000.

_____. *Entre paréntesis: ensayos, artículos y discursos (1998–2003)*. Ed. Ignacio Echevarría. Barcelona: Anagrama, 2004.

_____. *Estrella distante*. Barcelona: Anagrama, 1996.

_____. *La literatura nazi en América*. Barcelona: Seix Barral, 2005.

_____. *Monsieur Pain*. Barcelona: Anagrama, 1999.

_____. *Nocturno de Chile*. Barcelona: Anagrama, 2007.

_____. *Putas asesinas*. Barcelona: Anagrama, 2001.

Casanova, Pascale. *The World Republic of Letters*. Cambridge, MA: Harvard UP, 2004.

Damrosch, David. *What Is World Literature?* Princeton, NJ: Princeton UP, 2003.

Dove, Patrick. "The Night of the Senses: Literary (Dis)Orders in *Nocturno De Chile*." *Journal of Latin American Cultural Studies* 18.2 (2009): 141–54.

English, James F. *The Economy of Prestige: Prizes, Awards, and Circulation of Cultural Value*. Cambridge, MA: Harvard UP, 2005.

Hoyos, Héctor. *Beyond Bolaño: The Global Latin American Novel*. New York: Columbia UP, 2015.

López-Calvo, Ignacio, ed. *Roberto Bolaño: A Less Distant Star*. London: Palgrave Macmillan, 2015.

Manzoni, Celina. "Biografías mínimas/ínfimas y el equívoco del mal." *Roberto Bolaño: La escritura como tauromaquia*. Buenos Aires: Corregidor, 2002.

Mignolo, Walter. *Local Histories/Global Designs: Coloniality, Subaltern Knowledge, and Border Thinking*. Princeton, NJ: Princeton UP, 2000.

Moretti, Franco. *Signs Taken for Wonders: Essays in the Sociology of Literary Forms*. London: Verso, 1988.

_____. "Conjectures on World Literature." *New Left Review* 1 (Jan–Feb 2000): 54–68.

Nicholson, Brantley & Sophia McClennen. *The Generation of '72: Latin America's Forced Global Citizens*. Raleigh, NC: A Contracorriente Press, 2013.

O'Bryen, Rory. "Writing the Ghosts of Pierre Menard: Authorship, Responsibility and Justice in Roberto Bolaño's *Distant Star*." *Roberto Bolaño: A Less Distant Star*. Ed. Ignacio López-Calvo. London: Palgrave Macmillan, 2015. 17–34.

Patriau, Paz Soldán and Gustavo Faverón. *Bolaño Salvaje*. Barcelona: Editorial Candaya, 2008.

Pollack, Sarah. "Latin America Translated (Again): Roberto Bolaño's *The Savage Detectives* in the United States." *Comparative Literature* 61 (2009): 346–65.

Rohter, Larry. "A Chilean Writer's Fictions Might Include His Own Colorful Past." *New York Times*. The New York Times Company, 27 Jan 2009. Web.

Rueda, María Helena. "Dislocaciones y otras violencias en el circuito transncional de la literatura latinoamericana." *Revista de Crítica Literaria Latinoamericana* 69 (2009): 69–91.

Siskind, Mariano. *Cosmopolitan Desires. Global Modernity and World Literature in Latin America*. Evanston, IL: Northwestern UP, 2014.

The Other America: Influence of US Literature in Roberto Bolaño's Writing_____

José Javier Fernández Díaz

Roberto Bolaño had a vested interest in creating systems, networks of authors and books interconnected by boundaries that occasionally only he knew about. He has been considered the link between the Western canon and more peripheral forms of literature. It is precisely the breadth of his references that has made his works contemporary classics (Echevarría, "Bolaño Internacional"). This chapter aims to explore one of the common places in the author's critical reception: the influence[1] of US literature in his works. Despite obvious differences, from themes to tone and approach, names such as Edgar Allan Poe, Phillip K. Dick, Thomas Pynchon, or the Beats are frequently associated with him (Corral 36). Nevertheless, until recently, there was not any academic research on these influences, in contrast with the influence of other texts from the Western canon (Cáceres 21) or contemporary French literature (Bolognese 227–31). After the elaboration of a register of the more than one hundred explicit citations of US authors, this work reveals not only the names of these US authors, but also a new approach to Bolaño's works and criticism.[2]

These findings are structured in four parts: first, a focus on Bolaño's biographical context that dispels the myth of him as a noble savage. Instead, it postulates him as a learned writer; second, a systematization of the influences of US authors on the Chilean novelist through the explicit mentions he carries out and his devotion to lists of names; third, the drafting of a map of those influences, establishing its position and the values he attaches to each of the writers, with William S. Burroughs as one of his main models; and finally, the synthesis of a guide of Bolaño's style and literary motifs working in an intertextual dialogue with the US literary tradition.

The Portrait of the Noble Savage

Eleven years after his death, the reception and public image of Bolaño has suffered several mutations.[3] After the publication of *2666* and the growing interest in Bolaño abroad, particularly in the United States, a dichotomy between his fame and his literary values was created. It is fair to say that his personal charisma built a myth where his works were considered the product of a full-throttle life, nurtured by wild events, rather than the product of voracious reading or, perhaps more accurately, of being a connoisseur of the classics. In contrast to other biographical sketches, I propose to focus on the social context of his life and works.[4] As a member of the incipient Chilean middle class of the 1950s (Maristain 89), his home lacked a library where he could have been initiated into the world of literature: "I came from two families: one carrying five hundred years of constant and rigorous illiteracy and the other, my mother's, three hundred years of indolence"[5] (Braithwaite, *Bolaño por sí mismo* 34). From Bolaño's perspective, the art of writing is a way of self-fulfillment and a source of empowerment (*Entre paréntesis* 312). We find examples of this in many of his characters, including Carlos Wieder, from *Distant Star*, and Monsignor Ibacache, from *By Night in Chile*. In this sense, Bolaño's life is an example of the cultural democratization of the country. It can be read as the story of how the son of a truck driver and a primary school teacher finally achieves recognition as a writer, especially after his death. Still, it is convenient to nuance this statement, as I would not like to simplify his literary achievements through an edifying tale. My point is to consider all the factors that helped him fulfill a vocation. He left school early in life in order to commit himself full time to literature. This fact not only conditions his self-taught character, but also contributes to explain his placement on the margins and his will to become an outsider (Ríos Baeza 11–27).

The main conclusion is that Bolaño was more of an artisan than a savage. One just needs to note that, in a period of thirteen years, he published eleven novels. In contrast to several critics' comments, this is not just a case of a late genius, but the result of a creative methodology and of many years of an almost Spartan work discipline

(*Entre paréntesis* 331). This methodology relies on the collage approach, as essays such as "Un narrador en la intimidad" (*Entre paréntesis* 321–24) and "Consejos sobre el arte de escribir cuentos" (*Entre paréntesis* 324–26) imply. Furthermore, his notebooks, exhibited in *Archivo Bolaño 1976–2003*, showcase how he worked simultaneously on different manuscripts, taking arguments or ideas from the daily press or literally transforming or revisiting other books, in the same way as Borges did (*Entre paréntesis* 342).

As a result, Bolaño's works follow a strategy that could be labeled "fragmentary composition" and is built on three ideas: first, John Barth's notion of "literature of exhaustion," saturated by references to other authors and books; second, the author's playful perspective of these references; and third, the understanding of his works as a whole, a global vision of his life's works, which has resemblance precedent in Burroughs's books. The first aspect derives from Pozuelo Yvancos's essay on late twentieth-century fiction (35). It proves how, under Borges's influence and as part of contemporary narrative trends, Bolaño cites a wide range of names and references. It is not a metafictional approach, but a re-creation of Borges's works, where every aspect of life is subjected to a literary approach.

The second aspect revises Bloom's concept of the "anxiety of influence" and its application to Bolaño's poetics. If Bloom postulated that every author experiences an anxiety toward his predecessors (18), in Bolaño's case there is a different attitude: a sense of playfulness and invitation to the reader to guess these literary referents. Influence means joy rather than anxiety, as it creates a textual space where the juxtaposition of different narratives becomes possible. A good example of this can be found in *Nazi Literature in the Americas*, where different aesthetics and proposals cohabitate, from the homages to Poe (18–22) to the presence of the Beat poets (147–50) and the chapters dedicated to science fiction (109–21).

The third and last aspect is the idea of his work as an inter-linked universe. According to Burroughs, one of the major influences on Bolaño, each of his books can be conceived of as a piece of a jigsaw puzzle, requiring the reader to complete its deeper meaning. The Chilean author develops a similar dynamic by which his books, as with the works by Burroughs, evolve into variations on recurrent themes and characters. Furthermore, in some cases, there is a dialogue among them where the reader is offered different versions of the same story. I argue that what Ignacio Echevarría named "literatura fractal" ("Bolaño extraterritorial" 443) could be the product of the reading and influence of Burroughs, especially his *Nova Trilogy* and his experiments with the *Cut-up* and *Fold-In* techniques.[6] In both authors' bibliographies, life and literature are articulated in narrative fragments, with elements that travel from one book to another, are told in exactly the same way, and display a closed universe. In this sense, Bolaño himself mentions: "To understand one [of my books] you have to read all the others too, because they all refer to one another" (Braithwaite 127).

The Other America: The Evidence of the Explicit

One of Bolaño's most remarkable features as a narrator is his tendency to make lists of writers, which he uses as a simulation of storytelling. Thus, we find the following description of Nicasio Ibacache in *Distant Star* about:[7] "a very close friend of Neruda, before Huidobro, Gabriela Mistral's correspondent and favorite target of Pablo de Rokha and discoverer (according to him) of Nicanor Parra" (45). For this reason, I elaborated a list of the more than one hundred explicit citations of US authors extracted from his most acclaimed works.[8] The analysis verifies the importance of the influence and the substantial volume of explicit citations in his books, especially in his first novels. There is also an evolution throughout his career. Taking aside *Entre paréntesis*, the lists and the explicit mentions decrease as his production grows. *Nazi Literature in the America*s (1996), perhaps due to its encyclopedic nature, is the one containing more references. In *The Savage Detectives* (1998), the reader can find the longest list—there are three pages exclusively naming authors related to infrarrealism (218–20), but not as many authors as in the former example. Paradoxically, *2666*, his largest novel and one with a writer (Archimboldi) as its protagonist, contains fewer mentions. A possible explanation is his maturation as a writer. As

Bolaño grows and undertakes more ambitious projects, he does not have the need to quote other writers' names.

Then, one question arises: why the need of splashing his novels with so many names? One could understand it as a symbol of the impossibility of languages to encompass the world (Solotorevsky 163–71). It appears as an attempt to condense literature: a taxonomy of names and authors losing its sense by accumulation. However, its recurrent nature denies the possibility of a random use of these lists. The Chilean writer's works seem to be sustained by these lists of writers, which leads us to other reasons, such as an attempt to display his readings. Another motivation could be the invocation of different authors in order to find a dignified position among them (Manzoni 335–57). The last and perhaps the most plausible reason would be to consider the lists as part of his biographical and literary experience. From this perspective, Bolaño does not just want to exhibit his vast culture, but also to look for the reader's complicity through a shared reading experience. These mentions are a passport and an invitation to other books. In this sense, he is mainly addressing poets, novelists, philosophers, and literary critics. Proportionally, poets and genre writers (e.g., noir writers) are the ones with the strongest presence regardless of their real influence. For example, Walt Whitman is mentioned more often than any other US writer, which seems reasonable if one considers that all his main characters are poets. The explicit mention is also a way of taking over the classics, hence the role of William Carlos Williams's portrait in *Distant Star* (63–64).

Using the amount of references as criteria, the preeminent writers are the following: Whitman, Twain, Poe, Burroughs, Pound, Melville, Elliot, Hemingway, Dick, and Faulkner. Far from them, but still important are Malcom Lowry, Thomas Pynchon, and Hunter S. Thompson, all of them unquestionably part of the US literary canon. Their mention could obey, as pointed out, to Bolaño's wish of placing his works on the same sphere as those of these writers. Therefore, he links *The Savage Detectives* with *The Adventures of Huckleberry Finn* or presents *2666* as a novel coveting the literary status of *Moby Dick*, as seen in the passage of the conversation with the book-loving pharmacist in *2666* (289).

I will now outline the considerable differences between the works that Bolaño mentions and the ones that probably turned into literary models for him. In the case of Ambrose Bierce, he is only mentioned on the notebooks showcased on the exhibition *Archivo Bolaño*, but still a major influence. However, mentioning an author does not imply, due to the absence of verified links, a literary dialogue with him or her, as the next part will explain.

The Map and the Names

As previously mentioned, Bolaño has established different bonds between the Western canon and marginal forms of literature. Based on Bloom's theories, he conceives the definition of classic as the writer capable of "interpreting and rebuilding the canon" (Bolaño, *Entre paréntesis* 106). I will next present a list of Bolaño's main influences based on explicit references and Bolaño's analysis of their works. There is a stark contrast between the number of mentions of other writers and the mark they have left on his writing. For instance, although Whitman and Twain are recurrent names, the comparative analysis provides two other authors who are more likely to resound in the Chilean author's pages: Burroughs and Kurt Vonnegut.

The first one is a preeminent model in Bolaño's conception of what a writer is: he combines both a self-referential universe—characters, scenes, themes, and the groundbreaking idea of transcending one book in order to see all his production as a whole. Burroughs appears in Bolaño's notebooks early during his teenager years. In addition, he is frequently quoted in *Entre paréntesis* and news about his death are in the opening lines of a short story from *The Secret of Evil* (2007). *Nova Trilogy* and its edgy experimentalism seem to have been the seed of *Amberes*, one of Bolaño's most cryptic novels. Still, it should be noted that this particular structure and composition will not be repeated in later works. Finally, Burroughs should be mentioned as an inspiring example of how to create a legend that transforms an author into one of his own characters.

Until recently, Vonnegut's influence had not been recognized (Echevarría, "Bolaño Internacional" 191). However, his name already appears in *Nazi Literature in the Americas* (133). Vonnegut's narrators are distant, autobiographical, and have a flair for a confessional tone that is similar to the narrative voice in Bolaño's short stories. The careful reading of *Slaughterhouse-Five, Mother Night*, or *Breakfast of Champions* reveals most of the traits featured in Bolaño's books, such as *Distant Star* or *2666*. Some of them are the following: a cruel sense of humor when dealing with a controversial topic, such as Nazism; the insertion of images and graphic jokes, as in *The Savage Detectives*; or an anti-war stance featuring the candor of many of his main characters (respectively, Billy Pilgrim and Hans Reiter).

Two are the main ideas taken from Poe in Bolaño's poetic: one is the importance of composition when asking for a reader's reaction. There is a shared sense of imminence in both authors and horror seems to be always nearby. The second idea deals with characters: they are all perpetual seekers, beings of high intellectual capacity. Their lives depend on their ability to decipher the symbols of the world surrounding them, as was the case for Legrand in "The Gold Bug," Archimboldi's books in *2666*, or the poem entitled "Sion" in *The Savage Detectives*.

The eulogy of Twain comes from his attitude toward life; his sense of humor; and, most of all, his ability to write about outsiders and outcasts with tenderness. There are connections in both form and content between *The Adventures of Huckleberry Finn* and *The Savage Detectives*. Formally, there is a powerful and accurate imitation of conversational language that identifies their characters. Regarding content, Jim and Huck's escape from "civilization" matches the permanent escape of Belano and Lima from an ordinary life (Bolaño, *Entre paréntesis* 327).

In turn, Melville represents, for Bolaño, the twisted path of erudition and horror. *Moby Dick* works for him as both a novel and a symbol: it means the abyss. This is a concept the writer uses when talking about absolute evil and the dangers of literature (*Entre paréntesis* 269). Melville's novel shares with *2666* the literary aspirations of transcending the plot and propose an allegorical reading: Santa Teresa's femicide as the main symbol of the twentieth century.

The Beats, especially Jack Kerouac and Allen Ginsberg, are role models for the thinking of Bolaño's generation. In fact, Bolaño wrote a novel, *Los detectives salvajes*, in dialogue with Kerouac's *On the Road* in that there is no mystification, but just empathy for and parody of those lives consecrated to literature. In this sense, he admires poets, who seem heroic figures to him. Whitman, Pound, T. S. Elliot, or Ginsberg become names the narrator uses to situate the artistic attitude or projects of their characters, from the elegiac tone of *Howl* in *Los detectives salvajes* to the comical twist of the "anti-beatnik" Jim O'Bannon's life.

Among other remarkable influences, those by Hemingway, Henry Miller, and Faulkner should be mentioned. A comparative reading of "The Killers" and "Detectives" reveals a structure based on dialogues and ellipses. Both texts share a latent violence. Bolaño considers the author of *Tropic of Cancer* a master who contributed to his sentimental education (*Entre paréntesis* 182). His lessons are found in the Parisian episodes of *The Savage Detectives*. Likewise, Faulkner's *As I Lay Dying* or *The Sound and the Fury* are examples of extraordinary monologues that may have inspired Bolaño's narrators. Likewise, Heimito Künst's misfortunes in prison (*Los detectives* 306) may respond to a parodic version of the Benji's renowned tale.

The numerous nuances and variations used by a writer to modulate reality are the meeting point among Bolaño, Dick, and Thompson. Dick, the science fiction author, is profusely praised by the Chilean writer (Bolaño, *Entre paréntesis* 183; Braithwaite 133–38). He imitates a description of a landscape that seems to be more mental than physical. Regarding Thompson, the father of Gonzo journalism, rather than parallel universes or time-travel, his link with Bolaño resides in their use of a neurotic and sarcastic narrative voice. This made critics think about the possibilities of including Bolaño in what has been termed "hysterical realism" (Wood 2000).

Other less influential authors that could be mentioned are H. P. Lovecraft, whose characters share a common perspective of madness, and Cormac McCarthy, whose writing is reflected in Bolaño's literary treatment of violence and in his vivid landscape descriptions. Along these lines, Ambrose Bierce's use of irony could be tracked down in some of Bolaño's most bitter short stories, including "El regreso." Similarly, Raymond Carver may be the inspiration of Bolaño's melancholic tone, and Bolaño shares with Pynchon a common saturation of both marginal and learned references.

Mask and Mirrors: A Guide to Bolaño's Style

According to Ricardo Piglia, a writer's works of criticism are the "secret mirror" of his creative writing (141). Aiming to glimpse through that looking glass, this section attempts to unveil the not-so-secret paths linking US literature and Robert Bolaño's creations, taking into account "literary modalities" (Guillén 12) and literary themes. First, his texts were conceived as examples of transitional structures between avant-garde modernism and postmodern narrative schemes. Certainly, Bolaño has been considered an heir to avant-garde literature because of his fragmented narrative or his use of graphic elements (Gamboa 211–37). However, I believe that rather than a poetic proposal, it was an attitude toward literature. According to Echevarría, Bolaño mimics the avant-garde rhetoric as part of his personal vision, coated by nostalgia for a failed revolution and postmodern irony (qtd. in Maristain 186). These postmodern links can also be traced through his fascination for the science fiction genre.[9] Far from being just an "aesthetic motif" (Ríos Baeza 115–19), science fiction provides Bolaño with arguments, events, a model of narrative perspective, common motifs, and riddles for futures readers.

Second, another essential aspect of his novels is their ambiguous blend of autobiography and fiction. Instead of labels such as "metafiction," "self-fictional novel," or "faction," I argue that Bolaño's narrative is *autofictional*. I would like to use the term "art of ambiguity," coined by Philippe Lejeune and Manuel Alberca

(Alberca 15). These novels postulate different levels of textual existence. Therefore, *The Savage Detectives* and classics such as *On the Road* share a similar motivation: both are autobiographical fictions triggered by the personal obsession of a friendship—Neal Cassady in Kerouac's case and Mario Santiago in Bolaño's. In addition, the coincidence of the author's name with the narrator's, together with the invention of many avatars to play with (B, Bolaño, or Arturo Belano) is a strategy shared with Burroughs in books such as *Junkie* or *Nova Express*.

Third, novels such as *Amulet* or *2666* display the double nature of his use of the language (Cuevas Guerrero 61). Bolaño practices an almost conventional line, featuring dialogues that are very readable and have a regular rhythm. On the other hand, there is a hyperbolic line, full of oneiric images, risky metaphors and symbols: "It's kind of fun to write the word "silver" now: it sparks like an eye in the night" (Bolaño, *Estrella distante* 16). Regarding aspects of orality portrayed in his writing, the Chilean author does not draw inspiration from real-life conversational models, but from US canonical authors, such as such as Twain or Kerouac. In his quest for his own style, Bolaño avoids the literary emulation of slang or other expressions. Instead, he recreates the language so that his narrators can transport the reader, without losing his aesthetic goal, to the moment when the sentence was enunciated. In conclusion, the double nature of Bolaño's prose, colloquial and poetic, made his texts an ambivalent place: the verbal torrents of his eloquent characters contain the dreamlike gleam of someone who always thought of himself as a poet.

Fourth, there is a constant presence of humor. The same irony Melville displayed when narrating the tragedy of the Pequod can be found in Archimboldi's misadventures in the last part of *2666*. The use of comical elements in his books has a multi-purposed function: it balances the horror and atrocities narrated (e.g., the killings of *2666*), while simultaneously demanding a knowing smile from the reader through allusions or references. The mechanisms used to create this particular tone are repetitions; hyperbole; a dose of *costumbrismo*; de-familiarization; the use of graphic elements; the frustration of the reader's expectations; and, finally, a strong will of transgression.

Fifth, the "Great American Novel," a label that has been used to review *2666* (Goldman 2007) is an excellent point of departure by which to analyze Bolaño's main works. According to Bolaño, there are two structures or paths for a novelist who is hoping to write the "Great American Novel": the journey and the enigma, both represented respectively by *The Adventures of Huckleberry Finn* and *Moby Dick* (*Entre paréntesis* 269). This statement provides a field of connections between *The Savage Detectives* and *The Catcher in the Rye*; *Amulet* and *The Narrative of Arthur Gordon Pym*, *Moby Dick*, and *Slaughterhouse 5*.

As for the themes and topics of his literary world, I would consider at least three recurrent ones. The first one is the idea that failure has epic overtones. In Bolaño, the epic does not materialize a series of national virtues; quite the contrary, it is an exaltation of failure. As he stated, "Literature is danger" (Bolaño, *Entre paréntesis* 37). In his self-portrait as a writer, there is the notion of poetry as a heroic task. He is haunted by the destiny of failure that many of his adventures had, and most of all, by the death of the revolutionary dream of his youth in Chile. For this reason, his books confront the "official story" in Chile. The past is the source used by Bolaño to create a myth of his youth, but always throughout a conjectural and doubtful tale. In this regard, both *Distant Star* and *By Night in Chile* are metafictional devices designed to help readers to question the unstable nature of history.

The second topic is what Bolaño calls, in *El gaucho insufrible*, "the poetic learning" ("Literatura + Enfermedad" 146), a concept that encompasses three recurrent elements in his books: literature, sex, and illness. As mentioned, he believes that every work of art could be turned into symbol for his literary purposes. This is exactly the mechanism used in Bolaño's *Nazi Literature in the Americas* (21) and Poe's *Philosophy of Decoration*.

In turn, the narration of sex, far from being incidental, is a basic element of his novels. It is graphically displayed in almost all of his novels and it has generally been analyzed by critics in connection with X-rated films or as "degraded visual form" (Correa Pemjean 121–33). There are two ways in which sex works as a motif in Bolaño's writing. The first conceives of it as an intrinsic feature of his characters, who find in sex a way of dealing with the world. It helps to explain their motivations, as in Miller's *The Rosy Crucifixion*. It can also be understood, through Burroughs's influence, as an element related to transgression.

As to illness, more than an important biographical element,[10] it is almost a trademark of all his characters. It is also associated with madness. In this regard, Bolaño draws from illustrious precedents. Thus, the mother of all poets, Auxilio Lacouture, by the end of her monologue in *Amulet*, will be providing some intertextualities linking *The Narrative of Arthur Gordon Pym*, *Moby Dick*, and *At the Mountains of Madness*.

The third recurrent topic in Bolaño's work spreads through almost his entire oeuvre: the existence of pure evil and violence. For the novelist, evil is the inability to recognize others. In his own words, "Evil is basically selfishness narrated in different ways"[11] (Braithwaite 81). As a result, his fascination for an unjustifiable and overwhelming evil that is almost theological materializes in characters who play God. There is evidence in *Distant Star*'s main character, Carlos Wieder, whose behavior and totalitarian thinking reminds the reader of *Moby Dick's* Ahab and *Blood Meridian's* The Judge, a learned child-murderer. Related to evil, most academic research has studied the strong presence of violence in Bolaño's narrations. This has occasionally been depicted as the example and justification of some sort of political engagement in Bolaño's writing (Paz Soldán & Faverón Patriau 30). In my view, the writer's engagement is mainly with literature: he writes about political engagement in Chile's recent history or the femicide in Ciudad Juarez, but always through an aesthetical approach. In this sense, the repetition of violence is a motif whose shape has to do more with the forms of Tarantino's cinema or Brett Easton Ellis's poetics than with the social protest works of former generations. Hence, like the author of *American Psycho*, Bolaño seeks a hyperbolic and repetitive violence capable of touching a reader that has been anaesthetized by constant media exposure.

To conclude, this essay aims to be a guide and a proposal for future research. My intention has been to showcase the importance of US literature when it comes to analyzing Bolaño's writing. I devised a map of authors that indirectly reveals his analogies with other literature. My conviction is that each of his books contains traces of the precedent readings and the seeds of future writings.

Notes

1. I use the term "influence" based on Harold Bloom's *The Anxiety of Influence* and *The Western Canon*, which proved to be a major reference for Bolaño in his narrative (Cáceres 24).

2. This previous research is available in Spanish. (See Fernández Díaz 75–81).

3. An account of these changes is showcased in Corral's 2011 Bolaño traducido: nueva literatura mundial.

4. See Quezada (2007), Madariaga (2010), and Maristain (2012).

5. "provengo de dos familias: una que arrastraba unos quinientos años de analfabetismo constante y riguroso, y la otra, la materna, que arrastraba trescientos años de desidia."

6. Cut-Up and Fold-In are two complementary methods. They both consider cutting fragments from news, poems, or any kind of texts and then putting them together so they create a new meaning. In "The Cut Up Method," Burroughs unveils the practicalities of the process: "Cut the words and see how they fall. Shakespeare, Rimbaud live in their words. Cut the word lines and you will hear their voices" (Burroughs).

7. "Amigo personal de Neruda y antes de Huidobro y corresponsal de Gabriela Mistral y blanco predilecto de Pablo de Rokha y descubridor (según él) de Nicanor Parra" (45).

8. The books used for that list are as follows: *Nazi Literature in the Americas*; *Distant Star*; *The Savage Detectives*; *Entre paréntesis*; his articles and literary essays; and, of course, *2666*. In addition, I also included the proceedings from the exhibition "Archivo Bolaño" (2013) and the text *Tres*: "A Stroll through Literature," for obvious reasons.

9. Jameson considered this genre a degraded landscape or paraliterature that mesmerizes postmodernists in opposition to high literature (13). Regarding Bolaño's case, the influence of science fiction has always been commented on by reviewers as one of his sources.

10. It conditioned the writing and publishing of *2666* (Bolaño, *2666* 11).

11. "El mal es básicamente el egoísmo narrado de diferentes formas."

Works Cited

Alberca, Manuel. *El pacto ambiguo. De la novela autobiográfica a la autoficción*, Madrid: Biblioteca Nueva, 2007.

Bloom, Harold. *The Western Canon: The Books and School of the Ages* (*El canon occidental. La escuela y los libros de todas las épocas*). Trans. Damián Alou Barcelona: Anagrama, 2005.

Bolaño, Roberto. *2666*. Barcelona: Anagrama, 2004.

_____. *Los detectives salvajes*. Barcelona: Compactos Anagrama, 2006.

_____. *Entre paréntesis*. Barcelona: Compactos Anagrama, 2005.

_____. *Estrella distante*. Barcelona: Compactos Anagrama, 2005.

_____. *El gaucho insufrible*. Barcelona: Anagrama, 2003.

_____. *La literatura nazi en América*. Barcelona: Seix Barral, 2005.

Bolognese, Chiara, "París y su bohemía literaria: homenajes y críticas en la escritura de Roberto Bolaño." *Anales de la literatura chilena* 10.11 (2009): 227–39.

Braithwaite, Andrés. *Bolaño por sí mismo: entrevistas escogidas*. Santiago, Chile: Ediciones Universidad Diego Portales, 2006.

Burroughs, William S. "The cut-up method of Brion Gysin." *The New Media Reader*. (1961) Web 12 Jan 2015.

Cáceres, Alexis Candía. "La Universidad (des) conocida de Roberto Bolaño." *Mitologías hoy* 7 (2013): 19–2.

Cobas Carral, Andrea. "Déjenlo todo nuevamente: apuntes sobre el movimiento infrarrealista mexicano," 2006. Web. 27 Aug 2009.

Corral, Wilfrido. "Un año en la recepción anglosajona de 2666." *Roberto Bolaño: ruptura y violencia en la literatura finisecular*. Ed. Felipe Adrián Ríos Baeza. Mexico City: Eón/ Benemérita Univ. Autónoma de Puebla, 2010. 23–51.

_____, *Bolaño traducido: nueva literatura mundial.* Madrid: Escalera, 2011.

Correa Pemjean, Pablo Blas. "Dispositivos visuales en la narrativa de Roberto Bolaño." *Aisthesis: Revista chilena de investigaciones estéticas* 38 (2005): 121–33.

Cuevas Guerrero, Carlos. "Escritura e hipérbole: Lectura de *2666* de Roberto Bolaño." *Espéculo: Revista de estudios literarios* 34 (2007): 61.

Echevarría, Ignacio. "Bolaño extraterritorial" Ed. Paz Soldán & Faverón Patriau. Barcelona: Candaya. 2008. 431–47.

_____. "Bolaño Internacional: algunas reflexiones en torno al éxito internacional de Roberto Bolaño." *Estudios Públicos* 130 (Fall 2013): 175–202.

Gamboa, Jeremías. *"¿Dobles o siameses? Vanguardia y posmodernismo en* Estrella Distante" Ed. Paz Soldán & Faverón Patriau. Barcelona: Candaya, 2008. 211–37.

Goldman, Francisco. "The Great Bolaño." *The New York Review of Books* 54.12 (2007): n.p. Web. 3 Jan 2009.

Mandarriaga Caro, Montserrat. *Bolaño infra: 1975–1977. Los años que inspiraron* Los detectives salvajes. Santiago, Chile: RIL Editores, 2010.

Maristain, Mónica, *El hijo de Míster Playa.* Mexico City: Almadía, 2012.

Manzoni, Celina. "Ficción de futuro y lucha por el canon en la narrativa de Roberto Bolaño." Ed. Paz Soldán, Edmundo & Gustavo Faverón Patriau. Barcelona: Candaya, 2008. 335–57.

Paz Soldán, Edmundo & Gustavo Faverón Patriau, eds. *Bolaño salvaje.* Barcelona, Candaya, 2008.

Piglia, Ricardo. *Crítica y ficción.* Barcelona: Anagrama, 2001.

Pozuelo-Yvancos, José Marí. *Ventanas de la ficción. Narrativa hispánica siglos XX y XXI.* Barcelona: Península, 2004.

Quezada, Jaime. *Bolaño antes de Bolaño: Diario de una residencia en México.* Santiago, Chile: Catalonia, 2007.

Ríos Baeza, Felipe Adrián. *La noción de margen en la narrativa de Roberto Bolaño.* Barcelona: Universitat Autònoma de Barcelona, 2011. Web. 20 Oct 2012.

Solotorevsky, Myrna. "El espesor escritural en novelas de Roberto Bolaño." *Mitologías hoy: Revista de pensamiento, crítica y estudios literarios latinoamericanos.* 7 (2013): 163–71.

Roberto Bolaño's Queer Poetics_____

Ryan Long

I begin this essay with some trepidation. Approaching the work of Roberto Bolaño from the perspective of queer theory, I fear, risks simplifying the former and the latter; the former by suggesting that queer theory presents some kind of master key that unlocks the mysteries of his often enigmatic texts, not to mention the relations among them; the latter by suggesting that a practice of interpretation grounded in the work of one author and written by one critic can somehow contain the variety of critical tendencies often encompassed under the banner of queer theory, most notably feminism, gender studies, gay and lesbian studies, and sexuality studies. On the other hand, I begin this essay with enthusiastic inquisitiveness and a strong sense that the importance of not overlooking queerness in the work of Bolaño is directly proportional to what considering it can teach his readers, from general audiences to academic specialists. In fact, I am so convinced of the deserved interest in a queer reading of Bolaño that I am equally certain that anything I can say here will only be preliminary.

Though generally accepted in contemporary, progressive social and academic contexts, use of the term "queer" may still puzzle some readers. Its derogatory connotations and power to inflict harm persist. Yet its well-established, critical usage is an example of the way in which a marginalized group has reclaimed a pejorative term in order to define itself more than to let itself be defined by others, at once taking away the oppressor's moniker and recognizing the power of words. In an early consideration of the term's history and its importance for anti-homophobic politics, Judith Butler writes:

> If the term "queer" is to be a site of collective contestation, the point of departure for a set of historical reflections and futural imaginings, it will have to remain that which is, in the present, never fully owned,

but always and only redeployed, twisted, queered from a prior usage and in the direction of urgent and expanding political purposes. (19)

Butler emphasizes the tensions surrounding and produced by certain key words, like queer, whose meanings are subject to dispute and never completely controlled by any individual or group. Underscoring and working with the political nature of disputed terms, and disputes about terms, is a central aspect of queer theory, which tends to analyze such disputes as they occur in discussions of sexuality and power.

Elizabeth Freeman's more recent consideration of queerness in relation to cultural analysis underscores how queer theory continues to have anti-normative potential, that is, to exhibit challenges to that which is considered accepted and pertaining to so-called common sense. Freeman is specifically interested in examining how queer theory can disrupt dominant narratives about a global economic context characterized by a drive to normalize present-day power relations at the expense of understanding their historical formations or possible alternatives to them. Furthermore, in an attention to language similar to Butler's, Freeman queers what is often considered to be an overly traditional, if not entirely outmoded, way of analyzing literature or other forms of cultural representation, namely close reading. Associating close reading with contestation, Freeman writes, "To close read is to linger, to dally, to take pleasure in tarrying, and to hold out that these activities can allow us to look both hard and askance at the norm" (xvi–xvii). Arguing against a totalizing desire to contain and explain the immense variety of human experience by reproducing normative structures and the narratives that help justify and reproduce them, Freeman emphasizes excess over completeness, a distinction she reiterates when she separates erotics from desire. Erotics, writes Freeman, "traffics . . . in encounter, less [than desire] in damaged wholes than in interactions of body parts, less in loss than in novel possibility" (14). That which Freeman calls "queer intempestivity" (8) includes a "stubborn lingering of pastness" (8) with social and political consequences, wherein "repeating unproductive bodily behaviours [helps "deviants" use] pastness to resist the commodity-time of speedy manufacture and planned obsolescence" (9). Among the erotic encounters that Freeman discusses is to read closely, "to unfold, slowly" the texts she examines, and "to treat these texts and their formal work as theories of their own, interventions upon both critical theory and historiography" (xvii).

If Freeman's "deviants" are queer, then poets, at least according to two of Bolaño's characters who appear in three separate novels, are deviants, since they are queer, and queerly engaged in the "unproductive" task of writing poetry. In his discussion of "feelings irreducible to production and reproduction" (164) in Bolaño's short story, "El policía de las ratas" ("Police Rat," 2003), Brett Levinson emphasizes excess in the author's work, a "fragile surplus that both nature and society . . . strive to annihilate" (165). Of most interest to my queer reading of Bolaño is the way in which such "excess" feelings, activities, and thoughts are related with pastness, in general, and, in particular in the form of the failed politics of the Latin American left, especially in relation to the post-Allende Chilean diaspora. Notably, this particular form of pastness is associated with gay, male characters and homosocial and homoerotic desire in several texts that encompass the range of creative genres that Bolaño practiced, the novel, the short story, and the poem.[1]

Three of Bolaño's novels share an engagement with queerness that is also intertwined with a certain difficulty of relegating a literary object to the past, a difficulty due to what Freeman might call, "a stubborn lingering." I am referring to the 1998 novel *Los detectives salvajes* (*The Savage Detectives*);[2] the 1999 novel, *Amuleto* (*Amulet*), which is an expansion of a section of *Detectives*; and the posthumously published *Los sinsabores del verdadero policía* (*Woes of the True Policeman*, 2011). Both *Detectives* and *Woes* present a ribald parody of literary classification in the form of a taxonomy of different types of gay poets. In many instances, the passages in which the taxonomy appears are exactly the same in both novels. The character who presents it in *Detectives*, a young gay man named Ernesto San Epifanio, reappears in *Amulet*. He is absent from the section of *Detectives* that forms the initial basis of *Amulet*, but the context in which he appears prominently in *Amulet*—the return of Bolaño's alter-ego, Arturo Belano, from Chile after Pinochet's coup—is already outlined in the beginnings of *Amulet* that appear in *Detectives*. The order in which *Detectives* and *Amulet* were published is a known fact. Much less certain is the order in which the taxonomies of gay poets in *Detectives* and *Woes* were written, since the latter was only published by Bolaño's estate eight years after his death, and, according to the literary critic and professor Juan Antonio Masoliver Ródenas and Carolina López, Bolaño's widow, Bolaño worked on *Woes* from the 1980s until 2003, the year he died.[3] The return to the gay taxonomy in *Woes* might not be a return, but instead the first published appearance of the first version of it that Bolaño wrote. The queer themes that connect *Detectives*, *Amulet*, and *Woes* are all potentially returns of and returns to past moments of writing. They are clearly topics that persist, and that do not remain in the past in relation to Bolaño's oeuvre.

Trying to figure out what the persistence of queer themes in Bolaño's works might mean reminds me of the similarity shared by the concrete nouns in the titles of the novels in which the taxonomy of gay poets appear: detectives and policeman. Masoliver Ródenas quotes Bolaño in reference to the title of *Woes*: "The policeman is the reader, who tries in vain to organize this accursed novel" (*Sinsabores* 8).[4] Conceiving of the close reader as a detective or policeman is a seductive analogy, and I do not discard it completely. In fact, I believe that discussing a topic as understudied as queerness in Bolaño is detective work of a sort, whose task is to elucidate previously unnoticed or allegedly unimportant clues. Few critics have written about queerness in Bolaño, and they have discussed it either briefly or in relation to isolated texts, without engaging extensively with the valuable insights developed by queer theory over the past decades and without considering sufficiently how queer theory might serve as a means of interrelating several different texts.[5] But I am also wary of imagining the reader as policeman, since I aim to avoid a pitfall that Eve Kosofsky Sedgwick has identified in relation to queer readings of literary texts: a paranoid emphasis on sexual difference. In relation to the degree of vigilance and emphasis on disclosure that

Sedgwick associates with paranoia, she argues that theorists should be aware of "prejudicious gender reifications" ("Paranoid Reading" 11) that define in schematic ways human experience in relation to sexuality. Observing that "gender differentiation is crucial to human experience but in no sense coextensive with it" (1), Sedgwick focuses on contingency in order to avoid determinism: "For if . . . a paranoid reading practice is closely tied to a notion of the inevitable, there are . . . other features of queer reading that can attune it exquisitely to a heartbeat of contingency" (25). An important aspect of these features is excess, which Freeman and Levinson also theorize as something added to our understanding of experience that does not attempt to define the latter in complete terms.

The taxonomy of gay poets in *Detectives* and *Woes* seems excessive or contingent, in the sense of being unnecessary, in at least three ways, especially after the posthumous publication of the latter novel. First, the taxonomy itself traffics in parodic excess, as in the following list of different "types" of gay poets formulated by San Epifanio in *Detectives* and Joan Padilla, the lover of a fifty-year old Chilean widower and father named Amalfitano, in *Woes*. The list is exactly the same in both texts, and recounted, respectively, by the diarist Juan García Madero in *Detectives* and the narrator of *Woes*:

> Within the vast ocean of poetry he [San Epifanio or Padilla] identified various currents: faggots, queers, sissies, freaks, butches, fairies, nymphs, and philenes. Walt Whitman, for example, was a faggot poet. . . . Borges was a philene, or in other words he might be a faggot one minute and simply asexual the next. . . . Guillén, Aleixandre, and Alberti could be considered a sissy, a butch, and a queer, respectively. (*Detectives* 72; *Woes* 3)[6]

The image of the ocean suggests excess and denotes something uncontainable. The taxonomy, which seems to classify poets according to temperament and along a stereotypical and simplistic axis of sexual activity and passivity, plays with the totalizing impression of enumeration. A second type of excess appears from the relation between the taxonomy and the plots of each novel, in the sense that this relation is difficult to determine and seems superfluous.

One could say that the relation is less superfluous in the case of *Woes* since, as Masoliver Ródenas proposes, Padilla is arguably the main character (10), and the other principal character, Amalfitano, also engages in gay sex. On the other hand, defining *Woes* in any coherent sense is much more difficult than it is in relation to *Detectives*, for example, since the former was neither completed nor published by Bolaño. And this leads to the third type of excess: what to do with a posthumously published novel that repeats verbatim passages from a text that appeared thirteen years earlier?

At the risk of transforming excess into a clue that points toward a coherent system, I will highlight one notable difference between the taxonomies as they appear in both novels. Each taxonomy comprises about three pages, and they are mostly alike. The names of those who define them are different, as mentioned, and the version in *Woes* includes more Spanish poets than the version in *Detectives*, which includes more Mexican poets. In *Detectives*, San Epifanio is speaking to an audience at a party. In *Woes*, Padilla tells only Amalfitano. One particularly interesting change is the exchange of Amalfitano, in *Woes*, for Belano, in *Detectives*. In the midst of Padilla's and San Epifanio's almost exactly equal list of Latin American poets, both Amalfitano and Belano object to the same classification. The passage in *Woes* reads, "The Mexican Contemporaries are also queers (no, shouted Amalfitano, not Gilberto Owen!)" (5); and in *Detectives*: "'The Mexican Contemporaries are queers too...' 'No!' shouted Belano. 'Not Gilberto Owen!'" (74). Left unexplained, in excess, is precisely why there is such a vehement objection to Gilberto Owen's being identified as queer. More clearly suggestive is the substitution of Amalfitano for Belano, both of whom are characters who appear in more than one of Bolaño's texts (Amalfitano is also in the posthumous novel *2666*, published in 2004), and the latter of whom shares many experiences from Bolaño's biography, such as returning from Chile to Mexico after Pinochet's coup.[7] Furthermore, Amalfitano is also a Chilean exile.

The substitution of the man who expresses and acts upon homosexual desires at the age of fifty, Amalfitano, for Bolaño's frequently appearing alter-ego, presents a metonymically functioning centrality of queerness to Bolaño's work, which places in relation to one another several characters already mentioned (Amalfitano, Padilla, San Epifanio, and Belano) and more of whom I will discuss shortly. Queerness functions alongside and in relation to important characters and topics, such as Chile and its diaspora, without defining or explaining them exhaustively. My emphasis on the indirect and associative way that metonymy functions is informed by Sedgwick's warning against paranoid reading, and by her discussion of the "glass closet" (80), which appears in her pioneering work of queer theory *Epistemology of the Closet* (1990). The "glass closet" is a symbolic space that concentrates the different asymmetrical power relations that still tend to define homosexuality, and that speaks to the "radical uncertainty closeted gay people are likely to feel about who is in control of information about their sexual identity" (Sedgwick, *Closet* 79). The transparent, permeable space that these power-circuits surround functions in accordance with "the optics of the asymmetrical, the specularized, and the inexplicit" (80), and thus produce and sustain unequal power relations: "the position of those who think they *know something about one that one may not know oneself* is an excited and empowered one— whether what they think one doesn't know is that one somehow *is* homosexual, or merely that one's supposed secret is known to them" (80). The flip-side to the glass closet's destructive potential and its fostering of paranoid reading is another way of looking at or through it, developed by Sedgwick in her argument about how normative sexuality is inextricably linked with that which it sees as abnormal. At the close of her introduction, Sedgwick refers to a line in Proust from *Time Regained* that demonstrates a hope for knowing about the other that is not implicated in reproducing and/or enacting abusive relations of power: "'The book whose hieroglyphs are not traced by us is the only book that really belongs to us'" (63). Together with this observation is an insistence upon difference that resists normativizing categories and that allows critics to think productively about "the multiple, unstable ways in which people may be like or different from each other" (23).

The persistence of the past, the image of the glass closet, and unexpected affinities appear in surprisingly clear terms in the short story "El ojo silva" (Mauricio ["The Eye"] Silva) (2001). Its unnamed narrator shares similarities with Bolaño, such as living in Mexico City with his mother and sister in the early 1970s, frequenting the Café La Habana, having friends who are poets, and publishing books much later in life. The narrator describes the way his friend from his youth in Mexico City, Mauricio, returns to his life many years later, in Berlin, where Mauricio lives and hears that the narrator is visiting to give "a reading or a talk" (Bolaño, "Mauricio" 110). The narrator's fame as a writer allows Mauricio to return from his past and encounter him in a town square near the narrator's hotel.

Shortly after they meet again, Mauricio reminds the narrator of a conversation about the former's sexuality that they had at the Café La Habana years earlier, which the narrator has already described to the reader. The same night in Mexico City in which he tells the narrator that he is gay, Mauricio seemed, according to the narrator, "to be made of some kind of vitreous material. His face and the glass of white coffee in front of him seemed to be exchanging signals: two incomprehensible phenomena whose paths had just crossed at that point in the vast universe, making valiant but probably vain attempts to find a common language" (Bolaño, "Mauricio" 108). The following sentence reads, "That night he confessed to me that he was a homosexual, just as the exiled Chileans had been whispering" (108). The glassy figure of Mauricio and the communication between his face and the glass of coffee present an image of Sedgwick's glass closet that is very different from its earlier incarnation in the story, which describes how suspicions regarding Mauricio's sexuality circulated among members of the Chilean diaspora in Mexico City, a group that includes Mauricio and probably the narrator as well, although that fact is not made totally clear. Mauricio was different from other Chilean exiles. Unlike most of them, notes the narrator, "he didn't brag about his role in the largely phantasmal resistance; he didn't frequent the various groups of Chileans in exile" (106). In an observation about the dangerous power of the glass closet, which suggests the narrator's affiliation with the Chilean exiles, the latter writes, using Mauricio's nickname, "The Eye":

> At the time, The Eye was reputed to be a homosexual. By which I mean that a rumor to that effect was circulating in the various groups of Chileans in Exile, who made it their business partly for the sheer pleasure of denigration and partly to add a little spice to their rather boring lives. In spite of their left-wing convictions, when it came to sexuality, they reacted just like their enemies on the right, who had become the new masters of Chile. (Bolaño, "Mauricio" 107)

This serious condemnation of the Chilean left occurs within the context of the pernicious ways in which the glass closet functions in order to bolster the normativity of a group that defines itself in hostile opposition to a gay man.

The conclusion that the left are the same as the right in matters regarding sexuality is definitive. The language in this passage is thus very different from the one in the passage that I cited earlier, which describes Mauricio as if he were himself made of glass. That passage presents a moment of reflection (not conclusion) that occurs within a context of incomprehensibility and frustrated communication, a tentative moment that leads to the sharing of Mauricio's secret with the narrator. This moment of sharing creates a very different kind of affinity from the one ascribed by the narrator to most Chilean exiles, a group that, again, does not necessarily pertain to the narrator either. After Mauricio tells the narrator that he is gay, both of them end up "railing against the Chilean Left" (Bolaño, "Mauricio" 108). The narrator continues describing that night in Mexico City:

> at one point I proposed a toast to the *wandering fighters of Chile*, a substantial subset of the *wandering fighters of Latin America*, a legion of orphans, who, as the name suggests, wander the face of the earth offering their services to the highest bidder, who is almost always the lowest as well. But when we finished laughing, The Eye said violence wasn't for him. I'm not like you, he said, with a sadness I didn't understand at the time, I hate violence. I assured him that I did too. (Bolaño, "Mauricio" 108–09)

Like the reflection between Mauricio's face and his glass of coffee, the narrator finds himself reflected in Mauricio as well, and this perhaps explains his nickname, The Eye, the one who sees in others and in whom others see themselves, or who they would like to be, in this case, people who hate violence. As the narrator says at the story's outset, however, and regardless of how he or Mauricio may feel about it, "violence, real violence, is unavoidable, at least for those of us who were born in Latin America in the fifties and were twenty years old at the time of Salvador Allende's death. That's just the way it goes" (Bolaño, "Mauricio" 106).

When Mauricio meets him in Berlin, the narrator writes, "suddenly The Eye started talking, saying he wanted to tell me something he had never told anyone else" (Bolaño, "Mauricio" 111). This secret is not an open secret like the one that circulated among the Chilean exiles in Mexico City. The moment Mauricio shares it, therefore, it functions within a different relation of power from the moment Mauricio told the narrator that he was gay. Mauricio has the authority over the narrator, himself an author. Like the conclusion about the similarities regarding the Chilean left and right, the conclusion about the secret Mauricio tells the narrator in Berlin seems to be definitive: sometimes violence is necessary to correct an injustice.[8] In Mauricio's case, he has rescued from a brothel in India two young boys whose parents reject them after they have been castrated in a ritual ceremony. Mauricio rescues one who has already been castrated and saves another from that fate. The narrator writes with confidence about the violence this rescue required: "What happened next was all too familiar: the violence that will not let us be. The lot of Latin Americans born in the fifties. Naturally, The Eye tried to negotiate, bribe, and threaten, without much hope of success. All I know for certain is that there was violence and soon he was out of there" (117). As opposed to the Chilean exiles in Mexico City and their "largely phantasmal resistance" (106), Mauricio finds himself involved in an actual moment of resistance, which (even though it does not end with the ultimate salvation of the boys from the brothel, who die from disease about a year and a half later) is a significant act of bravery and defiance. The queer affinities described as part of the reflections, miscommunications, and incomprehensibilities that framed the encounter between Mauricio and the narrator in Mexico City create a relationship that functions differently from those in social spheres like the Chilean exile community. The conversation from the Café La Habana also provides the transition to Mauricio's secret, told many years later in Berlin. Queer affinity permits the story of a rescue.

A similar story occurs in *Amulet* and it involves none other than Ernesto San Epifanio, the gay character from *Detectives* whose somewhat ridiculous taxonomy of gay poets is at some less serious point along the spectrum of queer topics in Bolaño than the scenes of rescue in "Mauricio" and *Amulet*. At this point, I must also state something seemingly obvious: San Epifanio's name (which of course translates to St. Epiphany) serves as a clue to his importance not only as a repeated character in Bolaño's work, but also as a queer and queered character, if his parallel with Joan Padilla, the other gay poet taxonomist, is considered.

In *Amulet*, the narrator, Auxilio Lacouture, notes, when Belano returns from Chile, that "he was different" (76). As with the scene in the Café La Habana, perception and incomprehensibility play an important role in describing a character, this time in a novel practically defined by ambiguity and the stubborn refusal of the past to stay in the past.[9] Lacouture continues her explanation of Belano's difference in terms that also signal excess through an important repetition:

> What I mean is that although he was the same Arturo, deep down something had changed. . . . What I mean is that people, his friends, began to see him differently, although he was the same as ever. What I mean is that everyone was somehow expecting him to open his mouth and give us the latest news from the Horror Zone, but he said nothing, as if what other people expected had become incomprehensible to him or he simply didn't give a shit. (Bolaño, *Amulet* 76–77)

Clearly, Lacouture's need to repeat herself, and precisely the words, "what I mean," signals an inability to explain Belano's transformation in which the insistence upon his being "the same" seems like wishful thinking. Lacouture's description places Belano in a situation similar to Mauricio's when the latter appears to be made of glass. The narrator of "Mauricio" shares traits with Bolaño, and thus with Belano, adding another link to the queer metonymic chain of which Lacouture's description becomes more clearly a part when she writes about Belano's new friends, who sound like the young people Mauricio and his friend toasted in the Café La Habana: "he started hanging out with adolescent poets . . . who seemed to have graduated from the great orphanage of Mexico City's subway" (Bolaño, *Amulet* 77). Significantly, writes Lacouture, Belano "still kept up with one of his old friends, however. Ernesto San Epifanio. . . . What happened between them was very odd" (78–79).[10]

"Odd" is how Lacouture refers to the way in which Belano's story about being in Chile gives San Epifanio the strength to seek Belano's help. Lacouture invents stories about Belano in Chile for an ailing San Epifanio, "and with each repetition [San Epifanio] became more enthusiastic. What I mean is that as I talked and invented adventures, Ernesto San Epifanio's lethargy gradually fell away" (Bolaño, *Amulet* 81). Repetitions and the phrase "what I mean" connect excess with storytelling just before Lacouture recounts how San Epifanio approached Belano in a bar to ask for his help, when Belano, "sat alone at a table, accompanied only by his ghosts, staring at his last tequila as if a shipwreck of Homeric proportions were occurring in the bottom of the glass" (81). This encounter is almost a parallel of the narrator and Mauricio's in "Mauricio," and it, too, connects Chile and Chilean exiles with gay characters and a rescue from prostitution. After describing San Epifanio and Belano's encounter in the bar, Lacouture recounts the adventure that she, San Epifanio, and Belano, actually lived (or so it would seem) when they rescued another young man, Juan de Dos Montes, from the so-called King of the Rent Boys, at the same time that they release San Epifanio from an implicit contract with the pimp. In her tale of the end of De Dos Montes's "nightmare" (102), Lacouture describes San Epifanio as a "homosexual poet born in Mexico (and one of the two best poets of his generation, the other being Ulises Lima, who we didn't know at that stage)" (102); she describes Belano as "a heterosexual poet born in Chile" (102); De Dos Montes as "apparently bisexual" (102); and herself as being "of definitively indefinite age, reader and mother, born in Uruguay or the Eastern Republic, if you prefer, and witness to the intricate conduits of dryness" (102). Lacouture's labeling of different characters' sexuality reiterates the association between Chile and Chilean exiles and sexuality also apparent in "Mauricio." Her own brief taxonomy also takes place alongside the paradoxical description of her age as "definitively indefinite" and the practically inscrutable phrase "witnessing . . . dryness."

Throughout the novel, Lacouture is an indirect witness to the horrors of late-1960s and early-1970s Latin America, specifically the Tlatelolco Massacre of 1968 in Mexico City and Pinochet's coup in 1973. It is hard to imagine what it could mean to witness "the intricate conduits of dryness." But the image certainly implies a type of looking that poses a challenge, not unlike the reflections around and between Mauricio, Belano, and glasses in their respective bars and respective texts. Another reference to seeing (and we must remember Mauricio's nickname) occurs in *Amulet* as part of a connection to *2666*, the novel in which Amalfitano first appears in published form, although perhaps not in written form, since Bolaño began working on *Woes* long before *2666* appeared in print. As San Epifanio and Belano approach the house where the King of the Rent Boys has set up shop, and where they will realize he has imprisoned Juan de Dos Montes, Lacouture follows them down Avenida Guerrero, which, she writes, "at that time of night, is more like a cemetery than an avenue, not a cemetery in 1974 or in 1968, or 1975, but a cemetery in the year 2666, a forgotten cemetery under the eyelid of a corpse or an unborn child, bathed in the dispassionate fluids of an eye that tried so hard to forget one particular thing that it ended up forgetting everything else" (Bolaño, *2666* 86). Excess abounds in this dense image. The cemetery's date is practically ahistorical, beyond the reach of what anyone could reasonably imagine. It appears to be an eye, since it is under an eyelid; and it is an eyelid that belongs after death or before life, in places that are condemned to lie outside of history as the result of an obsessive focus on forgetting one thing.

If queerness in Bolaño can be summed up succinctly it is as something that rejects the very notion that "one particular thing" can exist at any point in time, left on its own to be remembered or forgotten. Representations of gay characters and homosexuality in *Detectives*, *Woes*, "Mauricio," and *Amulet* create networks of associations within and among texts that double back on and repeat themselves, thereby setting up encounters of openness, action, and bravery within contexts of political defeat that appear, at first or even second glance, to be hopeless.

Notes

1. Examples of topics I did not have room to explore here pertain to a poem and an additional short story. They are the homoerotic tension between Goux and Henric in the story "Laberinto" ("Labyrinth," 2007), and the strongly suggested homoerotic connection between the arguably autobiographical narrator of the poem "El burro" ("The Donkey" 1995) and Mario Santiago, fellow Infrarrealist poet and good friend of Bolaño's. A black motorcycle features prominently in both texts in relation to homoerotic encounters. Of course, there are several other examples from Bolaño's oeuvre that lend themselves well to queer readings.

2. Since I mostly cite the English translations of Bolaño's texts, I will refer to each text I cite with its English title after I have introduced it with its Spanish title unless I quote specifically from the Spanish-language version.

3. See Masoliver Ródenas's prologue to the Spanish-language original of *Sinsabores* (7) and López's "Editorial Note," which appears in both the Spanish-language original and the English translation (*Sinsabores* 321; *Woes* 249).

4. This is my translation from the Spanish-language original, which reads, "El policía es el lector, que busca en vano ordenar esta novela endemoniada."

5. The scarce number of academic publications about queerness and Bolaño include José Amícola's article, which places Bolaño as indebted to Manuel Puig in terms of how the latter has enabled the former, among others, to address homosexuality. In his discussion of the theory of homosexual poetry in *Sinsabores*, he notes, for example,

that the book is dedicated to Manuel Puig. Amícola praises Bolaño's novel for helping to critique traditional conceptions of masculinity and for presenting sexuality as mutable. *See also* Fischer, whose article compares Bolaño's figuration of the transgender performance artist, Lorenza Böttner, in *Estrella distante* (Distant Star, 1996) with that of Pedro Lemebel's *Loco afán: crónicas de sidario* (Crazy Desires: Chronicles of the AIDS Days) (1996), in the context of a critique of Chilean exceptionalism. Nicholas Birns mentions queerness briefly in his analysis of "Mauricio 'El Ojo' Silva" and other texts, presenting it, as does Amícola, as a way of critiquing dominant forms of masculinity (142-43).

6.   The Spanish original of the list of types reads, "maricones, maricas, mariquitas, locas, bujarrones, mariposas, ninfos y filenos" (*Detectives* 83; *Sinsabores* 21).

7.   For biographers' discussions of and their sources' references to Bolaño's journey to Chile, see Madariaga Caro (34-36) and Maristain (55, 98, 105, 148).

8.   See Andrews for a discussion about violence and the rescue of third parties in "Mauricio," *Amulet*, and other texts (132-42). Andrews does not address the topic of homosexuality in this discussion.

9.   See my article about *Amulet* for a discussion of the way in which the novel organizes time in relation to trauma.

10.   The Spanish original of the end of this quotation adds to the possibly queer valence of "odd": "Lo que pasó entre ellos es bien curioso" (70).

Works Cited

Amícola, José. "Roberto Bolaño o los sinsabores de la razón queer." *Léctures du genre* 10 (2013): 5–10.

Andrews, Chris. *Roberto Bolaño's Fiction: An Expanding Universe*. New York: Columbia UP, 2014.

Birns, Nicholas. "Valjean in the Age of Javert: Roberto Bolaño in the Era of Neoliberalism." *Roberto Bolaño, a Less Distant Star: Critical Essays*. Ed. Ignacio López-Calvo. New York: Palgrave Macmillan, 2015. 131–48.

Bolaño, Roberto. *Amuleto*. Barcelona: Anagrama, 1999.

_____. *Amulet*. Trans. Chris Andrews. New York: New Directions, 2006.

_____. *Los detectives salvajes*. Barcelona: Anagrama, 1998.

_____. "Mauricio ("The Eye") Silva." *Last Evenings on Earth*. Trans. Chris Andrews. New York: New Directions, 2006. 106–20.

_____. *The Savage Detectives*. Trans. Natasha Wimmer. New York: Farrar, Straus & Giroux, 2007.

_____. *Los sinsabores del verdadero policía*. Barcelona: Anagrama, 2011.

_____. *Woes of the True Policeman*. Trans. Natasha Wimmer. New York: Farrar, Straus & Giroux, 2012.

Butler, Judith. "Critically Queer." *GLQ* 1 (1993): 17–32.

Fischer, Carl. "Lorenza Böttner: From Chilean Exceptionalism to Queer Inclusion." *American Quarterly* 66.3 (2014): 749–65.

Freeman, Elizabeth. *Time Binds: Queer Temporalities, Queer Histories*. Durham: Duke UP, 2010.

Levinson, Brett. "Literature and Proportion in *The Insufferable Gaucho*." *Roberto Bolaño, a Less Distant Star: Critical Essays*. Ed. Ignacio López-Calvo. New York: Palgrave Macmillan, 2015. 149–67.

Long, Ryan. "Traumatic Time in Roberto Bolaño's *Amuleto* and the Archive of 1968." *Bulletin of Latin American Research*. 29.1 (2010): 128–43.

López, Carolina. "Nota editorial." *Los sinsabores del verdadero policía*. By Roberto Bolaño. Barcelona: Anagrama, 2011. 321–23.

_____. "Editorial Note." *Woes of the True Policeman*. By Roberto Bolaño. Trans. Natasha Wimmer. New York: Farrar, Straus & Giroux, 2012. 249–50.

Madariaga Caro, Montserrat. *Bolaño Infra 1975–1977: Los años que inspiraron Los detectives salvajes*. Santiago de Chile: RiL editores, 2010.

Maristain, Mónica. *El hijo de Míster Playa: Una semblanza de Roberto Bolaño*. Oaxaca de Juárez: Almadía, 2012.

Masoliver Ródenas, Juan Antonio. "Prólogo: Entre el abismo y la desdicha." *Los sinsabores del verdadero policía*. Barcelona: Anagrama, 2011. 7–13.

Sedgwick, Eve Kosofsky. *Epistemology of the Closet*. Berkeley: U of California P, 1990.

_____. "Paranoid Reading and Reparative Reading; or, You're So Paranoid, You

Probably Think This Introduction Is About You." *Novel Gazing: Queer Readings in Fiction*. Ed. Eve Kosofsky Sedgwick. Durham: Duke UP, 1997. 1–37.

Bolaño and Infrarealism, or Ethics as Politics[1]____

Rubén Medina

As has been repeatedly noted, in the last two decades, Roberto Bolaño has dominated the field of Latin American fiction and received overwhelming praise and critical attention. Jean Franco, in her article "Questions for Bolaño," offers an explanation for such an unusual reception and for his appeal to readers of literature. Franco astutely considers Bolaño's writing part of a Latin American generation born in the 1950s that would face several historical disasters since the late 1960s (military coups, massacres, failed revolutions, exile, state terror) and that, by the 1990s, would nostalgically see all their adolescent dreams of revolution and political engagement: "What marks this generation is that they grew up at a time of military governments when the guerrilla *focos* were being annihilated, where a dream of a changed society was no longer possible" (208). Thus in this social environment of failed dreams, politics, and disappearances, history becomes merely fragmented (or anecdotal or considered through random associations), and fiction turns into a substitute for the individual quest, corporal desire, or friendships among males. According to Franco, Bolaño's characters do not share common goals nor are they interested in pursuing state justice; instead, they are often characterized by a romantic anarchism. Bolaño, according to Franco, produces then a literature that fits well within the current post-political world:

> It is not so much that literature can do *anything* but rather that, in Bolaño's canon, there is not much left for it to do. Given that politics and religion are dead and carnal desire reduced to "coger" or "follar," literature or rather the search for the writer behind the masks substitutes as a quest. Destitute of belief after the disasters of the twentieth century, Bolaño's characters have little left to amuse themselves besides occasional friendships and trivial pursuits

including literature. Survivors of a great disaster, they are left chasing an always elusive real. (208)

Rather than arguing against Franco's analysis, I will instead reconsider that early historical moment in which Bolaño emerges as a writer. I will also address his relationship to infrarealism, a neo-avant-garde movement he helped create along with other young Latin American poets in Mexico City in the mid-seventies. This early experience (a moment when infrarealism turns politics into ethics) is central to understanding Bolaño's later approach to literature and politics. As I will argue in the following pages, ethics is fundamental to infrarealism and a central trait in Bolaño's writing. Ethics is an "attitude" infrarrealists adopt for their everyday life, an attitude that Foucault defines as "a mode of relating to contemporary reality; a voluntary choice made by certain people; in the end, a way of thinking and feeling; a way, too, of acting and behaving that at one and the same time marks a relation of belonging and presents itself as a task" (309–10).

Before proceeding, I should note that I was a founding member of infrarealism in Mexico City, and my identities as a poet, academic, and infrarealist inform my approach. I never had any doubt that Bolaño would become one of the major poets of his generation, but throughout the years, I was indeed surprised by the prominence that his narrative achieved over his poetry. I was not prepared for his early death, for the increasing interest in his writing afterwards, or for the subsequent cult that developed around him as a writer. For several years after his death, I turned down invitations to speak about him, but in 2010, I finally decided to do so and to reconstruct my peer's journey within infrarealism.

Bolaño's early writing period, before his commercial success and recognition as a writer as a result of the publication of *Los detectives salvajes* (*The Savage Detectives*, 1998), has been generally overlooked.[2] Given the biographical references that are constantly repeated in articles, Bolaño's prehistory has become part of the writer's legend. It is not surprising that Jean Franco would question the validity of those biographical references: "Was he a heroin addict? Was he imprisoned after Pinochet's coup? Did he really learn from Roque Dalton's assassins exactly how the unfortunate poet met his death?" (208). As part of the legend, Bolaño appears as a writer who travels around Latin America as a very young man as part of his initiation experience (similar to that of young Che Guevara in Walter Salles's film *Diarios de Motocicleta* [*The Motorcycle Diaries*, 2004], to whom he has been compared). Then, back in Mexico City, he creates the neo-avant-garde infrarealist movement before arriving in Barcelona two years later. There, he leads quite a lonely, anonymous life, writing poetry and novels, until fame transforms him into a literary phenomenon. In this approach, the figure of the poet or his activity as a poet is merely circumstantial or temporal; at best, it represents the road Bolaño has to travel in order to discover his talent for fiction. Yet, if we consider Bolaño's writing within infrarealism's ethics and aesthetics, his trajectory as a writer becomes a clearer political project. In fact, Bolaño's writing cannot be separated from infrarealism or from the group's ethics, particularly in that Bolaño was instrumental in articulating an ethical and aesthetic approach to writing in his 1976 manifesto "Déjenlo todo, nuevamente" ("Leave Everything Behind, Again").

The figure of the poet is central to the infrarealists' activity. For infrarealism, poetry resists being part of the game (the market) and can manage to have a full life outside the literary establishment; the poet, therefore, fully embodies contemporary rebellion. Bolaño considers himself first and foremost a poet, and by the time he leaves Mexico in 1977, he has published his long poem *Reinventar el amor* (*Reinventing Love*, 1976); has a couple of unpublished poetry collections, including one entitled *Overol Blanco y otros poemas* (*White Overall and Other Poems*), and another one, in collaboration with Bruno Montané, titled *Gorriones cogiendo altura* (*Sparrows Gaining Altitude*) (Bolaño's collection is entitled *Visión pornográfica del capitalism* [*Pornographic View of Capitalism*]); and has submitted for publication an anthology of Latin American poetry, *Muchachos desnudos bajo el arcoiris de fuego* (*Naked Boys Under the Rainbow of Fire*). The poet, as his long poem *Reinventing Love* indicates, wants to grasp social totality through the many fragments that the lyrical subject observes in his surroundings: "All of a sudden everything exists beyond the startled eye... All of a sudden everything weighs on the back... All of a sudden everything exists between the vegetables and the flies of the markets in ruins..., All of a sudden everything takes on substance and appears..."[3] (19–24). Within that observation, the poem discloses the intense and difficult relationship between young lovers and social reality:

> The poet is a Parrot, the poet is a Monkey, the poet is a Lizard.
> And the space of my mind was populated by planets that sang:
> Flowers to eat, violent flowers dragged by the wind.
> The desperate recognize one another in the night and embrace.
> My dream is a music that is recognized in adventure.
> Happiness and not humiliation.
> I saw children of prehistoric towns wish me luck with their hands raised
> or ask me for a soda water while the *Lulú Refreshments* truck
> got lost amidst the sunshine of the road, inexorably.
> Little volcanoes on the shore of life
> Little delicate trees on the shore of panic.
> Because today the heart rests, hard and deep,
> on the tongue of monsters"[4] (22)

The poem ends expressing uncertainty about reinventing love in the future:

> And if I don't love you why do I count the beds where we have fornicated?
> And love will come with Class Struggle
> at a decisive point
> > Bang! Bang!
> > We come from infrareality. Where are we going?[5] (24)

As I have argued elsewhere,[6] Bolaño is a poet who resorts to writing fiction (short stories and novels) with the purpose of broadening his income sources. Over the years, he originally and creatively transfers his neo-avant-garde poetics to the writing of fiction, developing one of the most unusual narrative oeuvres since

---

the so-called Latin American Boom. Since his arrival to Barcelona in 1977, Bolaño continues to fill notebooks with poems and notes on what he is reading and all that draws his attention. The notebooks he eagerly writes on, represent, since the early 1970s, a kind of diary in which the infrarealist poet records diverse aspects of his everyday life, such as his adventures with fellow infrarealist poets, notes on travels, readings and aesthetics issues, dreams and nightmares, as well as poems, his own stories, or stories that his friends share with him. Within a single week, Bolaño would write, for example, about the Paris Commune's writers, *Les pas perdus* (*The Lost Steps*) and the surrealist manifestos, Witold Gombrowicz, infrarealists' storming into public poetry readings, and the daily conversations with them during the long night walks throughout Mexico City. Such writing reveals two traits of his personality and writing activity. On the one hand, there is an evident obsession with recording every aspect of his life that he finds meaningful; on the other, an interest in extreme and extraordinary situations related to life in the "dark holes" (the dark side of modernity). In connection with his subsequent novels, these notebooks configure a creative exercise of fragmented and apparently random writing—not linear or successive due to the physical limitations of the notebooks—in which he writes, with precision and clarity, digressions, news, and anecdotes from his friends that call for a storyline. His notebooks, often characterized by the presence of digressions, represent embryonic forms of his stories. Yet these are not direct transcriptions, as in the case of Jack Kerouac.

During the 1980s and the first part of the 1990s, Bolaño's lifestyle is similar to the one he had in Mexico. His approach to living is intimately connected to his attitude and identity as a marginal and unknown writer, far removed from an easy and comfortable middle-class life, and refusing to belong or to be integrated into the literary structures of power, with all their perks. Bolaño, then, accepts the jobs that are available to him in Barcelona—selling costume jewelry, unloading freighters, working in the harvest or as a night watchman in a campground—and writes whenever he has time or for a couple of months whenever he has enough savings from those jobs. During those years in Spain, Bolaño continues to send his poems to literary competitions, as he did in Mexico. His existence is precarious, but the poet does not need much as long as he can read and write; he only needs a place to sleep, eat, some money to help his mother, buy books (if he cannot steal them), and go to the movies or to a bar with friends. As his letters to fellow infrarealists indicate, his life is characterized by anti-consumerism and a material minimalism. Notably, however, Bolaño seeks additional income by submitting, with positive results, short novels such as *Consejos de un discípulo de Morrison a un fanático de Joyce* (*Advice for a Morrison Disciple from a Joyce Fanatic*, co-authored with Antoni García Porta in 1984) and *La pista de hielo* (*The Skating Rink*, 1993) to literary competitions. In 1984, he wins the Ámbito Literario Narrative Competition, and in 1993, he receives the Félix Urabayen Narrative Prize for *La senda de los elefantes* (which he later published under the title of *Monsieur Pain*). Bolaño's narrative, in this context and as part of his entire writing activity, represents a tool for additional income. Yet, his novels and short stories develop the ethical and aesthetic concerns expressed in his poetry, as well as his particular approach to reality and literature. From 1992 on, Bolaño is fully dedicated to writing—now with the additional responsibility of having to provide for his first child—but it is not until the publication of *La literatura nazi en América* (*Nazi Literature in the Americas*, 1996) in a commercial publishing house that the poet and narrator can begin to sell his manuscripts instead of sending them to literary competitions.

Bolaño's entry into the publishing market and his success as a writer do not change his writing, worldview, or ethical stance. It is true that, as a recognized writer with an increasing prestige since the publication of *The Savage Detectives* and the Rómulo Gallegos Award (1998), Bolaño made some controversial and paradoxical statements about writers he considered important or whom he abhorred. At this point, Bolaño feels and acts like a literary protagonist, and he meticulously articulates an alternative approach to narrative in various brief essays that were later collected in *Entre paréntesis: ensayos, artículos y discursos, 1998–2003* (*Between Parenthesis:*

Essays, Articles and Speeches, 1998–2003). He identifies several writers from his generation, whom he considers part of a new fiction, such as Pedro Lemebel, Rodrigo Rey Rosa, Horacio Castellanos Moya, Juan Villoro, César Aira, Rodrigo Fresán, among others. Such a leading role was not new for Bolaño, as he did the same in a 1976 article on poetry published in the literary magazine *Plural*, where he proposed a list of poets that, for him, represented the new Latin American poetry. Bolaño also creates, in his narrative, his own myth as a writer through the character and alter ego Arturo Belano (the narrator in his main novels). In doing so, he assumes a privileged position in the literary construction of infrarealism, for his own benefit. In fact, in various interviews, he reduces infrarealism to a movement made up by Mario Santiago Papasquiaro and himself and considers it a prehistoric Mexican experience, even though in the mid-1990s he still publishes the poetry collection *El último salvaje* in Mexico City and is aware of the existence of a growing and active contingent of infrarealists there. In any case, Bolaño never tried to create his own literary mafia or to become part of one, and neither did he pursue a position within cultural institutions for personal benefit, or use his own literary prestige and power to have his friends' works published or to destroy a rising writer. Moreover, all his writing is characterized by the constant and virulent critique of the literary institution. It is an exploration of ethical questions and diverse forms of narrating the twentieth century's chasm and brutality. In this sense, Bolaño, like the other members of infrarealism in Mexico City and in the diaspora, never abandons the ethical principles of the neo-avant-garde movement.

Infrarealism emerges in 1975, bringing together a group of several Latin American young poets living in México.[7] It proposes a unification of poetry and life, a new ethics for writing, a constant movement between the margin and the center, a rupture with the traditional *modus operandi* of poets, and a nomadic existence. In the social context, the emergence of infrarealism coincides with the massification of higher education in Mexico after 1968, resulting from the mass migration from the countryside to the city during the previous two decades; the increasing politicization and polarization of Latin American culture in the 1970s; the initial euphoria for the Cuban Revolution and the critique of Stalinism; the growing consciousness of the middle class; and the subaltern groups' disappointment with local modernity and its cosmopolitans (Paz's creed, "For the first time in our history, we are contemporaries of all mankind" [194]); and the complicity of the official left. Those years also see the birth of a new conception of the body, desire, and sexuality; a significant change in the perception of the sexual and ethnic Others; a critique of the left from the left; and the collapse of the boundaries between high and popular culture. Infrarealists pay close attention to these changes and subjective formations and seek to create a new structure of feelings. Their particular interest lies in pursuing a new relation between the poet and the reader/listener, and in creating a different image of the poet, shaped by the interaction between center and the margin, and the rejection of hegemonic forms of writing.

From its beginnings, infrarealism is not only a movement that opposes a poetic tradition, but, more broadly, it is a movement against the literary and cultural establishment. Thus infrarrealism questions dominant conceptions of the poet, language, and poetry, including traditions from which it emerges, as well as its mechanisms of expression and legitimacy. One of the main tenets of infrarrealism is the rejection of the traditional practice by Mexican writers throughout the twentieth century of depending upon the State by pursing job positions in their institutions. This was conceived of as a way to facilitate their writing activity. Infrarrealism considers this *modus operandi* a way to destroy the poet's true creativity, reproducing instead literary hegemony and literary groupings of power. Thus infrarealism seeks to break up with such dependency and with the image of the writer as a social climber or as apolitical. As Bolaño noted in his 1976 manifesto, infarrealism is quite aware of the most appealing avant-garde movements of the first part of the twentieth century that end up integrated into the official canon. They become part of a stable, complacent, and renowned literary family. Two of these movements are Dada and surrealism, which form an additional chapter in European literary history. Infrarealists are attracted to their virulent and radical approach to artistic practices, which results in a new power strategy and aesthetic exploration. Even André Breton lamented seeing all Dada's activity and rebellion reduced to the bookstore's store window. Infrarealism is conscious of not being or becoming a mere movement of aesthetic renewal or an adolescent expression of rebellion disputing the symbolic power of the Father. For infrarealists, poetry and the poem as an neo-avant-garde practice are not the only battleground; they also resort to public confrontation in the form of book presentations disruptions, poetry readings, and literary cocktail parties.[8] In their disregard for poets from previous generations, Infrarealism assumes a patricide attitude and explores other ways to be a poet at a time when all paths appear to be closed or to end up in the same place.

In his 1976 manifesto, Bolaño calls to "leave everything behind, *again*." The main thing to abandon, in his view, is the path that each generation of young poets chooses in search for recognition, literary godfathers, social position, publications, and acceptance into the dominant tradition and literary power groups. Bolaño challenges young poets to overcome their fear of losing privileges, social comfort, and dependency. Given their ethics and marginal position, poets embody an absolute Otherness and difference. In Bolaño's own words,

> —The infrarealists propose Indianism to the world: a crazy, timid Indian.
> —A new lyricism that is beginning to grow in Latin America sustains itself in ways that never cease to amaze us. The entrance to the work is the entrance to adventure: the poem as a journey and the poet as a hero who reveals heroes. Tenderness as an exercise in speed. Breathing and heat. Experience shot, structures that devour themselves, insane contradictions. (7)
> If the poet is interfering, the reader will have to interfere for himself. 'erotic books full of misspellings'

The poet not only emerges from a different social background and experience, but that difference becomes a guide marking her or his life:

These are hard times for poetry, some say, sipping tea, listening to music in their apartments, talking (listening) to the old masters. These are hard times for mankind, we say, coming back to the barricades after a workday full of shit and tear gas, discovering/creating music even in apartments, spending all day watching the cemeteries-that-expand, where they hopelessly drink a cup of tea or get drunk on pure rage or the inertia of the old masters. (7–8)

Infrarealism conceives of this new ethics as transformative because it represents a rupture with the "normative" modus in which culture operates in society. Such ethics, informing each of the writer's actions and defining her/his political and material position in society, has been absent in art production regarding artist's agency and social positioning even in the earlier avant-garde.

It has been noted that Bolaño, in his 1976 manifesto, takes up Breton's declaration "Lâchez tout." That which has not been noted, however, is the strategic way Bolaño uses such a statement in order to underscore another moment of radical rupture that affects infrarealism in the mid-1970s. Included in *Les pas perdus*, Breton's text is part of a series of testimonies and reflections on the avant-garde, which rationalizes his breakup with Dada, all the while setting forth various aesthetic elements of surrealism. Breton proposes a nomadic attitude for the poet and urges him/her to experiment the intellectual, mental, and everyday imbalances in order to find a more profound revolution whose purpose is to break the boundaries between the private and the public, fantasy and reality, dream and reason. These activities would produce a new subjectivity. "Lâchez tout" ends with the following declaration, summing Breton's breakup with Dada:

Leave Everything.
Leave Dada.
Leave your wife, leave your mistress.
Leave your hopes and fears.
Drop your kids in the middle of nowhere.
Leave the substance for the shadow.
Leave behind, if need be, your comfortable life and promising future.
Take to the highways. (78–79)

Breton is highly critical of Dada's anarchism and its non-dialectical opposition to every art and literary activity. He finds a lack of efficiency in the *dictadure de l'espirit* (dictatorship of the spirit), as Tzara defines Dada. Breton argues, instead, that he is most interested in the permanent transformation of the human being ("*je songe à ce que je puis encore devenir* [I'm thinking of what I could still become]"), which represents a way to subvert bourgeois society constantly. Surrealism thus proposes a nomadic practice (he takes this idea from Picabia) that requires the surrealist writer to give up everyday life's logic, behavior, habits, and even memory in order to inquire into other realities, all the while managing to avoid fixing them as systems and identities. However, surrealism leaves out the question of ethics as well as the social and material position of the writer. It sees art as a form of alternative knowledge and the sole space of significance. In relinquishing everyday life's logic and mental patterns, surrealism privileges the aesthetic field, and as a result, the writer remains within the same tradition he/she rejects or seeks to destroy. Therefore, surrealism's ethics are not an active agent in the avant-garde activity and do not participate in the pairing of life-art. Within the social position of the writer, there is not internal or external tension in connection with the writer's thoughts and actions. Breton's nomadic attitude does not include the writer's life (his existence as ethical subject), thus turning the surrealist adventure into a simple intellectual experience within the poem or literary text. It then becomes a literary practice with all the familiar resources (collage, ideograms, black humor, automatic writing, play) and familiar obsessions (eroticism, exploring the unconscious, spiritualism, and convulsive beauty).

A surrealist's poem or text is the fundamental place of adventure, search, and the nomadic intellect. It is in the text where artists try to unmask the conflicts and mysteries of the world. Surrealists' daily rejection of the bourgeois world is purely textual. In spite of Breton's criticism to traditional sites of culture (museums, academia, galleries), surrealism remains confined to the aesthetic sphere.

Whereas in his text "Lâchez tout" Breton highlights his breakup with Dada, in "Déjenlo todo, nuevamente," Bolaño stresses infrarealism's rupture with the historical avant-garde (mainly surrealism and Dada), as well as with the notion of avant-garde that dominates Western culture since the 1920s. Historically speaking, the interest in uniting art and politics that emerges with the Commune writers would be articulated within the Marxist-Leninist paradigm in the following revolts and revolutions of the emerging century. Avant-garde is conceived of as an advanced or leading group (intellectual aristocracy) that knows and explains to the masses everything that has been and is still to come in order to guide them toward utopia. According to Poggioli,

> the very metaphor of "avant-garde" points precisely to the activist moment (rather than to the antagonistic.) Within the military connotations of the image, the implication is not so much of an advance against an enemy as a marching toward, a reconnoitering or exploring of, that difficult and unknown territory called no-man's land, in which the intellectual is having a planned approach, spearheading "action, the deployment of forces, maneuvering and formation. (27–28)

This view in its every day implementation not only provides privileges to the intellectual leaders, but also defines the limits of the field of intellectual action. Infrarealism questions it (as was lived by several members in their political militancy) and proposes to overcome it by placing at the center of action the social and economic being of the poet as source of ethics. During the same years in which infrarealism emerges, Foucault explains this problem regarding the intellectual's theory and practice, questioning the traditional idea of avant-garde:

> The intellectual spoke the truth to those who had yet to see it, in the name of those who were forbidden to speak the truth: he was conscience, consciousness, and eloquence. In the most recent upheaval the intellectual discovered that the masses no longer need him to gain knowledge: they know perfectly well, without illusion; they know far better than he and they are certainly capable of expressing themselves. But there exists a system of power which blocks, prohibits, and invalidates this discourse and this knowledge,

a power not only found in the manifest authority of censorship, but one that profoundly and subtly penetrates an entire societal network. Intellectuals are themselves agents of this system of power-the idea of their responsibility for "consciousness" and discourse forms part of the system. The intellectual's role is no longer to place himself "somewhat ahead and to the side" in order to express the stifled truth of the collectivity; rather, it is to struggle against the forms of power that transform him into its object and instrument in the sphere of "knowledge," "truth," "consciousness," and "discourse." (n.p.)

Infrarealism knows well those who block, nullify, and distort the expressions of others, including Infrarealists themselves, in the case of Mexico. Within Marxist theory, Gramsci has an important role in questioning the rising of Stalinism inside and outside Moscow. From jail, he reformulates the concept of the intellectual by breaking apart the traditional division between manual and intellectual labor. He indirectly suggests that a professor and a miner do not join the (Communist) party simply as a professor and miner, since their own militancy would dissolve those traditional categories or professions. For Gramsci, both become intellectuals and active agents of revolution. However, in spite of his efforts and theorization, the traditional division of labor and the vertical social structures continue during the next decades, keeping privileges, hierarchies, social behaviors, elitism, and anti-intellectualism within the leftist parties. For infrarealism, ethics (defining the social positioning of the poet as well as her/his actions) becomes constitutive of politics. Infrarealism relocates the notion of avant-garde to the margins (searching for other historical subjects and political collectivities).

The following may seem paradoxical, but it is not: Bolaño is a marginal writer and consistently acts against the literary establishment. Upon entering the powerful publishing market and receiving recognition, he still continued to act as a marginal writer, viscerally rejecting the literary establishment. In his writing, he aimed to provide another vision of the literary canon. Bolaño is the guest who would not be invited again, but his presence as a writer can no longer be disregarded. Bolaño's criticism, perspectives and ethical position can be corroborated in his essays, interviews, and above all in his poetry and (short or monumental) narrative. In what follows, I provide some examples from his novels.

As has been noted, in *Nazi Literature in the Americas* Bolaño reveals the cultural, psychological and social fabric in which extremist ideologies are "naturally" expressed in society. This permeates Western culture, spoiling the modern project. The very existence of a Nazi literature demystifies literature as a space of human significance and the "sacred" order of signs. This novel shows the way various social and sinister groups provide meaning to literature, by transforming it into a form of social mobility, a masking of or escape from reality, or a power strategy. For this reason, at a certain moment, the narrator comments about a Haitian journalist:

> He soon realized that there were two ways to achieve his aim [to belong to the upper classes of the city]: through violence, which was out of the question, since he was peaceable and timorous by nature, appalled by the mere sight of blood; or through literature, which is a surreptitious form of violence, a passport to respectability and can, in certain young and sensitive nations disguise the social climber's origins" (127–28).

Thus the young and ambitious journalist chooses literature and begins to plagiarize other poets. Soon he is noticed by the powerful, who consider him a "treasured poet," and is rewarded with the post as cultural attaché in Boon. *Llamadas telefónicas* (1997)[9] is a collection of short stories that deals mostly with the marginal lives of writers and their complex relationship to the literary establishment. Bolaño pays attention to the experience of the "dark holes," which, as the narrator explains in the beginning of the short story "Sensini" are experiences of exile, poverty, the stubbornness to keep writing, the shadow of politics lurking constantly, minor and failed writers, and writers lost somewhere in the world. In many of the stories, the writing activity is assumed as any other job, but is considered "terrible," "painful," "ridiculous," and a constant challenge in which the writer knows in advance that he is defeated. And this is so because the individual activity is always minor to the devastated impositions of external/internal reality.

Along these lines, in *The Savage Detectives*, Bolaño provides a fictionalized account of infrarrealism. It is quite significant that in almost six-hundred pages the poems of the visceral realists are never mentioned or dealt with, as these are poets without poems. What is important in the novel is not their poems, but the ways they survive throughout the years (two decades) in their desire to write and dignify a new image of the poet in the second part of twentieth century. The author underscores the connection between life and art and the challenges to avoid becoming a social climber, a coward, or a cannibal. As the novel indicates, intelligence, knowledge, and sensibility are not sufficient to be a poet; rather, what matters is the ethical poetic outburst and the way one deals with everyday events. For this reason, adventure and contingencies dominate the narrative, instead of destiny. In this regard, Bolaño coincides with the situationists, who refuse to participate in the cultural establishment in order to translate poetics to everyday life and to reinvent it.

Another work by Bolaño, *Amuleto* (*Amulet*, 1999), tells us about the legendary life of Alcira Soust Scaffo (the Uruguayan mother of Mexican poetry) and, at the same time, about Bolaño's biography during his stay in Mexico. In this way, the novel also functions as a fragmented and fictional genealogy of infrarrealism (of the lost children, a concept articulated by Guy Debord). Auxilio Lacouture, in her dislocated voice, explains the generational gap between infrarealists and the poets who emerge during the Tlatelolco massacre in 1968 (as is the case of Orlando Guillén, Julián Gómez, and Juan José Oliver, all of them quite close to the infrarealists; in many ways, they can be regarded as older brothers).

Likewise, in his two more obviously political novels, *Estrella distante* (*Distant Star*, 1996) and *Nocturno de Chile* (*By Night in Chile*, 2000), Bolaño offers a powerful critique of the complicity of literature, including neo-avant-garde expressions, with state terror, torture, murder, disappearances, and cultural elites. *Una novelita lumpen* (*A Little Lumpen Novelita*, 2002), in my own reading, is an allegory of writing, particularly about the relationship between the publishing market and the writer's ethic. The plot involves a young woman named Blanca (symbol of purity and innocence), who becomes an orphan along with her brother and faces two options during her process of maturation: to become a delinquent or a prostitute. The novel's epigraph by Antonin Artaud is clearly deliberate and a clue in the narrative: "All writing is garbage. People who come out of nowhere and put into words any part of what goes on in their mind are pigs. All writers are pigs. Especially writers today." *A Little Lumpen Novelita* is the only novel that Bolaño writes on request given his recognition and success, and he clearly responds to that situation with the fictional story, underscoring an ethical position. It is interesting that ethics in the novel are associated to the term "lumpen," which identifies the writer as a lumpen, and that Blanca chooses to be a criminal instead of a prostitute. Writing cannot be reduced to only skills, precision, and exploratory form. Above all of these attributes are ethics, and this drives the narrative.

Bolaño's focus and ethical concerns do not change or are downplayed with the passing of time, but are instead strengthened. This is evident in *2666,* a novel and testament, given the fact that he was well aware of his upcoming death. He sets forth two main concerns of his life-writing: first, to secure the economic future of his children and then, to formulate his aesthetic-ethics concerns through a look into the massive abyss of the twentieth century, which in the novel is associated with Ciudad Juárez. In *2666*, four European academics search for the enigmatic novelist, Benno von Archimboldi, which foreshadows the current search for Bolaño by many academics today. Yet those four literary professors appear constrained by their intellectual and institutional limitations ("fear of the unexpected instability and of unknown spaces?") as they are incapable of go inside the dark holes of life. After two decades since his departure from Mexico, however, Bolaño once again exposes the modus operandi of Mexican intellectuals. He voices it through another Chilean alter ego living along the US-Mexican border, who is also deeply concerned by avant-garde art and the failed revolutions of the twentieth century:

> "I don't really know how to explain it," said Amalfitano. "It's an old story, the relationship of Mexican intellectuals with power. I'm not

saying they're all the same. There are some notable exceptions. Nor am I saying that those who surrender do so in bad faith. Or even that they surrender completely. You can say it's just a job. But they're working for the State. In Europe, intellectuals work for publishing houses or for the papers or their wives support them or their parents are well-off and give them a monthly allowance or they're laborers or criminals and they make an honest living with their Jobs. In Mexico, and this might be true across Latin American, except in Argentina, intellectuals work for the state. It was like that under PRI and it'll be the same under the PAN. The intellectual himself may be a passionate defender of the state or a critic of the state. The state doesn't care. The state feed him and watches over him in silence. And it puts this giant cohort of essentially useless writers to use. How? It exorcises demons, it alters the national climate or at least tries to sway it. It adds layers of lime to a pit that may or may not exists, no one knows for sure. Not that it's always this way, of course. An intellectual can work at the university, or, better, go to work to an American university, where the literature departments are just as bad as in Mexico, but that doesn't mean they won't get a late-night call from someone speaking in the name of the estate, someone who offers them a better job, better pay, something the intellectual thinks he deserves, and intellectuals *always* think they deserve better. This mechanism somehow crops the ears off Mexican writers. It drives them insane. Some , for example, will set out to translate Japanese poetry without knowing Japanese and others just spend their time drinking. Take Almendro–as far I know he does both. Literature in Mexico is like a nursery school, a kindergarten, a playground, a kiddie club, if you follow me...[10] (120–21).

To this long account by Amalfitano to the four academics who are in search of Archimboldi, Norton replies: "I do not understand a word you've said" (121).[11] Norton reveals not only a lack of understanding of the social environment in which writers live in certain societies, but also an interest in those issues as a researcher.

Within infrarrealism, poetry is the privileged genre, a literary form far removed from the publishing market. This makes the connection between art and poetry easily available. Poets can maintain that union and resist any kind of (monetary, institutional post) mediations to facilitate writing. The poet, according to infrarrealism, is "a microbe / a spoken virus," a body in flames, a Savage adolescent "driving a locomotive towards the Fine Art Palace" (Peguero 254). The poet (Mario Santiago Papasquiaro/ Ulysses Lima) is the protagonist of the ethical and aesthetic infrarealist's rebellion. Bolaño extends the paradigm to the novelist, as can be seen in the trajectory between his own large novels. While *The Savages Detectives* is about the poet's adventure and the search of Cesárea Tinajero through the model of Rimbaud (Arturo Belano is lost in Africa), *2666* configures the search of a novelist as a trip to the unknown or Nazi brutality and Ciudad Juárez.

In sum, Bolaño never moves away from infrarealism's ethics. In all of his narrative, his principles, the critique to the literary establishment, the ethics of the group, and a simultaneous position within the margin and the center lie beneath. Bolaño's narrative takes the reader to the dark holes, as he claims in his 1976 manifesto. However, the figure of the poet who embodies the artistic rebellion of his generation does not disappear from his writing. This image still emerges in his poetry, as it is evident in the poem "The Donkey":

> Sometimes I dream that Mario Santiago
> Comes looking for me on his black motorcycle.
> And we leave behind the city and as
> The lights are disappearing,
> Mario Santiago tells me we're dealing with
> A stolen bike, the last like
> Stolen to travel through the poor
> Northern lands, toward Texas,
> Chasing an unnamable dream,
> Unclassifiable, the dream of our youth,
> Which is to say the bravest of all
> Our dreams. And put that way
> How could I deny myself a ride on that fast back
> Northern bike, breaking out on those roads
> Long ago traveled by Mexican saints,
> Mendicant Mexican poets,
> Taciturn leeches from Tepito
> Or la colonia Guerrero, all on the same path,

Where times are mixed up and confused,
Verbal and physical, yesterday and aphasia. (121)

Notes

1. I want to thank Eve Pujol, John Burns, and Ignacio López-Calvo for their comments to my essay and for correcting my awkward English.

2. With the exception of two critics, Andrea Cobas Carral and Nibaldo Acero, who have explored Bolaño's connection to infrarrealism. I should add Francisco Goldman's review "The Great Bolaño" (*New York Times Book Review*, July 19, 2007) to the list.

3. "Todo de pronto existe más allá del ojo azorado…, Todo de pronto pesa en la espalda…, Todo de pronto existe entre las verduras y las moscas de los mercados en ruinas…, Todo de pronto cobra substancia y aparece…" Translated into English by John Burns.

4. "El poeta es el Loro, el poeta es el Mono, el poeta es el Lagarto.
   Y el espacio de mi mente se pobló de planetas que cantaron:
   Flores para comer, flores violentas que el viento arrastra.
   Reconócense los desesperados en la noche y se abrazan.
   Mi sueño es una música que se reconoce en la aventura.
   La felicidad y no la humillación.
   Vi niños de pueblos prehistóricos decirme buena suerte con las manos levantadas
   o pedirme un agua de soda mientras el camión de *Refresquerías Lulú*
   se perdía entre el sol del camino, inexorablemente.
   Pequeñísimos volcancitos a la orilla de la vida.
   Arbolitos delicados a la orilla del azoro.
   Porque hoy el corazón reposa, duro y profundo,
   en la lengua de los monstruos"

5. "¿Y si no te amo porque enumero las camas donde hemos fornicado?
   Y amor vendrá con Lucha de Clases
   en un punto decisivo
   ¡Bang, Bang!
   De la infrarrealidad venimos, ¿a dónde vamos?"

6.   See my article "Un poeta latinoamericano: la incesante aventura de Roberto Bolaño," *Quimera* 314 (Jan. 2010): 34–38.

7.   The group is integrated by the Chileans Bruno Montané, Roberto Bolaño, and Juan Esteban Harrington; the Peruvian José Rosas Ribeyro; the Argentine Claudia Kerik; and the Mexicans Mario Santiago Papasquiaro, Mara Larrosa, José Peguero, Rubén Medina, Cuauhtémoc Méndez, Guadalupe Ochoa, and Jorge Hernández Piel Divina. Later, in the early and mid-1980s, additional members joined the movement in Mexico City.

8.   Due to their disruption of literary events, infrarealists immediately receive general condemnation (some public, mostly private among writers), and the group retreats to the margins. During the late 1970s and 1980s, infrarealists had very few and occasional publications and public acts, and some of them started to leave Mexico as early as 1977. Yet Mario Santiago Papasquiaro kept the group active and even recruited more members for the movement during the 1980s and 1990s.

9.   Some of the stories of *Llamadas telefónicas* have been included on *Last Evenings on Earth*. Trans. Chris Andrews. New York: New Directions, 2006.

10. "—En realidad no sé cómo explicarlo —dijo Amalfitano—. La relación con el poder de los intelectuales mexicanos viene de lejos. No digo que todos sean así. Hay excepciones notables. Tampoco digo que los que se entregan lo hagan de mala fe. Ni siquiera que esa entrega sea una entrega en toda regla. Digamos que sólo es un empleo. Pero es un empleo con el Estado. En Europa los intelectuales trabajan en editoriales o en la prensa o los mantienen sus mujeres o sus padres tienen buena posición y les dan una mensualidad o son obreros y delincuentes y viven honestamente de sus trabajos. En México, y puede que el ejemplo sea extendible a toda Latinoamérica, salvo Argentina, los intelectuales trabajan para el Estado. Esto era así con el PRI y sigue siendo así con el PAN. El intelectual, por su parte, puede ser un fervoroso defensor del Estado o un crítico del Estado. Al Estado no le importa. El Estado lo alimenta y lo observa en silencio. Con su enorme cohorte de escritores más bien inútiles, el Estado hace algo. ¿Qué? Exorciza demonios, cambia o al menos intenta influir en el tiempo mexicano... Por supuesto, esto no siempre es así. Un intelectual puede trabajar en la universidad o, mejor, irse a trabajar a una universidad norteamericana, cuyos departamentos de

literatura son tan malos como los de las universidades mexicanas, pero esto no lo pone a salvo de recibir una llamada telefónica a altas horas de la noche y que alguien que habla en nombre del Estado le ofrezca un trabajo mejor, un empleo remunerado, algo que el intelectual cree que se merece, y los intelectuales *siempre* creen que se merecen algo *más*. Esta mecánica, de alguna manera, desoreja a los escritores mexicanos. Los vuelve locos. Algunos, por ejemplo, se ponen a traducir poesía japonesa sin saber japonés y otros, ya de plano, se dedican a la bebida. Almendro, sin ir más lejos, creo que hace ambas cosas. La literatura en México en como un jardín de infancia, una guardería, un kindergarten, un parvulario, no sé si lo podéis entender…" (161).

11.   "No entiendo nada de lo que me has dicho" (164).

Works Cited

Bolaño, Roberto. *2666*. Trans. Natasha Wimmer. New York: Farrar, Straus & Giroux, 2004.

_____. *Amuleto*. Barcelona: Anagrama, 1999.

_____. "Déjenlo todo, nuevamente." *Correspondencia infra* (1977): 7–8.

_____. *Estrella distante*. Barcelona: Anagrama, 1996.

_____. *Last Evenings on Earth*. Trans. Chris Andrews. New York: New Directions, 2006.

_____. *La literatura nazi en América*. Barcelona: Anagrama, 2005.

_____. *A Little Lumpen Novelita*. Trans. Natasha Wimmer. New York: New Directions, 2014.

_____. *Llamadas telefónicas*. Barcelona: Anagrama, 1997.

_____. *Nazi Literature in the Americas,* Trans. Chris Andrews. New York: New Directions, 2008.

_____. *Nocturno de Chile*. Barcelona: Anagrama, 2000.

_____. "Reiventar el amor." *Punto de Partida*. Mexico City: UNAM, 1977. 51–52.

_____. *The Romantic Dogs*. Trans. Laura Healy. New York: New Directions, 2006.

Breton, André. "Leave Everything." *The Lost Steps*. Trans. Mark Polizzoti. Lincoln: U of Nebraska P, 1996.

Franco, Jean "Questions for Bolaño." *Journal of Latin American Cultural Studies: Travesia* 18 (2009): 2–3.

Foucault, Michel. "Intellectuals and Power: A Conversation Between Michel Foucault and Gilles Deleuze." *libcom.org.* libcom.org, 8 Aug. 2015. Web.

_____. "What Is Enlightenment?" *Ethics. The Essential Works of Michel Foucault.* Vol. 2. Ed. Paul Rabinow. Trans. Robert Hurley & others. New York: Penguin Books, 1997.

Paz, Octavio. *The Labyrinth of Solitude. Life and Thought in Mexico.* Trans. Lysander Kemp. New York: Grove Press, 1961.

Peguero, José. "Callejón sin Esperanza. Contra la poesía nada / contra el poeta todo." *Perros habitados por las voces del desierto. Poesía infrarrealista entre dos siglos.* Ed. Rubén Medina. Mexico City: Aldus, 2014.

Poggioli, Renato. *The Theory of the Avant-Garde.* Trans. Gerald Fitzgerald. Cambridge, MA: U of Harvard P, 1968.

Why Didn't *Amberes* Embarrass Roberto Bolaño? The Reification of Anti-Realism and an Interest in Disinterestedness

Ignacio López-Calvo

In the second chapter of his *Roberto Bolaño's Fiction: An Expanding Universe*, Chris Andrews argues that "Bolaño's work insistently invites us to construct a figure of the author, which we should distinguish conceptually from the writer Roberto Bolaño" (x). In this essay, I use the sociologist Pierre Bourdieu's theories to contend that, while it is true that the Chilean often invites his readers to construct a mental image of the author, we should not always distinguish this author in his texts from real-life Bolaño himself. In fact, in several texts, and particularly in the opening remarks of *Amberes* (*Antwerp*, 2002), a sort of preface tellingly titled "Anarquía total: veintidós años después" ("Total Anarchy: Twenty-Two Years Later"), the real-life author does strive to portray himself (or a certain stage of his writing career) as a Latin American bohemian or *poète maudit*, hoping that the marginality that marked many years of his life will add to his credibility as a "pure" and "disinterested" writer. Along these lines, Andrews denies any sort of nostalgia for marginality or any desire to remain pure from corruption by honors and commercial success on the part of Bolaño: "I think it would be wrong to draw such a conclusion, for two reasons. First, Bolaño was closely acquainted with the practical discomfort of a marginality unsupported by cultural institutions. And second, in his work, marginality is no guarantee of aesthetic achievement or ethical integrity" (7). Yet, this is not what transpires from Bolaño's descriptions of his own life in interviews or in the preface to *Amberes*, for example, where, in my view, the recollection of his idealist youth, bohemian lifestyle, and economic insecurities (living "A la intemperie" ["Out in the Cold"], as the title of one of the essays in *Entre Paréntesis* [*Between Parentheses*] defines it) is aimed precisely at gaining credibility as a "pure" writer.

Bolaño is better known for his masterpieces *2666* (2004), *Los detectives salvajes* (*The Savage Detectives*, 1998), *Nocturno de Chile* (*By Night in Chile*, 2000), and *Estrella distante* (*Distant Star*, 1996). His eighth published novel (or novella), *Amberes*, has not received similar critical attention mostly because, among other factors, it is not as reader-friendly as the other ones. The illegibility and hermeticism of *Amberes* was apparently intentional, as evidenced by one of Bolaño's answers in an interview with Felipe Ossandón appearing in the Chilean journal *El Mercurio* on February 14, 2003:

> I like *Amberes* very much, perhaps because when I wrote that novel I was another person, in principle much younger and perhaps braver than now. And the exercise of literature was much more radical than today, because now I try, within certain limits, to be intelligible. Back then, I didn't give a damn if I was understood or not."[1]

In Bolaño's mind, therefore, the experimental form and structure of this novella reflected his view of a type of personal writing that was pure, devoid of conventions, and far from traditional, realist models in which successful communication with the reader was a priority. *Amberes*, in other words, reminded Bolaño of his youth, which he associated with radicalism, bravery, innocence, and selflessness.

In this essay, I explore plausible reasons Bolaño claimed that *Amberes* was the only one of his novels that did not embarrass him (and, by extension, why he also stated, in an interview with Mónica Maristain, that his poetry collections embarrassed him less than his prose books). I argue that one of the reasons is that *Amberes* embodies the radical, anti-realist novel that Julio Cortázar proposed in the "dispensable" chapters of *Rayuela* (*Hopscotch*, 1963), even though the Argentine author fell short of implementing his own rules in the rest of the novel, leaving the challenge for his experimental novel *62 modelo para armar* (*62: A Model Kit*, 1968). Indeed, Bolaño declared his admiration for Cortázar in his 2004 volume *Entre paréntesis. Ensayos, artículos y discursos (1998–2003)* (*Between Parentheses. Essays, Articles, and Speeches, [1998–2003]*), edited by his friend Ignacio Echevarría. Writing about Argentine literature in the essay "Derivas de la pesada" ("The Vagaries of the Literature of Doom"), included in this book, he states: "there's Cortázar, best of them all" (20).[2] In particular, as we see in another essay of this collection titled "*Bomarzo*," he admires his originality ("the most forward-looking in devising literary structures that could make strides into undiscovered territory [like Borges and Cortázar]" [316]),[3] which he finds in *Rayuela*: "My generation, it goes without saying, fell in love with *Hopscotch,* because it was exactly what we needed, our salvation" (317).[4]

Language and aesthetics have similar centrality in both *Amberes* and *Rayuela*. Whereas *Rayuela* is not known as a reader-friendly novel, *Amberes* pushes the boundaries even further, forcing active readers to collaborate in the creation of meanings and challenging them to make sense of its disordered and non-linear structure. Its fragmented narrative, rather than a story, is a collage of sketches, motifs, and drifting, marginal characters that reappear time and again. Bolaño blends together impressionistic brush strokes of different stories in a confusing manner and without paying much attention to the conventions of traditional plot or narrative perspective. While in some passages Bolaño approaches the epistolary genre, others are close to a surrealist automatic writing and oneiric prose poetry, as seen in the following passage: "With the first puff, it occurs to him that monogamy moves with the same rigidity as the train. A cloud of opaline smoke covers his face. It occurs to him that the word 'face' creates its own blue eyes. Someone shouts. He looks at his feet planted on the floor. The word 'shoes' will never levitate. He sighs" (5–6).[5] Or later, "The boss pays in heroin and the farm workers snort it in the furrows, on blankets, under scrawled plan trees that someone edits away" (10).[6]

Some passages flirt with incoherence, in part because some sentences are left hanging, seemingly disconnected with the rest of the paragraph, as if they were verses extracted from an unrelated poem. These loose sentences, according to Enrique Salas Durazo, sometimes "signal the reported speech of a character," while other times they are part "of the written notes of an elusive author working on his text" (196). Along these lines, the almost telegraphic use of asyndeton typifies the strange language of this text, which shares similarities with stream of consciousness and the surrealists' automatic writing technique: "I wanted to be alone too. In Antwerp or Barcelona. The moon. Animals fleeing. Highway accident. Fear! (*Amberes* 68).[7] And although the avant-gardist Vicente Huidobro, one of the greatest Chilean poets, was not among Bolaño's favorites, several passages of *Amberes* are certainly reminiscent of the metaphysical poem "Altazor o el viaje en paracaídas" ("Altazor or Voyage in Parachute" 1931).

Besides including what seem to be passages from letters, verses from poems, synopses, scattered thoughts, memories, and dreams ("Yesterday I dreamed that I lived inside a hollow tree— soon the tree began to spin like a carousel and I felt as if the walls were closing on me" [51]),[8] there are asides throughout the plot of *Amberes* explaining that someone applauds, thus suggesting that we are reading a dramatic text. The feeling of spontaneity and even improvisation is enhanced in some passages, where one of Bolaño's narrators, using the present tense, reviews his own life and his expatriate condition, often from a negative and pessimistic perspective. The plot also creates intertextualities with epigraphs about the end of life by seventeenth-century French philosopher Blaise Pascal and American filmmaker David O. Selznick, included before the preface and the first chapter respectively. Through all this experimentalism, Bolaño avowedly tries to avoid the narrative techniques of realism and of "bourgeois literature" in general.

There is no logical plot development or denouement in *Amberes*. Although the editors of Anagrama, Bolaño's publishing house, go to great pains to establish some sort of plot in the back cover of the edition, their summary is somewhat misleading. We find out that there is a policeman (who becomes a first-person narrator in some chapters) lost en route between Castelldefels and Barcelona; a mysterious red-haired woman lost in a campsite everyone talks about, but no one has seen; a hunchback homeless man who lives in the forest; mysterious murders that only a few locals remember; a few scattered sadomasochistic scenes with the policeman and the red-haired woman; people walking by the ocean; and a film someone is projecting on a cloth hung between trees in the forest that may hide to the key to the story. This blurb may mislead the reader into assuming that it is a typical detective novel, rather than a loosely connected collection of fragmentary sentences and texts whose tenuous plot is full of narrative silences and, as is typical in Bolaño's writing, eventually leaves the mystery unresolved. In addition, all characters in *Amberes* are underdeveloped and flat. But it is precisely the text's lack of readability, its inaccessibility for readers without the literary competence to decode complex structures, which makes its author so proud.

Bolaño, therefore, brings to fruition the anti-realist advice provided by Cortázar in *Rayuela*. This anti-realist approach is noticeable in the misleading title of the novella, since the action does not take place in Antwerp, but in Catalonia. Only chapter 49 mentions that a man was killed in Antwerp after being run over by a truck full of pigs. Bolaño blends this information with a dialogue, in Barcelona, between an inebriated man and a woman who wants to be alone. Unsuccessful communication among human beings, the topic of this chapter, turns out to be a *leitmotif* throughout the novella. *Amberes* is, after all, a metatext about language, the role of the writer, and writing itself, as evidenced in chapter 47: "All writing on the edge hides a white mask. The rest: poor Bolaño writing at a pit stop. . . ('Tell that stupid Arnold Bennet that all his rules about plot only apply to novels that are copies of other novels') (64).[9] In this passage, we first find Bolaño's self-assessment of the autobiographical nature of his own writing. He then rejects realist models and announces a quest for uniqueness and originality that is noticeable throughout the novella. Completing this approach, the "Post scriptum," signed in Barcelona in 1980, turns into a manifesto about writing as a tool for immortality as well as about the inseparability of life/ethics and writing/aesthetics:

> Of what is lost, irretrievably lost, all I wish to recover is the daily availability of my writing, lines capable of grasping me by the hair and lifting me up when I'm at the end of my strength. (Significant, said the foreigner.) Odes to the human and the divine. Let my writing be like the verses by Leopardi that Daniel Biga recited on a Nordic bridge to gird himself with courage. (78)[10]

The Chilean author eliminates the realist novel's dependence on cause and effect, turning instead confusion and disorder (rather than realist order) into acceptable parameters. As Andrews points out, Bolaño, even though he would eventually become an outstanding storyteller, spent decades trying to escape the art of storytelling, which he considered an "atavism": "He had been writing and publishing postsurrealist poetry for twenty years. He had written, but not published, *Antwerp*, in which the story is pulverized thoroughly enough to satisfy the most radical advocates of the 'new novel'" (70). *Amberes* is, indeed, as self-reflective and auto-referential as *Rayuela* and even more experimental, less linear. Within this apparent disorder, however, the implicit author and his alter ego see in their writing a representation of reality, which they perceive as always already fragmented: "All I can come up with are stray sentences, he said, maybe because reality seems to me like a swarm of stray sentences" (42).[11]

Amberes and *Rayuela* also share philosophical leanings, as they approach the topics of love and life from a metaphysical perspective. Characters that feel overwhelmed by a barely veiled pessimism, existential angst, and sense of impotence populate both texts. Thus, perhaps marked by Bolaño's precarious health and sense of mortality, one of his narrators in the second chapter confesses: "Then all that's left is emptiness" (4).[12] Later, in the eighth chapter, we read: "When you think about it, we're not allowed much time here on Earth to make lives for ourselves: I mean, to scrape something together, get married, wait for death" (11).[13] Characters in both texts also share an inability to communicate with others: "The language of others is unintelligible to me" (7),[14] states a narrator also called Roberto Bolaño in *Amberes*.

Although in the preface to *Amberes* Bolaño claims that it took him several years to write the novella, in a note he wrote for the posthumous poetry collection *La universidad desconocida* (*The Unknown University*, 2007) the author states that it was written in 1980, while working as a night watchman at the Estrella de Mar campground in Casteldefels (443–56). However, it was not published until 2002, a year before his death, when the publishing house was aware that Bolaño's fame would guarantee its sales. That he uncritically describes *Amberes*, a fragmented and disordered poetic narrative, as a novel is also noteworthy. In reality, none of his other novels is closer to his poetry collections than this novella, which he wrote when he was still mostly devoted to poetry. Tellingly, in 2007, an almost identical text to *Amberes* (but now titled "Gente que se aleja" ["People Walking Away"]) was included as poetry in *La universidad desconocida*. This ambivalence suggests that *Amberes* could be considered the missing link between Bolaño's poetry writing and his narrative.

As Enrique Salas Durazo and other scholars have pointed out, one of the most interesting traits of *Amberes* is the way in which it reveals, in a condensed fashion, many of the topics, tones, and traits of Bolaño's writing. For this reason, the Argentine writer Rodrigo Fresán has called this novella the "Big Bang" of Bolaño's literary world. In *Amberes*—as in *2666*, *Los detectives salvajes*, and other texts written by Bolaño—there are crimes, violence, and unresolved murders in a world of frustrated, misfit poets, who constantly write, overwhelmed by a romantic melancholia. We also find corrupt policemen who foreshadow the ones in *2666*; chapter 20 is the synopsis of a plot that is reminiscent of those in *La literatura nazi en América* (*Nazi Literature in the Americas*, 1996); and chapters 21 and 22 include similar drawings to the ones found in *Los detectives salvajes*. Moreover, in the preface to *Amberes*, we learn that the original manuscript had many more pages: "the text tended to multiply itself, spreading like a sickness" (ix).[15] This type of expanding literature is, of course, typical of Bolaño's oeuvre. Many of Bolaño's paragraphs are recycled (sometimes verbatim, others as non-hierarchical variations) in different texts without falling into self-plagiarism, expanding rhizomatically without a clear conclusion and gaining additional connotations as they move from one text to the text. In fact, even in this short final version that ended up being published under the title *Amberes*, there are repetitions of the same scenes (like the first sentence in chapter 31), anecdotes, and motives, which resurface in other parts of the novella from a different perspective.

An Interest in Disinterestedness

But there is a second reason *Amberes* did not embarrass Bolaño, as his other works allegedly did: it reifies his interest in disinterestedness, as did his poetry collections. Bolaño shared this attitude with the rest of the *infrarrealista* movement, as Rubén Medina explains:

> Publication was never the main goal of *Infrarrealismo*. In fact, on several occasions—during the final years of the 1970s and the entire following decade in Mexico—we, the *infrarrealistas*, consistently refused to be included in the anthologies and magazines of that time, either as a group or individually. The goal, to be precise, was to maintain our ethics: the ethics of writing even if it implied self-marginalization, a fragile existence as poets, remaining unpublished and in the black holes, not having a "legitimate" presence in the Mexican literary space or being seen as the expression of a Romantic infantilism for our intransigent position, as happened to the Dadaists. Rather than publishing, the fundamental thing was to explore the binomial life-writing as far as the senses, the forms would allow it.[16]

Following these *infrarrealista* premises, in his interviews, autobiographical writings, and declarations, Bolaño made it clear how his life and his writing (poetry writing initially) were inseparable. He wanted to make sure that his readers understood that the ethical-aesthetic mantra of *infrarrealismo* had guided his life as well as his writing. In fact, his literary career, notwithstanding his lack of publications, *was* his life. Thus, addressing the ethical principles written by Bolaño in the *infrarrealista* manifesto "Déjenlo todo, nuevamente" ("Leave Everything, Again"), Medina clarifies: "The poet is characterized, in this context, by a precarious life, but not as a pre-condition to his true identity and search…but as a result of keeping one's ethics while still being surrounded by the imposing economy of the modern and global world."[17]

In the prologue to *Amberes*, Bolaño seems to claim that—in line with what he declared in the *infrarrealista* manifesto—he always fought against the norms of the cultural world: throughout his life he kept his ethics intact, always refusing to make writing just another profession and rejecting opportunism, always refusing to acquire respect, social mobility, and privilege through his writing in order to join a guild of people who feel superior to the rest of society. In other words, he went well beyond the changes that were limited to the aesthetic realm, as supposedly André Breton proposed in his 1922 surrealist manifesto "Lâchez tout" (Leave Everything). Yet, as Medina reminds us, at one point, writing did become Bolaño's profession, in contrast with his best friend, Mario Santiago, who continued with his marginal life until his death in 1998: "Bolaño assumes writing as his profession since the mid-1990s, he enters a powerful editorial market and during the last five years of his life, he reaches a great worldwide recognition for his writing, particularly for his narrative."[18] Bolaño even wrote *Una novelita lumpen* (*A Little Lumpen Novelita*, 2002), the last novel he published while still alive, to fulfill his contract obligation with a publishing house. In Medina's view, "Bolaño's entry to the editorial market, however, does not transform either his writing or his ethical position as a writer."[19] Indeed, he continued to be critical of the literary world and never took advantage of his new fame and prestige: "At no moment did Bolaño seek to create a literary mafia, obtain a position in a cultural institution for his personal benefit, or use his power to publish his friends' texts or to destroy a fledgling writer."[20]

In line with these principles of interest in disinterestedness, Bolaño expressed on several occasions his disregard for either his critics' or his readers' opinions. For instance, he predicted, during a 1998 televised interview in Chile, that the publication of *Los detectives salvajes* would create many enemies for him. In Chris Andrews's view, this suggests that the author "was working against his own success in the final years of his life. Another such indication is the choice he made in 2002 to publish the jagged and disoriented *Antwerp*, a manuscript dating back to 1979 and published posthumously in 2010. Of *Antwerp* he said in his last interview that it was the only novel of which he was not ashamed, perhaps because it remained unintelligible" (6). In the same vein, in the preface to *Amberes*, Bolaño declares that he had no target readers when he wrote this novella: "I wrote this book for myself, and even that I can't be sure of. For a long time these were just loose pages that I reread and maybe tinkered with, convinced I had no *time*... I wrote this book for the ghosts, who, because they're outside of time, are the only ones with time" (ix).[21] Similarly, he assured Maristain, in an interview, that he almost never thought about his readers (*Between Parentheses* 363). Regardless of their probable sincerity, all these answers, in my view, form part of the careful construction of his public persona.

Bolaño complemented the construction of this public persona in interviews with his autobiographical writing. Although, in his opus, one must be cautious not to assume the existence of autobiographical traits, one of the main narrators in *Amberes* (there is un unclear number of narrative voices) is seemingly autobiographic, a young Bolaño living in Barcelona in 1980: he is a South American expatriate in Catalonia named Roberto Bolaño, who works at night as a security guard at a campground, has had numerous odd jobs, foresees his upcoming death, suffers from insomnia, writes poetry, and smokes. Yet in chapter 19, another narrator suddenly speaks about Roberto Bolaño in the third person, making the reader wonder whether there has been a sudden change in narrative perspective or whether the narrator until this point in the novella was not really Bolaño. In any case, it is in the preface to *Amberes* where there is no doubt that the real-life Bolaño is painting a picture of himself for his readers, highlighting a rebellious attitude as a writer that, for many years, was translated to his daily life. He states, for example, that in his last year in Barcelona, thinking that he would not live much longer, he led the same bohemian and antisocial life of his admired *poètes maudits*, including Arthur Rimbaud: "In those days, if memory serves, I lived exposed to the elements, without my papers, the way other people live in castles" (ix).[22] And a few paragraphs later, he adds, "Those things (rage, violence) are exhausting and I spent my days uselessly tired. I worked at night. During the day I wrote and read. I never slept. To keep awake, I drank coffee and smoked" (ix–x).[23] Writing his preface in Blanes in 2002, twenty-two years after the events took place, Bolaño summarizes his irreverent way of being in the world by recalling the two words written in Polish on a paper, "Total anarchy,"[24] which he stuck on the wall by his bed one day. Bolaño claims that at the time he was happy, as if the lack of attachment to material things or nationalities ("I felt equally distant from all the countries in the world [x])[25] had freed his soul. As Salas Durazo points out, "One of the main themes in *Antwerp* is the relationship between the aspiring writer and the world, along with his attempt to express it" (194) and, indeed, this is a tortuous relationship in which the author repeatedly makes it clear that, for many years, he refused to abide by the rules of bourgeois society.

In this context, Pierre Bourdieu, in *The Field of Cultural Production: Essays on Art and Literature* (1993), describes a similar disposition: "Gladiator or prostitute, the artist invents himself *in suffering*, in revolt, against the bourgeois, against money, by inventing a separate world where the laws of economic necessity are suspended, at least for a while, and where value is not measured by commercial success" (169). Bourdieu explains this phenomenon by studying the "habitus" of authors and artists, which he describes as lasting, acquired schemes of perception, thought, taste, and action. These patterns or dispositions, according to him, are the result of their individual or collective internalization of social structures or culture. In Bolaño's case, it could be described—to use Bourdieu's vocabulary again—as "a feel for the game" of literature, which provided him with the practical skills to navigate it without necessarily abiding by prescribed rules.

In this sense, I argue that Bolaño's avowed decision to disregard his critics' or readers' opinions, declaring his "interest in disinterestedness," is intimately associated to his desire for an associated symbolic capital in the field of literature. Thus, in the first page of the preface to *Amberes*, he proudly explains: "I never brought this novel to any publishing house, of course. They would've slammed the door in my face and I'd have lost the copy" (ix).[26] By initially turning his back to the sanction of the market; cultural agents (publishers, critics, editors); and cultural institutions ("literary mafias," academies, prizes, honors)—and, therefore, to economic profit—the Chilean author assumes to be gaining a "credit" that may eventually bring him recognition, once his "authenticity" and reputation have been established (in his case, with the recognition, also came celebrity and economic profits). This is evident in the preface, where he explains that his disease back then was rage, violence, and pride (could this pride be related to his detachment from literary circles?): "The scorn I felt for so-called official literature was great, though only a little greater than my scorn for marginal literature. But I believed in literature; or rather, I didn't believe in arrivisme or opportunism or the whispering of sycophants. I did believe in vain gestures. I did believe in fate" (x).[27] This fondness for "gestos inútiles" (vein gestures) is reminiscent of what Bourdieu termed "interest in disinterestedness." Along these lines, the Chilean's belief in "fate" perhaps refers to his faith in achieving literary recognition by following this path, which he considers the one chosen by genuine writers. His resentment against the literary world reappears in the seventh chapter, when one of the narrators states: "I'm alone, all the literary shit gradually falling by the way-side—poetry journals, limited editions, the whole dreary joke behind me now…" (10).[28] As Andrews points out, Bolaño's work "stigmatizes attraction to institutionally vested power and prestige" (186).

To return to Bourdieu's theories, in contrast to the principles of ordinary economy, in the artistic and literary fields a lack of monetary gains, honors, or academic training may be considered actual virtues. Indeed, in Bolaño's mind, the disinterested approach becomes a *sine-qua-non* condition for the path to becoming a consecrated writer. In his interview with Maristain, for instance, he declares not to care at all about the sales rankings of his books. Also for this reason, he cultivates a rebel image in his interviews and writings, as well as in his antagonistic interactions with most established artists during his youth—a sort of struggle to make his own mark (although the *infrarrealista* Rubén Medina claims that Bolaño was rarely present among the *infrarrealistas* who boycotted poetry readings [Andrews 22]). Bolaño's initial decision to choose poetry and drama instead of more economically profitable literary genres, such as the novel and the essay, may also obey to this same frame of mind. Along these lines, one can sense an obvious pride in his having withstood so many hardships for so many years. Thus, in his interview with

Maristain, he answers the question, "Have you experienced terrible hunger, bone-chilling cold, choking heat?," with a veiled sense of pride: "I quote Vittorio Gassman from a movie: In all modesty, yes" (360).[29] In the 1990s, however, his precarious economic situation and his desire to support his family would force him to go against his *infrarrealista* principles: he first turned to short narrative (even though, in a televised interview in Chile, he half-jokingly stated that writing in prose was in bad taste) in order to win Spanish regional literary awards and, once his health began to deteriorate, to the novel, excelling at a more traditional style of storytelling, which at one time he had considered archaic.

For Bolaño, therefore, *Amberes*, unlike his other novels, represents the work of a pure writer in a confrontational relationship with the bourgeoisie, cultural agents, and institutions of the republic of letters. In this sense, according to Bourdieu,

> the works produced by the field of restricted production . . . are "pure" because they demand of the receiver a specifically aesthetic disposition in accordance with the principles of their production. They are "abstract" because they call for a multiplicity of specific approaches . . . They are "esoteric" for all the above reasons and because their complex structure continually implies tacit reference to the entire history of previous structures, and is accessible only to those who possess practical or theoretical mastery of a refined code, of successive codes, and of the codes of these codes. (120)

Amberes consciously displays these traits summarized by Bourdieu: besides boasting novelty, originality, and the marks of rupture with its antecedents, it is a pure text because it demands a literary preparation and competence on the readers' part, including an ability to accept a non-linear, non-realist narrative; it is also pure because, in its open and open-ended nature, it accepts multiple approaches and readings; and it is definitely esoteric in its hermeticism, only accessible to or decipherable by the initiated in both Bolaño's writing and the principles or codes of the avant-garde.

Among other rituals in this almost ontological search for the image of the pure writer, Bolaño performed the typical prophetic denunciations, such as his derogative proclaims against Octavio Paz, the Boom and Post-Boom authors, or against the Chilean literature in exile, for example. Behind the rebellious demeanor, therefore, this provocative stance and the presumed disregard for material gratification were probably aimed, whether consciously or unconsciously, at accumulating a symbolic and cultural capital that would gain him the desired recognition among literary peers and, consequently, literary prestige and legitimacy. It would not be too far-fetched to assume that these lifestyle and demeanor were part of the life performance of the *poète maudit* personage that he so admired. But this disposition was, of course, not new. Bourdieu reminds us how advocates of pure art, such as Charles Baudelaire, invented "art for art's sake" and a

> social personage without precedent—the modern artist, full-time professional, indifferent to the exigencies for politics and morality, and recognizing no jurisdiction other than the specific norm of art. Through this they invented pure aesthetics, a point of view with universal applicability, with no other justification than that which if finds in itself... Against bourgeois art, they wanted ethical freedom, even transgression, and above all distance from every institution, the state, the Academy, journalism. (199)

Overall, *Amberes*, and particularly its preface, is a testimony to Bolaño's careful construction of a rebellious public persona that aligned itself with his image of the French *poètes maudits*, whom he admired. But as Bourdieu has demonstrated, these choices, rather than rebellious or atypical, are in fact in line with the artistic and literary fields, where priorities actually run counter to societal economic rules. While it is true that it would be a mistake to identify all characters called Bolaño, Belano, or B with the author himself, it is also true that the Chilean author did construct a detailed bohemian image of himself through his interviews, prefaces, and fiction that has undoubtedly contributed to the so-called Bolaño myth.

Notes

1. "*Amberes* me gusta mucho, tal vez porque cuando escribí esa novela yo era otro, en principio mucho más joven y quizás más valiente y mejor que ahora. Y el ejercicio de la literatura era mucho más radical que hoy, que procuro, dentro de ciertos límites, ser inteligible. Entonces me importaba un comino que me entendieran o no" (113).

2. "Está Cortázar, que es el mejor" (Braithwaite 24).

3. "El más adelantado en concebir estructuras literarias capaces de internarse en territorios ignotos (como Borges y Cortázar)" (292).

4. "Mi generación, de más está decirlo, se enamoró de *Rayuela*, porque eso era lo justo y lo necesario y lo que nos salvaba" (293).

5. "Cuando exhale la primera bocanada piensa que la fidelidad se mueve con la misma rigidez que el tren. Una nube de humo opalino cubre su rostro. Piensa que la palabra 'rostro' crea sus propios ojos azules. Alguien grita. Observa sus pies fijos en el suelo. La palabra 'zapatos' jamás levitará" (19).

6. "El patrón paga con heroína y los campesinos esnifan en los surcos, tirados sobre las mantas, bajo palmeras escritas que alguien corrige y hace desaparecer" (26).

7. "También yo quise estar solo. En Amberes o en Barcelona. La luna. Animales que huyen. Accidente en la carretera. El miedo" (106).

8. "Ayer soñé que vivía en el interior de un árbol hueco, al poco rato el árbol empezaba a girar como un carrusel y yo sentía que las paredes se comprimían" (81).

9. "Toda escritura en el límite esconde una máscara blanca. Eso es todo. Siempre hay una jodida máscara. El resto: pobre Bolaño escribiendo en un alto en el camino. . . : ('¡Díganle al estúpido de Arnold Benner que *todas* las reglas de construcción siguen siendo válidas sólo para las novelas que son copias de otras')" (102).

10. "De lo perdido, de lo irremediablemente perdido, sólo deseo recuperar la disponibilidad cotidiana de mi escritura, líneas capaces de cogerme el pelo y levantarme cuando mi cuerpo ya no quiera aguantar más. (Significativo, dijo el extranjero.) A lo humano y a lo divino. Como esos versos de Leopardi que Daniel Biga recitaba en un puente nórdico para armarse de coraje, así sea mi escritura" (119).

11. "Sólo me salen frases sueltas, le dijo, tal vez porque la realidad me parece un enjambre de frases sueltas" (69).

12. "Después sólo resta el vacío" (17).

13. "Bien mirado, es poco el tiempo que nos dan para construir nuestra vida en la tierra, quiero decir: asegurar algo, casarse, esperar la muerte" (27).

14. "El lenguaje de los otros es ininteligible para mí" (22).

15. "El texto tendía a multiplicarse y a reproducirse como una enfermedad" (10).

16. "La consigna del infrarrealismo nunca fue la de publicar. De hecho, en varias ocasione—durante los años finales de los setenta y toda la siguiente década de los ochenta en México—los infrarrealistas nos negamos de manera consistente a ser incluidos en antologías y revistas de la época, como grupo o individualmente. La consigna, para ser precisos, era mantener una ética: una ética de la escritura aun si ésta implicaba la auto-marginación, una frágil existencia como poetas, permanecer inéditos y en los agujeros negros, no tener una presencia 'legítima' en el espacio literario mexicano y ser vistos como la expresión de un infantilismo romántico por nuestra posición intransigente, a la manera de los dadaístas. Más que la publicación, lo fundamental era explorar el binomio vida-escritura hasta donde lo permitieran los sentidos, las formas" (17).

17. "El poeta se caracteriza, en este contexto, por una vida precaria pero no como precondición de su verdadera identidad y búsqueda . . . , sino como resultado de mantener una ética en la impositiva economía del mundo moderno y global" (23).

18. "Bolaño asume la escritura como profesión desde mediados de los 90, entra a un poderoso mercado editorial y durante los últimos cinco años de su vida alcanza un gran reconocimiento mundial por su escritura, particularmente por su narrative" (44).

19. "La entrada de Bolaño al mercado editorial, no obstante, no transforma su escritura ni posición ética como escritor" (51).

20. "En ningún momento Bolaño busca crear alguna mafia literaria, conseguir alguna posición en instituciones culturales para beneficio personal, ni usar su poder para publicar a sus amigos o destruir a un naciente escritor" (Medina 52).

21. "Escribí este libro para mí mismo, y ni de eso estoy muy seguro. Durante mucho tiempo sólo fueron páginas sueltas que releía y tal vez corregía convencido de que no tenía *tiempo*. . . . Escribí este

libro para los fantasmas, que son los únicos que tienen tiempo porque están fuera del tiempo" (9).

22. "En aquellos días, si mal no recuerdo, vivía a la intemperie y sin permiso de residencia tal como otros viven en un castillo" (9).

23. "Estas cosas (rabia, violencia) agotan y yo me pasaba los días inútilmente cansado. Por las noches trabajaba. Durante el día escribía y leía. No dormía nunca. Me mantenía despierto tomando café y fumando" (10).

24. "Anarquía total."

25. "Me sentía a una distancia equidistante de todos los países del mundo" (11).

26. "Por supuesto, nunca llevé esta novela a ninguna editorial. Me hubieran cerrado la puerta en las narices y habría perdido una copia. Ni siquiera la pasé, como se suele decir, a limpio" (9).

27. "El desprecio que sentía por la llamada literatura oficial era enorme, aunque solo un poco más grande que el que sentía por la literatura marginal. Pero creía en la literatura: es decir no creía ni en el arribismo ni en el oportunismo ni en los murmullos cortesanos. Sí en los gestos inútiles, sí en el destino" (10).

28. "Estoy solo, toda la mierda literaria ha ido quedando atrás, revistas de poesía, ediciones limitadas, todo ese chiste gris quedó atrás..." (25).

29. "¿Ha experimentado el hambre feroz, el frío que cala los huesos, el calor que deja sin aliento?"; "Cito a Vittorio Gassman en una película: Modestamente, sí" (335).

Works Cited

Andrews, Chris. *Roberto Bolaño's Fiction: An Expanding Universe*. New York: Columbia UP, 2014.

Bolaño, Roberto. *2666*. Barcelona: Anagrama, 2008.

——. *Amberes*. Barcelona: Anagrama, 2002.

——. *Amuleto*. Barcelona: Anagrama, 1999.

——. *Antwerp*. Trans. Natasha Wimmer. New York: New Directions, 2020.

—————. *Between Parentheses. Essays, Articles, and Speeches, 1998–2003*. Ed. Ignacio Echevarría. Trans. Natasha Wimmer. New York: New Directions, 2011.

—————. *Los detectives salvajes*. New York: Vintage Español, 1998.

—————. *Entre paréntesis. Ensayos, artículos y discursos (1998–2003)*. Ed. Ignacio Echevarría. Barcelona: Anagrama, 2004.

—————. *Estrella distante*. Barcelona: Anagrama, 1996.

—————. *La literatura nazi en América*. Barcelona: Seix Barral, 2005.

—————. *Nocturno de Chile*. Barcelona: Anagrama, 2000.

—————. *Los sinsabores del verdadero policía*. Barcelona: Anagrama, 2011.

—————. *La universidad desconocida*. Barcelona: Anagrama, 2007.

Borges, Jorge Luis. *Ficciones*. Madrid: Alianza Editorial, 1996.

Bourdieu, Pierre. *The Field of Cultural Production: Essays on Art and Literature*. New York: Columbia UP, 1993.

Braithwaite, Andrés, ed. *Bolaño por sí mismo: entrevistas escogidas*. Santiago, Chile: Ediciones Universidad Diego Portales, 2006.

Cortázar, Julio. *Rayuela*. Nanterre, France: ALLCA Xxe, 1991.

López-Calvo, Ignacio. "Roberto Bolaño's Flower War: Memory, Melancholy, and Pierre Menard." *Roberto Bolaño, A Less Distant Star: Critical Essays*. Ed. Ignacio López-Calvo. New York: Palgrave Macmillan, 2015. 35–64.

Maristain, Mónica. "Final: 'Estrella distante' (Entrevista de Mónica Maristáin)." *Entre paréntesis. Ensayos, artículos y discursos (1998–2003)*. Ed. Ignacio Echevarría. Barcelona: Anagrama, 2004. 329–43.

Medina, Rubén. *Perros habitados por las voces del desierto: Poesía infrarrealista entre dos siglos*. Mexico City: Aldus Biblioteca José Sordo, 2014.

Salas Durazo, Enrique. "Roberto Bolaño's Big Bang: Deciphering the Code of an Aspiring Writer in *Antwerp*." *Roberto Bolaño, A Less Distant Star: Critical Essays*. Ed. Ignacio López-Calvo. New York: Palgrave Macmillan, 2015. 189–209.

Liminal Spaces in Roberto Bolaño's *Una novelita lumpen* and Alicia Scherson's Film Adaptation *Il futuro*

Traci Roberts-Camps

According to Chris Andrews, longtime translator of Roberto Bolaño's novels into English, "The sympathetic characters in Bolaño's fiction tend to share [an] aimlessness, and are rarely inclined to fashion selves through storytelling or to live their lives in a narrative mode, as if they were . . . the protagonists of stories" (95). This begs the question of how to approach characters who do not act as such, characters who are unaware of any importance to the telling of their lives. Bianca, the protagonist of *Una novelita lumpen* (*A Little Lumpen Novelita*, 2002), belies the aimlessness Andrews describes. What is more, the way she tells her story defies any sense of concrete storytelling or narrative mode, underlining the idea that she herself does not see her story as worthy of much mention. Bianca is a marginal protagonist, if that is possible; her story is not necessarily noteworthy, but is, in this way, representative of life, which hardly ever follows a narrative arc. Scherson's film *Il futuro* (*The Future*, 2013), the screen adaptation of Bolaño's novel, shares the original's aimlessness and captures Bolaño's antagonism to tight endings and traditional storylines. The protagonist in the novel and film exists in a liminal space during the narration, a space between the young girl she was before her parents' death and her later life as an adult and mother, only briefly mentioned in the opening lines of the novel. This essay explores the various liminal spaces in *Una novelita lumpen* and *Il futuro*, including emerging adulthood, interactions between print and moving image cultures, languages and countries represented, and the relationship between the two genres.

The theory of liminal spaces is central to this discussion of Bolaño and Scherson's texts. While theorists such as Néstor García Canclini in *Cultural híbridas* (*Hybrid Cultures*, 1990) or Gloria Anzaldúa in *Borderlands/La frontera* (1987) have adopted the theory of liminality in cultural and literary studies to discuss the US-Mexico border, these theories differ from the present one in the sense that they are examining cultural hybridity where there is no permanent movement through the liminal space; the cultural liminal space they speak of is in fact permanently liminal.[1] In the case of Donna Haraway in *Simians, Cyborgs, and Women* (1991), the liminal nature of identity is also seen as an essential and not a transitional phase from one step to another. On the other hand, the idea of liminality in this essay deals with a temporary stage, a liminal space in the developmental process that is transitory. Thus, it is more akin to the anthropological sense of liminality observed by theorists such as van Gennep and Turner.

In their work, cultural anthropologists Arnold van Gennep— and, later, Victor Whitter Turner—explore the idea of liminality as it directly relates to rites of passage and cultural ceremonies. For van Gennep, the rite of passage is a transitional space between two stages of life and is worthy of investigation: "Because of the importance of . . . transitions, I think it legitimate to single out *rites of passage* as a special category, which under further analysis may be subdivided into *rites of separation, transition rites*, and *rites of incorporation*" (10–11). For van Gennep, this space in between deserves focus in and of itself. Turner also sees the importance of these transitional stages and later develops his work on symbolism and rituals.[2] Van Gennep's and Turner's theories of liminality focus on cultural practices that become rites of passage between two stages or spaces. Their significance to the current discussion is the emphasis on their in-between nature, not the beginning or the end. In other words, these cultural anthropologists valued the in-between moments previously neglected by theorists. Bolaño and Scherson do the same in their treatment of Bianca, and this essay relies on the same attentiveness to the liminal space as in-between, yet valuable as a focus of discussion.

One of the liminal spaces apparent throughout *Una novelita lumpen* and *Il futuro* is Bianca's stage in life—between childhood and adulthood. One theory in particular mirrors the depiction of Bianca in the novel and film. Jeffrey Jensen Arnett elaborates on his theory of the developmental period between adolescence and adulthood in *Emerging Adulthood: The Winding Road from the Late Teens Through the Twenties* (2015), identifying the following characteristics: identity exploration, instability, self-focus, feeling in-between, and being aware of possibilities (ix). He clarifies that feeling in-between in this stage is the sense of no longer being an adolescent, but not yet feeling like an adult (Jensen Arnett 14–15). For many of the subjects interviewed, entering adulthood had much less to do with full-time work and marriage and more to do with "accepting responsibility for one's actions, making independent decisions, and becoming financially independent" (xiv). As Jensen Arnett indicates, this represents a shift from earlier generations, who typically finished school and got married at an earlier age and who also associated these two factors with entering adulthood. For the purposes of this chapter, Jensen Arnett's theory of emerging adulthood relates to the idea of liminal spaces, as the emerging adult is in the liminal space between two stages—this is evident in the protagonist, Bianca. Specifically, the idea of emerging adulthood embodies Bianca's ambiguity about her present place in the world and her future.

Una novelita lumpen and *Il futuro* follow Bianca (played by Manuela Martelli in the film) and her brother, Tomás (only named in the film, played by Luigi Ciardo), after the death of their parents in a car accident. Both express a shifted perception of reality after the accident, including continuous light and no distinction between night and day: "Suddenly, the night no longer existed and everything was a continuum of sun and light" (Bolaño 15).[3] They spend their time watching television, leaving it on even while sleeping. When Tomás's friends come to stay, the newcomers suggest a plan in which Bianca seduces a rich, older man, Maciste (Rutger Hauer), so that they can rob him of the money they imagine he hides in his rundown mansion. In the process of visiting Maciste, Bianca develops feelings for him and realizes that she can no longer carry out the plan. The protagonist subsequently asks the two young men to leave.[4]

Perhaps the most striking examples of Bianca in the liminal space between adolescence and adulthood are in Scherson's film.

Two scenes in particular embody this sense of being in between: the ones in which Bianca has intercourse with one of the young men her brother brought home. In the first scene, the camera films them from above and, after the act, directly cuts to a snow globe. We can see Bianca's eyes in the snow globe as the glitter swirls around inside, eventually settling to the bottom. Scherson has used symbolic images in this way before; for example, in her first feature-length film, *Play*, the director incorporates the image of a plate of melting butter. In both cases, the snow globe and the butter, there is an awareness of the passing of time, as the butter melts quickly and the glitter in the snow globe falls to the bottom. Specific to *Il futuro*, this image could also be a visual representation of the alternate perceptions of reality that the protagonist and her brother experience after their parents' death. The siblings start to notice a change in the light, where it no longer gets darks at night and they feel that time is passing in a different way. While all of this is significant to the film and novel, what is noteworthy for the current analysis is the act of looking at the snow globe as something that a child would enjoy doing. The contrast is stark between the first image, filmed from above, of the couple making love and panting and the second image of Bianca's eyes reflected in the snow globe as she contemplates the glitter. While the first image relates more to adulthood, the second is more akin to childhood. Shortly following this scene, there is another one of Bianca in bed with the other young man. We can tell it is the other friend because of the tattoo on his back. Again, this scene is filmed from above, showing the protagonist sitting up in bed; the young man is asleep with his arm draped over her legs. Bianca sits in the semidarkness eating candy. Once more, we see the contrast between adulthood and childhood in the young man's post-coital sleep and Bianca's candy-eating. As with the snow globe, the candy represents a link to childhood and the ambiguity of Bianca's space between adolescence and adulthood. These moments are reminiscent of Arnett's theory of emerging adulthood, a space between adolescence and adulthood. A significant part of this stage is the feeling of being in-between. This is certainly relevant to Bianca and her forays into the adult space, after which she retreats to childish or adolescence acts.

There are other Latin American films directed by women that explore images of young girls in a very similar way to the aforementioned scenes with Bianca. For example, in Mexican director Marisa Sistach's films, there are key scenes that juxtapose the protagonist's youth and innocence with images of adult sexuality. The tension often lies between the young girl's youthful appearance and actions and an image of a sexual act. In *Perfume de violetas* (*Violet Perfume*, 2001), Sistach intersperses images of a rape scene with those of the young girl's bag filled with such items as school notebooks, glitter, and fingernail polish. This is similar to the scenes in *Il futuro* of Bianca eating candy or staring into a snow globe following intercourse. Of course, the two sexual acts are very different—one is consensual and the other one is not. However, the emphasis on opposing images of girlhood and sexuality are clearly intentional. In Sistach's film *La niña en la piedra* (*The Girl on the Stone*, 2006), the protagonist suffers sexual and physical assault, and the film ends with an image of her holding a doll and singing a childhood song while looking down at her sister kissing a boyfriend. Her childish demeanor is meant to contrast with earlier images of her budding adolescent sexuality and the harsh reality of the sexual and physical assaults. Argentine director Lucrecia Martel also explores these ideas in her films. Specifically, in *La niña santa* (*The Holy Girl*, 2004), the film alternates scenes of the protagonist acting like a young girl with others of her trying to seduce one of the doctors at a convention in her family's hotel. All of these examples parallel Bianca's scenes in *Il futuro*, all of which underline the in-between nature of the young girl's identities as both child and adult. As with Bianca, each of them exists in a liminal space between childhood and adulthood. Furthermore, they sense the ambiguity as much as the viewer does. And this, finally, leads back to Andrews's comments about Bolaño's characters and their disinclination toward telling their stories in a traditional narrative mode or living their lives as if they were protagonists of a story. In fact, they are evasive and doubtful about their own story because they inhabit a liminal space.

Returning to Jensen Arnett's theory of emerging adulthood, the feeling of having become an adult only comes after making decisions for oneself, taking responsibility for those actions, and being financially independent. At the end of the novel and the film, Bianca resolves to confront the two young men in her house, discontinue the search for hidden money, and move on with her life, allowing her brother to do so as well: "After a while I again told them to leave. That they could watch the program until the end and then they should pack their bags and go."[5] Thus, her actions foretell the future adult Bianca, who has learned to make decisions and take responsibility for them. As for being financially independent, Bianca orchestrates it so that at least they will not be financially beholden to the two young men. In this way, the ending is a reminder that the narrative is one of transition—namely, the liminal space between childhood and adulthood.

Another liminal space worthy of exploration in the novel and film lies between print culture and moving image and pop culture. While the novel is a product of print culture, the film is based on the novel, guided by a written script, and shows Bianca reading to Maciste.[6] On the other hand, Bolaño's text repeatedly refers to pop culture. Thus, from the beginning of this novel, the television is on in Bianca and Tomás's apartment:

> But I'll talk about that later. Television and video are a large part of this story. Even today, when I turn on the TV, in the afternoon, when I don't have anything else to do, it seems like I see on screen the young delinquent that I was, but the vision doesn't last long, only the time it takes the device to turn on.[7]

At first, they watch television to "kill time," but then it becomes a companion in the apartment and is on all night. In Scherson's film version, there is a recurrent image of characters sitting on the couch watching or falling asleep to a television program. At first, it is just Bianca or Tomás, and then it is both of them. When Tomás's friends arrive, the four of them fall asleep on the couch watching shows. In a way, the television attracts them all to the same space in the apartment and provides the illusion of companionship. At times, they even interact with the programs, such as the quiz show, during which they try to answer as many questions as possible. However, the characters remain solitary and never make any real connections with one another, a comment on the futility of human relations. There is also a scene in Scherson's film that focuses on the image of a myriad of satellite receivers on the apartment roof transmitting television shows to all of the surrounding apartments. The image reinforces the idea of the pervasiveness of pop culture in modern life.[8]

At a certain point, Bianca and Tomás begin visiting video rental stores and occasionally using their leftover money to rent films, thus introducing film as another element of pop culture. When Bianca begins to visit Maciste, she learns that he is a former Mr. Universe and film star, appearing in such films as *Maciste Versus the Living Dead*. Even the opening credits of *Il futuro* imitate the block letters and music of Maciste's films.[9] Macarena Areco discusses this intertextuality: "the intertextuality with the B movies—not only the Peplum movie and films by Maciste, but also the pornography that Bianca's brother watches and the romantic movies Bianca prefers—tell of the multi-colored intertextual fabric of the work" (11).[10] Scherson continues this intertextuality in her film adaption. There are several sequences in *Il futuro* that include clips from Maciste's movies. This is reminiscent of Scherson's film *Play*, in which the character plays the video game "Streetfighter" and then enacts a scene from the video game later in the film. As a further example, Bianca—in Bolaño's text and Scherson's production—takes a quiz in a popular magazine about which movie stars to marry and other superficial questions for readers to answer: "What actor do you want to have as your boyfriend/husband/lover/father?" (62).[11] Not only do these questions—and her Hollywood answers—underscore the importance of pop culture as a theme in this novel, but they also highlight Bianca's in-between stage. She considers no real prospects for boyfriends or husbands and only muses about the impossible. Even Bianca's clothing in the film is representative of pop culture and of her pre-adult stage—she is mostly shown wearing a Masters of the Universe T-shirt.

Another liminal space is the numerous languages and countries represented in *Una novelita lumpen* and *Il futuro*. Roberto Bolaño and Alicia Scherson are both native speakers of Spanish. *Una novelita lumpen* is in Spanish in its entirety, aside from the titles of the Italian newspapers and magazines Bianca imagines one of her brother's friends browsing, remembers her father reading, or buys herself: *L'Osservatore Romano*, *Il Messagiero*, *La Repubblica*, and *Donna Moderna* (36–37). *Il futuro* is in Italian in its entirety, except for the scenes with Maciste, which are in English. Bolaño and Scherson are from Chile; however, Bolaño moved to Mexico at the age of fifteen, traveled extensively, returned to Chile briefly, and eventually settled in Spain.

Of Bolaño, Siddhartha Deb has said: "After a brief period of imprisonment, the young man begins a wanderer's existence, crossing countries and continents, finding fellow exiles scattered in large cities and provincial towns, gathering moments of existential qualm that are transmuted into fiction" (ix). Scherson lives in Chile, but has spent significant time in Cuba and the United States. Both novel and film are set in Rome, Italy.[12] At first glance, setting is insignificant and the novel could have been set elsewhere. However, the streets of Rome play a key part in Bianca's wanderings. Additionally, because of its visual nature, Rome figures more prominently in *Il futuro*. There are panning images of Rome when Bianca wanders the streets of the city, comparable to Cristina in Scherson's film *Play*, who walks the streets of Santiago listening to her headphones. The film also explicitly compares Bianca's contemporary Rome to the images of Rome in Maciste's films—the feel of Bianca's story in Rome is very different from the epic feel of Rome in Maciste's movies.

A final liminal space in the current analysis is the space between the original novel and the film adaptation. *Una novelita lumpen* is the last novel Bolaño published during his lifetime, and he dedicated it to his children, Lautaro and Alexandra Bolaño. This work has been relatively ignored by critics, in favor of such novels as *Estrella distante* (*Distant Star*, 1996); *Los detectives salvajes* (*The Savage Detectives*, 1998); and *2666* (2004).[13] However, *Una novelita lumpen* lends itself well to the aesthetic mood of Alicia Scherson's films, making it an excellent foundation for her adaptation. While Scherson has commented that she was nervous about adapting from such a well-known author, the feel of the novel is evocative of the director's earlier work in *Play*.[14] For example, the protagonist Cristina [Viviana Herrera] wanders the streets of Santiago, Chile, before going on her search for the man whose briefcase she finds in the dumpster. In the course of the film, Cristina enters the man's girlfriend's house, tries on her clothes, sits in her restroom, and rests in her living room.

The aimlessness and muted mood of these scenes parallel Bianca's own life following the death of her parents. Bianca wanders the streets of Rome and rambles through Maciste's house, just as Cristina does in *Play*. In her film adaptation, Scherson captures this sense of futility or emptiness in her depiction of Bianca, someone who even questions the possibility of the future.[15] Andrews indicates: "Bolaño's fiction values an improvising openness over concentrated striving to attain objectives and to 'make something of one's life'" (95). Thus, we have the ironic title of the film, *Il futuro*, referring to Bianca's reflections as a nebulous idea that holds no relevance for her. In the novel, the protagonist questions her brother's attempts at preparing for the future: "Finally I told him that I didn't care about the future, that ideas came to me, but that those ideas, if I really thought about it, never projected themselves into the future."[16] Later, after fantasizing about a future life with Maciste, Bianca comes to the conclusion that these thoughts are futile and useless. Also similar to Scherson's *Play*, *Una novelita lumpen* and *Il futuro* have relatively open endings. In the novel, Bianca worries—as the reader does—that there will be retribution for her decision not to keep searching for Maciste's supposed hidden money; however, there is no clarification and the ending insinuates that nothing dramatic occurs. Furthermore, we know from the beginning of the novel that Bianca moves on, as the first line is "Now I am a mother and also a married woman."[17] In the film version, the last scene is of the protagonist looking out her window and then the image of a flock of birds zigzagging over Rome at night. Symbolically, the birds mirror the wanderings of the characters themselves. The open ending and the protagonist's thoughts on the future reflect what Ignacio López-Calvo calls the "futile search for meaning and closure in some of Bolaño's works" (5). This also corresponds to Andrews's comments on Bolaño's characters and their reluctance to see themselves in a narrative way.

The title given to the novel is significant as well. *Una novelita lumpen* refers to lumpen: the socio-economically marginalized or "lumpenproletariat." In this novel, Bolaño presents the protagonist and her brother as abruptly entering the working classes after the death of their parents. Much of the first part of the novel considers their search for jobs and their gradual departure from school. As the novel develops, Bianca's thoughts about her future are either pessimistic or vacant. In a sense, the two young people have been left with fewer possibilities for the future, and their struggles in the novel represent them coming to terms with this loss. Luis Íñigo-Madrigal also considers the word "lumpen" in the title of Bolaño's novel:

> Because it tells of a brief delinquent episode in the life of an adolescent; because its characters belong to the exploited stratums of the population and have no sense of class; because it is a commissioned novel, a quasi betrayal of what is thought (what Bolaño thinks) that literature should be: an act of prostitution homologous to that of Bianca.[18]

The novel is about the socioeconomically disenfranchised, and it is "a little novel," something to turn in to fulfill a responsibility to an editor. However, this diminutive is misleading, as the novel has much more to offer than the title implies. Furthermore, this literary act of prostitution, as Íñigo-Madrigal calls it, mirrors Bianca's own experiences with Maciste, which also offer more meaning than their beginnings would indicate. Bianca does grow in her relationship with Maciste, and it is through her involvement with him that she finds the strength to confront the two young men living in her house and to put an end to their collective search for an alternate future with the supposed hidden fortune.

In conclusion, there are several liminal spaces in *Una novelita lumpen* and *Il futuro*, including the relationship between the two genres; the many languages and cultures represented; the interactions between print and moving image culture; and emerging adulthood as an in-between stage of life. The idea of liminal space is essential to an understanding of Bolaño and Scherson's work, as it highlights the importance both creators place on in-between spaces. Bianca is the most prominent example, as she exists throughout the narration in a liminal space; the narration itself is of a liminal time in her life between childhood and adulthood and between her life before her parents' death and her later life as a "mother and a married woman." Bianca's first words in the novel and her actions at the end of the novel imply that she eventually leaves this liminal state; however, this in-between space is important enough to merit filling the entire narration. Although Bianca, as with other Bolaño characters, neither acts in a narrative mode nor tells her story as though she were the protagonist in a grand narrative—as Andrews contends—Bolaño's short novel and Scherson's film nevertheless center on her in-between story and give it the significance it deserves.

Notes

1. See Subha Mukherji's introduction to *Thinking on Thresholds: The Poetics of Transitive Spaces* (2011) for a brief history of the theory of liminality or threshold spaces.

2. Turner develops his theories in such works as *The Forest of Symbols: Aspects of Ndembu Ritual* (1967).

3. "De pronto la noche dejó de existir y todo fue un continuo de sol y luz." [All translations into English are mine.]

4. *Il futuro* won the following festival awards: Sundance Film Festival Grand Jury Prize for World Cinema–Dramatic; Rotterdam International Film Festival KNF Award; Huelva Latin American Film Festival Silver Colon Best Actress for Manuela Martelli; and Best Director for Alicia Scherson (all in 2013).

5. "Al cabo de un rato volví a decirles que se fueran. Que vieran el programa hasta el final y que luego hicieran las maletas y se fueran" (149).

6. This is similar to the scenes of Cristina reading to the older gentleman for whom she cares in Scherson's *Play*.

7. "Pero de eso hablaré más tarde. La tele y el video ocupan un lugar importante en esta historia. Aún hoy, cuando enciendo la tele, por la tarde, cuando ya no tengo nada que hacer, me parece ver en la pantalla a la joven delincuente que una vez fui, pero la visión no dura mucho, sólo el tiempo que tarda el aparato en encenderse" (17).

8. In its treatment of popular and techno-cultures, Bolaño's *Una novelita lumpen* is similar to the novels of Edmundo Paz Soldán, such as *Sueños digitales* (2000) and *El delirio de Turing* (2003). Paz Soldán, like others of the McOndo generation, explores themes related to technology and the media. The presence of pop culture in Bolaño's novel is comparable; however, he is not considered part of the McOndo movement.

9. Many of Maciste's films are "Hercules" or Peplum movies that have a Biblical setting and a main character who is strong like Hercules.

10. "la intertextualidad con el cine clase B—no solo con el péplum y las películas de Maciste, sino que también con las pornografías que ve el hermano de Bianca y las de amor que prefiere ella—da cuenta del abigarrado tejido intertextual de la obra."

11. "De qué actor de cine te gustaría ser novia/esposa/amante/hija?"

12. *Una novelita lumpen* is part of a series, edited by Claudio López of Mondadori Editorial, in which the novels are set in different cities.

13. Juan Miguel López Merino, in his article "Bolañismo," only mentions *Una novelita lumpen* very briefly. The other small numbers of reviews and articles analyzing this work are included in this chapter.

14. In an interview with *Indiewire*, Scherson comments: "This is my first literary adaptation after writing always my own material. It's based on a Roberto Bolaño novel *Una novelita lumpen*. This was clearly the biggest challenge not so much because it was hard to adapt—in fact the novel is full of images—but because everyone thought I should be very scared and intimidated. So I was" (*Indiewire*).

15. "personajes menores de dramas también menores, a lo mucho héroes de calamidades comunes y corrientes" (Piché). Bruno H. Piché sees Bolaño's novel as a reminder that we are only "minor characters in dramas that are also minor, at most heroes of everyday calamities"

16. "Finalmente le dije que a mí el futuro no me importaba, que se me ocurrían ideas, pero que esas ideas, si lo pensaba bien, nunca se proyectaban hacia el futuro" (18)

17. "Ahora soy una madre y también una mujer casada" (13).

18. "Porque cuenta un breve episodio delictual de la vida de una adolescente; porque sus personajes pertenecen a los estratos explotados de la población y no tienen conciencia de clase; porque es una novela hecha por encargo, una cuasi traición a lo que se piensa (Bolaño piensa) que debe ser la literatura: un acto de prostitución homólogo al de Bianca" (Chao). Curiously, in his review of *Una novelita lumpen*, Ramón Chao writes of the title and use of the word "lumpen": "Porque cuenta un episodio delictual de la vida de una adolescente; porque sus personajes pertenecen a los estratos explotados de la población y no tienen conciencia de clase; y porque es una novela hecha por encargo: un acto de prostitución semejante al de la protagonista de la novela, Bianca, para ganarse la vida" [Because it tells of a brief delinquent episode in the life of an adolescent; because its characters belong to the exploited stratums of the population and have no sense of class; and because it is a commissioned novel: an act of prostitution similar to that of the protagonist of the novel, Bianca, in order to make a living" (Chao). With the exception of a few lines, Chao's wording (in 2009) is a direct copy of Íñigo-Madrigal's from 2003. López Merino cites Íñigo-Madrigal's review in his article "Bolañismo."

Works Cited

Andrews, Chris. *Roberto Bolaño's Fiction: An Expanding Universe.* New York: Columbia UP, 2014.

Bolaño, Roberto. *Una novelita lumpen.* Barcelona: Anagrama, 2009.

Chao, Ramón. "La sexualidad y el engaño." Rev. of *Una novelita lumpen* by Roberto Bolaño. *Le Monde diplomatique.* Le Monde diplomatique, 29 Dec. 2009. Web. 10 Sept. 2015.

Deb, Siddhartha. "Foreword: On Roberto Bolaño." *Roberto Bolaño, A Less Distant Star: Critical Essays.* Ed. Ignacio López-Calvo. New York: Palgrave, 2015. ix–xxi.

Íñigo-Madrigal, Luis. "*Una novelita lumpen.*" Rev. of *Una novelita lumpen* by Roberto Bolaño. *La Nación.* Comunicaciones Lanet S.A., 20 Jul. 2003. Web. 10 Sept. 2015.

Jara, Cristián. "'El Futuro,' primera cinta basada en una obra de Bolaño." Rev. of *Il futuro*, by Alicia Scherson. *24horas.cl*. Televisión Nacional de Chile. 27 May 2013. Web. 10 Sept. 2015.

Jensen Arnett, Jeffery. *Emerging Adulthood: The Winding Road from the Late Teens Through the Twenties*. Oxford: Oxford UP, 2015.

López-Calvo, Ignacio. "Introduction." *Roberto Bolaño, A Less Distant Star: Critical Essays*. Ed. Ignacio López-Calvo. New York: Palgrave, 2015.

López Merino, Juan Miguel. "Bolañismo: 2005–2008." *Iberoamericana* 9.33 (2009): 191–200.

Macarena, Areco. "Lo que queda de la utopia: La absolutización de la vida privada en tres relatos breves de Roberto Bolaño y Alejandro Zambra." *Espejos y prismas: Tradición y renovación en la narrativa breve moderna de España e Hispanoamérica*. Ed. Kutasy Mercédesz, Gabriella Menczel, & Lásló Scholz. Budapest: University of Eötvös, 2011. 7–17.

Mukherji, Subha, ed. *Thinking on Thresholds: The Poetics of Transitive Spaces*. London & New York: Anthem Press, 2011.

Oliver, Kelly, ed. *The Portable Kristeva*. Rev. ed. New York: Columbia UP, 2002.

Pérez, Fernando. "Roberto Bolaño: Melancolía y delirio en tres novelas breves." *Cyber Humanitatis: Revista de la facultad de Filosofía y Humanidades Universidad de Chile* 43 (2007). Web.

Piché, Bruno H. "Una novelita salvaje." Rev. of *Una novelita lumpen* by Roberto Bolaño. *Letras Libres*. *letraslibres.com*. Editorial Vuelta, Aug 2003. Web. 19 Sept. 2015.

Scherson, Alicia, dir. *Il futuro*. Strand Releasing Home Video, 2013. DVD.

Scherson, Alicia. Interviewed by Indiewire Staff. "Meet the 2013 Sundance Filmmakers #44: Alicia Scherson Adapts Bolaño in 'Il Futuro'." *Indiewire*. Indiewire, 2013. 21 Jan 2013. Web.

van Gennep, Arnold. *The Rites of Passage*. Chicago: U of Chicago p, 1960.

Una novelita lumpen's Roman Posthumous Future_____

Alicia Ramos-Jordán & Marco Valesi

Between Past and Present: Federico Fellini, Pier Paolo Pasolini, and Roberto Bolaño Imagining Rome

Of all the islands he'd visited, two stood out. The island of the past, he said, where the only time was past time and the inhabitants were bored and more or less happy, but where the weight of illusion was so great that the island sank a little deeper into the river every day. And the island of the future, where the only time was the future, and the inhabitants were planners and strivers, such strivers, said Ulises, that they were likely to end up devouring one another. (Bolaño, *The Savage Detectives* 334–35)

Una novelita lumpen (*A Little Lumpen Novelita*, 2002) was the last novel published by Roberto Bolaño while he was still alive. With it, the author participated in the Mondadori project "Year 0," in which seven Latin American writers responded to the task of writing a novel about one of today's major world capitals. Bolaño chose Rome, known as "Caput Mundi" and "La Citta Eterna," thus showing his timeless vision of contemporaneity (Fig.1).[1] The novella takes its name from *Tres novelitas burguesas* (*Three Bourgeois Novelitas*) by José Donoso, who, like Bolaño, was a Chilean author who lived in both Mexico and Spain. Bolaño sets his novella in the city that was also so often chosen by the Italian filmmakers Federico Fellini and Pier Paolo Pasolini. In fact, the reader can feel their subtle presence in this story, almost as an homage to them. In inimitable Bolaño fashion, it forces us to look at the province of the uprooted—a bewildering place where we might otherwise not go.

The image of Rome is so recurrent in Western culture that it is not surprising that it has played such a major role in literature and film. As to the seventh art, in the twentieth century, Rome became the filmmaking center of Italy and one of the biggest in the world.

A city full of ancient buildings (the Forum, the Coliseum, the Via Appia, the Catacombs, the Pantheon, the Baths of Caracalla), it became a unique inspiration to filmmakers. In *Una novelita lumpen*, Bolaño sees Rome as a bridge between the past and the future. *La Città Eterna* has been a source of inspiration for filmmakers such as Roberto Rossellini (*Roma città aperta*); Vittorio De Sica (*Ladri di biciclette*); Pier Paolo Pasolini (*Accattone, Mamma Roma*); Federico Fellini (*Roma, Satyricon*); William Wyler (*Roman Holiday*); Nanni Moretti (*Caro Diario*); Ettore Scola (*Gente di Roma*); Woody Allen (*To Rome with Love*); and Paolo Sorrentino (*La Grande Belleza*).

In the following pages, we analyze the relation between two of the most important Italian directors, Fellini and Pasolini, and Rome. Then, we compare it with the relation between this city, *Una novelita lumpen*, and the film *Il Futuro*, Alicia Scherson's adaptation.

In this context, when considering the film career of Italian director Fellini, one must keep in mind the influence of Rome on his creative development as an artist and as a source of endless inspiration. Settings his films in ancient Rome, Fellini created something entirely different from the traditional Hollywood productions or the Italian-Roman epics movies. In Fellini's 1969 *Satyricon*, loosely based on the work of the Roman author Petronius Arbiter, the cinematic Rome, "bears absolutely no relationship to the Rome we learned about in school books. It is a place outside historical time, an area of the unconscious in which the episodes related by Petronius are relived among the ghosts of Fellini" (Grazzini 75). Although set during Nero's reign, Fellini's film made no effort to be historically accurate. Instead, the filmmaker was attempting to create an analogy between ancient Rome and contemporary society. At the same time, he wanted to depict "A voyage, between past and present but toward the future, into total obscurity!" (Grazzini 75)

Just like Fellini created a "post-Hollywood epic," Bolaño portrayed the character of Maciste in *Una novelita lumpen* as a post-Hollywood movie star by rejecting Hollywood conventions: "Then, as we talked that afternoon about what we would do, they told me that for a while, probably before my brother and I were born, Maciste had been a movie star and his movies were seen all over the world.

Then he'd had the accident and retired, and after that he'd gradually been forgotten" (54).[2] Rome, in Fellini's films, also reflects Italy's postwar status, having lost its imperial or military aspirations, but boasting a more prosperous society of which the Italian director decries its moral and spiritual decay: "From a pre-Christian to a post-Christian one: Christ has disappeared and we've got to get along without him. This is the relevance of the film today" (Mora), Fellini averred in one of his many statements about *Satyricon*.

In the film *Roma*, we saw instead a deeper exploration of a style that paid homage to a legendary city that was the filmmaker's muse and teacher. "In *Roma*," Fellini stated, "I wanted to get across the idea that underneath Rome today is ancient Rome" (Borin 56). In this sense, film historian Fabrizio Borin observes that Fellini's "subconscious is Roman and composed of progressive stratifications like the seven layers of earth below it" (70).

Along these lines, for Pier Paolo Pasolini, Rome was not only a cinematographic set or a place to live in; the great writer and director had a passionate relationship with the city, which was characterized by mixed feelings of love, attraction, inspiration on one hand and rejection and estrangement on the other. Pasolini's life in Rome determined his friendships, literature, politics, love affairs, and filmmaking. But he did not just dwell in the suburbs; he was also attracted by the anti-clerical mood that fired up some downtown neighborhoods (Fig. 2),[3] in Italian "le borgate" (townships), such as Trastevere, Quadraro, and Casal Bertone. In two major films, *Accattone* (1961) and *Mamma Roma* (1962), one can notice Pasolini's obsession with the interrelations between postwar Roman urban planning and the sociopolitical conditions of the marginalized classes that filled the housing projects in the 1950s and 1960s.

The question of whether *Una novelita lumpen* is a Roman novel or at least a spatial novel has been one of the most critically addressed subjects so far. Whereas for Patricia Espinosa, in this novel Rome is "almost a character, almost a protagonist and more than a reference" (22), in our view, Rome, a repressive space, marked by boredom and routine, is the only possible location for the novella. It gives us a snapshot of a Roman metropolis through locations (Ponte Garibaldi, the Tiberina Island, Campo de Fiori), as well as local newspapers (*L'Osservatore Romano, La Repubblica, Il Messaggero*). More importantly, there is a search for a European tradition lost among the many yet-to-be-addressed problems shared by European and, by extension, Western culture in general in the twentieth century: "At the same time economic conditions were deteriorating. Not much, but on TV they said they were deteriorating. Somethimes was wrong in Europeo or Italy, I think. Or Rome. Or our neighborhood" (Bolaño, *Lumpen* 36).[4] The mechanism that Bolaño uses to translate this sad image is the portrayal of globalizing media and traces of mass culture. In the novel, they are exemplified by the incorporation of pornographic film, videos, magazines, newspapers, and television. The same feeling of loneliness, of lack of values affects Bianca, the main character in Bolaño's book, when she walks around, trying to find herself, lost in a society that she does not understand: "There were cars that passed with the windows already rolled down and kids inside yelling—'Fascism or barbarism!'–and they'd keep going too. I didn't look at them. I stared at the river and my videos and tried to forget the few things I knew" (13).[5] Rome, as expressed by Fellini in the film *Le notti di Cabiria*, is also a lumpen space where the main character is a prostitute who tries to survive, roaming the streets in search of love. As Rome is dramatically and passively living this condition, Bianca is also open to accepting her new status, in spite of being scared: "I was afraid of becoming a prostitute. I didn't like the idea of it. But I sensed that it was all a matter of getting used to it. Sometimes while I was working at the salon, I clenched my fists and tried to imagine my future" (48).[6]

In fact, even though Bolaño's *Una novelita lumpen* is set in another historical period than the Fellini and Pasolini cultural productions, we relive the same feelings of loneliness and aimlessness in scenes where Bianca and her brother, two high school dropouts, waste time watching talk shows and X-rated movies. This concept of lumpen, which appears in both the English title and the original Spanish, brings us back to the question of reality. The lumpen, as portrayed by Fellini and Pasolini's characters, refer to the dispossessed, to those who have been severed or displaced from

---

their status in society. Bolaño's interpretation, on the other hand, takes also us into a bizarre world of bodybuilding, a world without much conversation, without literature or intellectual culture. Rome, being a timeless reality floating between an imperial past and decadent present, becomes the perfect scenario for a social-artistic analysis.

Bolaño's Roman Lumpen

La marginalidad es vivida en diversos planos. *Una novelita lumpen* no es precisamente la narración de una mujer que guarda dentro de sí expectativas de igualdad—promovidas por el ascenso laboral o estudiantil, tampoco posee conciencia de los costosos avances en el ámbito del derecho que se contraponen a una realidad de desigualdad en el área del trabajo y la familia—; su ubicación y configuración penden y dependen de un borde (borroso, innominado, confinado y asentado en una periferia que se concibe desde lo mínimo, y desde allí articula una narrativa de origen signada por la pobreza). (Lucero Bustos)

Following Lucero Bustos's description, one can see Bianca dispossessed of any desire or agency of her own, except in brief instances. As she recounts this time in her life, we enter a dreamlike reality where she moves through the dark, labyrinthine world that she has entered with absolute indifference. Bianca's personhood is not established until near the end of the novel; we only know what she told us at the very beginning: her life goes on as a "mother and a married woman" (3).

Bianca is a veiled and exaggerated version of Bolaño, as so many of his other characters, because she is an outsider, surviving on the fringes of society, settling into the fact that her life has no meaning and no aiming for any great goal beyond her daily routine. She seems to live, as the Chilean author, in exile from herself; even at her own house, the foreigners—the Libyan and the Bolognan— invade and colonialize her territory, leaving her helpless to do anything but accept the world that is closing in on her.

This quiet, but powerful, story demonstrates that we all live on the edge of other kinds of lives. It illuminates the borders of other ways of existing and shows how easily the neatness of that existence can radically, suddenly change, as has happened to Rome throughout its history. For this reason, Bolaño portrays Rome, the cradle of Latin civilization, as a city blurred and fragmented by globalization, hidden behind the shadow of neoliberalism, representing its decadence, the final sunset of Western society and literature. Our interpretation of the novel establishes a connection between Bolaño and Maciste,[7] an old star of the popular sword-and-sandal movies turned into a *blind* and obese bodybuilder: "These days," says Maciste, "bodybuilding is considered a sport but when I practiced it, it was an art . . . Like magic . . . There was a time when it was an art and magicians were artists . . . Now it's just part of the show" (78).[8] Bolaño's use of bodybuilding here could be compared to contemporary literature. For this reason, we argue that he portrays Maciste as a symbol of a nationalism that is concomitantly euphoric and degraded, anchored in a past built on illusions, and full of weaknesses. This creates a unique Roman reality that, together with the rest of Bolaño's ouevre, has brought comparisons with Jorge Luis Borges, often underlining how they both embraced the "unreality of literature." In fact, the narrator of the novel states:

> After that, the days were different. Or the passing of the days. Or the thing that joins one day and the next but at the same time marks the boundary between them. Suddenly the night stopped existing and everything was constant sun and light. At first I thought it was exhaustion, or the shock or our parent's sudden disappearance, but when I told my brother about it he said that he dad noticed the same thing. Sun and light and an explosion of windows.
> I began to think that we were going to die (3).[9]

Through this passage, we immediately understand that Bolaño argues against the unreal narrative flatness, masked by everyday realism, which characterizes the representation of the world in today's so-called mass culture. In this sense, his story is an unforgettable blend at three different levels. The first one deals with the squalor of the protagonists' daily life:

My brother said that if I could dream of owning a mini-salon, he had the right to dream of a better future too. That was the word he used: *future*. I went into the kitchen and got our dinner started. Spaghetti. Then I set out the plates and silverware. Still thinking. At last I said that I didn't care about the future, that I had ideas, but those ideas, if I really thought about it, never extended into the future.

"Where do they go, then?" howled my brother. "Nowhere." (17)[10]

The second one could be represented by the artificial, ruthless, and almost baroque attempted conspiracy: "They had a plan. That much I do remember. A hazy plan on which each of them, my brother included, had gambled his future, and to which each had added his bit, his personal touch, his vision of fate and the turns of fate" (16).[11] And the third one deals with the unresolved story of the interwoven romance: "I dreamed that Maciste was my boyfriend and we were talking a walk around Campo de' Fiori. At first I was madly in love with him, but as we walked, he didn't seem like an interesting person to me anymore" (105).[12] This tension between reality and surreality continues in other passages of the novel: "And in the dream I thought: this is a movie, he's not really sleeping, he's just pretending to sleep, and in fact he's awake, and only then did I realize that Maciste, making the movie, was in the present, and I, watching the movie or dreaming that I was watching it, was in the future, Maciste's future, or, in other words, nothingness. Then I woke up (80).[13] Overlapping dreams and wakefulness, Bolaño creates an almost apocalyptic representation of society, just like Alicia Scherson in her cinematographic adaptation of the novella.

Il futuro

The film *Il Futuro* depicts a modern, chaotic, collapsing Rome and, by extension, Europe. It relates a bizarre, twisted, and contemporary story. Narrated from the future, the dreamlike drama focuses on a pair of teenage orphans in Rome. After siblings Bianca (Manuela Martelli) and Tomás (Luigi Ciardo) lose their parents in a car accident ("Accidents release such energy they modify the universe," we are told; in fact, when the siblings go to see the car in which their parents died, it has changed from yellow to white), they stay at the family apartment, trying to survive financially, all the while waiting for some vaguely promised governmental assistance.

The film takes on a "Beauty and the Beast" mood (Cocteau rather than Disney) when Bianca enters Mr. Bruno's crumbling mansion. A former movie star, Maciste (Hercules), who starred in titles such as "Maciste in Hell" and "Maciste vs. the Living Dead," is now the disheveled, but surefooted Mr. Bruno, as much of a ruin as Rome's most famous sites. Yet by spending long nights in Mr. Bruno's embrace, Bianca gains the confidence to break free from the numbness that has engulfed her since the accident.

Throughout the film, Scherson cleverly pays tribute to various film genres of the past. Bianca's opening narration, "I'm now a mother and also a married woman, but not that long ago I was a criminal," sets a film-noir tone, as do the opening orchestral score and title graphics. Later, when Bianca sees an unexplained light, the film recalls 1950s science fiction. After meeting Mr. Bruno, she tours the epic sets of film studio Cinecitta' and rents old Maciste films. The ancient world still holds sway in *Il Futuro*, where the newly orphaned siblings must begin to care for themselves amid the ruins of Rome and other faded splendors.

Considering that Bolaño's works are only now beginning to inspire film adaptations, Scherson made the right decision by starting with a minor work, seeping with classic Bolaño tropes: dislocation, literature, and crime. In its best moments, *Il Futuro* catches the weird quirks and anxieties of life in the new millennium. This imaginative film creates entire metafictional worlds within the text through interplays between the real and the unreal. One of the best scenes of *Il Futuro* has the group of youngsters huddled around a supposed Maciste picture. In it, we see the young Mr. Universe rescue a vestal virgin from the barbarians. Sometimes, small visual clues can be enough to evoke something much bigger. For all of its preoccupation with pushing the present away with the past, this thoughtful film revels in its elegance. *Il Futuro* subtly contemplates not only its own characters' futures via the past, but also cinema's own future.

Conclusion

Bolaño, through his many novels and short stories, explores the history and literature of dozens of countries, as well as the politics of Europe, Mexico, Central and South America. His books examine religion, the nature of death, drama, academia, games, World War II, the lives of the poets, drinking, sex, the police, oceans, disappearances, murder, sports, and film, just to name a few of the topics. His work in general operates on a hyper-realistic model of everything-at-once. By contrast, *A Little Lumpen Novelita* is unique in his fictional universe because it is set in Rome. Mysterious, claustrophobic, and haunting, Bolaño's novella, is at the same time an uncomfortable excursion into the somnambulistic existence of an orphaned teenage girl and also a metaphoric flaneuristic voyage through our glorious past and uncertain future. It is in the fog of Bianca's storytelling that we have to make our way through, on a path of discovery. Both Bolaño and Scherson lead us to believe that we might be part of a detective story, but, when all is said and done, we discover that we are co-conspirators of our present world.

Both cultural productions, suspended in time and having as background Rome, *la Città Eterna*, describe anonymous lives, using an epic sword-and-sandal movie's hero (Maciste); Pasolinian realism (bodybuilders, hair-dressers); magic realism (the sun that never sets); and Fellini-esque surrealism (escapes into desert) as *neo-mythological* point of departure hoping for a new future.

Both the novel and the film are obsessive and ambiguous, yet they reflect the open-ended nature not only of the protagonists, but of Bolaño himself. At the denouement of both, for example, Bianca tells, in an existential passage, of discovering oneself in "the space between planets, a noiseless, eyeless storm from another world, a world that not even the satellites in orbit arount the Earth could capture, a world where there was a place that was my place, a shadow that was my shadow" (109).[14] In conclusion, this essay reveals the space of the precarious balance that Bolaño creates between posthumous past ("Any thoughts about the word 'posthumous'?" an interviewer asked him. He answered "It sounds like the name of a Roman gladiator, an unconquered gladiator" [Vadles 58]) and uncertain future. Rodrigo Fresán uses the word "cosmic," which seems appropriate to describe the ambition and the radically open-ended quality of Bolaño's vision. Indeed, Rome was the perfect space for Bolano's last cosmic vision.

Notes

1. The picture "Zeus solo" by Luca Locatelli/Institute, published in the French version of *National Geographic* on January 1, 2015, symbolically represents the passage between Rome's glorious past and the terrible future.

2. "Después, por la tarde, mientras seguíamos dándole vueltas a lo que íbamos a hacer, me contaron que durante una época, probablemente antes de que mi hermano y yo naciéramos, Maciste había sido una estrella de cine y que sus películas habían dado la vuelta al mundo. Luego tuvo el accidente y se retiró. A partir de ese momento fue entrando poco a poco en el olvido" (67–68).

3. The French artist Zilda's wonderful project 'Io sono una forza del passato' ('I am a force of the past') places figures from classic Roman cinema of the 1950s and 1960s in Rome. As movie characters, they are part of Romans' collective history and through Zilda's work, they are brought into modern life.

4. "Por aquellos días la situación económica había empeorado. No mucho, pero en la tele decían que había empeorado. Creo que algo le pasaba a Europa o a Italia. O a Roma. O a nuestro barrio" (47).

5. "Había coches que pasaban con las ventanillas ya bajadas y con jóvenes en su interior que gritaban 'fascismo o barbarie' y que también seguían de largo. Yo no los miraba. Yo miraba las aguas del río y las carátulas de mis películas y trataba de olvidar las pocas cosas que sabía" (24).

6. "Tenía miedo de ser una puta. No me hubiera gustado ser una puta. Sin embargo intuía que todo era cuestión de acostumbrarse. A veces apretaba los puños, mientras estaba en la peluquería, trabajando, e intentaba imaginar mi futuro" (56).

7. The character of Maciste first appears in the film *Cabiria* (1914), whose screenplay was written by the fascist poet Gabrielle D'Annunzio. This film allowed other filmmakers, such as Federico Fellini and Jesús Franco, to become interested in the figure of Maciste.

---

8. "Ahora el culturismo es considerado un deporte, cuando yo lo practicaba era un arte . . . Igual que la magia . . . Hubo un tiempo en que fue considerada un arte y los magos unos artistas . . . Ahora sólo es parte del espectáculo" (78).

9. "A partir de ese momento los días cambiaron. Quiero decir, el transcurso de los días. Quiero decir, aquello que une y que al mismo tiempo marca la frontera entre un día y otro. De pronto la noche dejó de existir y todo fue un continuo de sol y luz. Al principio pensé que era debido al cansancio, al shock producido por la repentina desaparición de nuestros padres, pero cuando se lo comenté a mi hermano me dijo que a él le pasaba lo mismo. Sol y luz y explosión de ventanas. Llegué a pensar que nos íbamos a morir" (2).

10. "Mi hermano me respondió que así como yo soñaba con tener una minipeluquería, él también tenía derecho a soñar con un futuro mejor. Ésa fue la palabra que empleó: futuro. Fui a la cocina y puse la comida en el fuego. Spaghetti. Luego llevé los platos y cubiertos a la mesa. Siempre pensando. Finalmente le dije que a mí el futuro no me importaba, que se me ocurrían ideas, pero que esas ideas, si lo pensaba bien, nunca se proyectaban hacia el futuro. —¿Y hacia dónde, entonces?—chilló mi hermano.—Hacia ninguna parte" (17).

11. "Tenían un plan. Eso lo recuerdo. Un plan borroso en el que todos, mi hermano también, habían cifrado su destino y puesto su grano de arena, su aporte personal, su visión de la suerte y de los giros de la suerte" (21).

12. "Soñé que Maciste era mi novio y que íbamos a pasear por el Campo dei Fiori. Yo al principio estaba locamente enamorada de él, pero conforme paseábamos Maciste dejaba de parecerme una persona interesante" (116).

13. "Y en el sueño yo pensaba: es sólo una película, él no duerme de verdad, está fingiendo que lo hace, pero en realidad está despierto, y sólo entonces me daba cuenta que Maciste, mientras filmaba esa película, estaba en el presente y que yo, que veía la película o que soñaba que veía la película, estaba en el futuro, en el futuro de Maciste, es decir en la nada. Entonces me desperté" (93).

14. "El espacio que media entre planeta y planeta, una tormenta sin ruido y sin ojos que venía de otro mundo, un mundo que ni los satélites que giran alrededor de la Tierra pueden captar, y donde existía un hueco que era mi hueco, una sombra que era mi sombra" (120).

Works Cited

Accattone. Dir. Pier Paolo Pasolini. Perf. Franco Citti, Franca Pasut, & Silvana Corsini. Prod. Alfredo Bini. 1961.

Barnes, Joshua. "Translating Bolaño: An Interview with Natasha Wimmer." *Sampsonia Way*. City of Asylum/Pittsburgh, 17 Jan. 2013. Web.

The Belly of an Architect. Dir. Peter Greenaway. Perf. Brian Dennehy & Chloe Webb. Metro Golden Meyer, 1987. Film.

Bolaño, Roberto. *2666*. Trans. Natasha Wimmer. London: Picador, 2009.

_____. *Amulet*. Trans. Chris Andrews. London: Picador, 2010.

_____. *Between Parentheses*: *Essays, Articles and Speeches, 1998–2003*. Ed. Ignacio Echevarría. Trans. Natasha Wimmer. New York: New Directions, 2004.

_____. *By Night in Chile*. Trans. Chris Andrews. London: Vintage, 2009.

_____. *Distant Star*. Trans. Chris Andrews. London: Vintage, 2009.

_____. *The Savage Detectives: A Novel*. Trans. Natasha Wimmer. New York: Picador/ Farrar, Straus & Giroux, 2007.

_____. *The Third Reich*. Trans. Natasha Wimmer. London: Picador, 2012

_____. *Una novelita lumpen*. Barcelona: Random House Mondadori, 2002.

_____. *Woes of the True Policeman*. Trans. Natasha Wimmer. New York: Farrar, Straus & Giroux, 2012.

The Bicycle Thieves [Ladri di biciclette]. Dir. Vittorio De Sica. Perf. Lamberto Maggiorani, Enzo Staiola, & Lianella Carell. P.D.S, 1948. Film.

Borin, Fabrizio. *Federico Fellini. A Sentimental Journey into the Illusion and Reality of a Genius*. Roma: Gremese, 1999.

Casanova, Pascale. "Literature as a World." *New Left Review* 31 (Jan.–Feb. 2005): 71–90.

Dear Diary [Caro diario]. Dir. Nanni Moretti. Perf. Nanni Moretti & Giovanna Bozzolo. Sacher Film, 1993. Film.

Deckard, Sharae. "Bolaño and the Global Remapping of Literature" *Academia*. Academia.edu, 16–17 May 2013. Web. 20 Jun. 2015.

Espinosa, Patricia. "Roberto Bolaño: metaficción y posmodernidad periférica." *Revista Quimera* 241 (Feb 2004): 21–23.

Fresán, Rodrigo. "Borges and Me, and Me." *Granta*. Granta, 14 Apr. 2009. Web. 20 Jun 2015.

Gente di Roma. Dir. Ettore Scola. Perf. Valerio Mastandrea & Stefania Sandrelli. Instituto LUCE, 2003. Film.

Giles, Paul. *The Global Remapping of American Literature*. New Jersey: Princeton UP, 2011.

Grazzini, Giovanni. *Federico Fellini Intervista sul cinema*. Roma: Laterza, 1983.

The Great Beauty [*La grande bellezza*]. Dir. Paolo Sorrentino. Perf. Toni Servillo, Carlo Verdone, & Sabrina Ferilli. Indigo Film, 2013. Film.

Il Futuro [Una novelita lumpen]. Screenplay by Roberto Bolaño. Dir. Alicia Scherson. Perf. Manuela Martelli & Rutger Hauer. Movimiento Film, 2013. Film.

Kurnick, David. "Bolaño to Come." *Public Books*. Public Books, 5 Sept. 2012. Web. 1 Aug. 2015.

La Dolce Vita. Dir. Federico Fellini. Perf. Marcello Mastroianni & Anita Ekberg. Riama Film & Pathé Consortium Cinéma. 1960. Film.

L'Eclisse. Dir. Michelangelo Antonioni. Perf. Alain Delon & Monica Vitti. Prod. Robert & Raymond Hakim. Cineriz, 1962. Film.

Lucero Bustos, Ana Karina. "Novelita, lumpen, testimonio: coordenadas y variables de un Ejercicio." *Trinidaddecuatroesquinas*. Daniel Rojas Pachas/Blogger.com, 30 May 2013. Web. 20 Jun 2015.

Mamma Roma. Dir. Pier Paolo Pasolini. Perf. Anna Magnani & Ettore Garofolo. Prod. Alfredo Bini. Arco Film, 1962. Film.

Maristain, Mónica. "The Last Interview." *Stop Smiling* 38 (Jul 2003): 50–59.

Mora, Carl. J. "The Image of Ancient Rome in the Cinema." *Publicacions U.B.* n.p. Web. 20 Jun 2015.

Murdoch, Jim. "*A Little Lumpen Novelita.*" *The Truth About Lies*. Jim Murdoch/Blogger.com, 14 Dec. 2014. Web. 20 Jun 2015.

Roma. Dir. Federico Fellini. Perf. Peter Gonzales & Fiona Florence. Les productions artistes Associés, 1972. Film.

Roma, Open City [*Roma città aperta*]. Dir. Roberto Rossellini. Perf. Anna Magnani, Aldo Fabrizi, & Marcello Pagliero. Minerva Film SPA, 1946. Film.

Roman Holiday. Dir. William Wyler. Perf. Gregory Peck & Audrey Hepburn. Paramount Pictures, 1953. Film.

Satyricon. Dir. Federico Fellini. Perf. Martin Potter & Hiram Keller. Produzioni Europee Associati, 1969–1970. Film.

To Rome with Love. Dir. Woody Allen. Perf. Woody Allen, Alec Baldwin, & Roberto Benigni. Medusa Film, 2012. Film.

Young, Stephenie. "Roberto Bolaño's *A Little Lumpen Novelita.*" *Asymptote*. Asymptote, 2015. Web. 20 Jun 2015.

Homo Bolañus: Missing Link or the Last Dodo

Ignacio Padilla (trans. Ignacio López-Calvo)

If it were possible (it is not) to establish a central date to understand Latin American literature, I would choose June 17, 2003. And if it were indispensable—which, luckily, it is not—I would specify that it happened between midnight and one in the morning.

That day, in the morning, Palabra de América, a meeting of relatively young Latin American writers, began. It had been convened by the paradigmatic Seix Barral publishing house and the Lara Foundation, although other institutions and publishers also participated. The meeting had its singularities: it was to be a closed-door event where only twelve participants—an apostolic number—would present their concerns, thoughts, and digressions about what it meant for them to be or not to be new Latin American writers. Furthermore, it would be godfathered by two paradigmatic authors: Guillermo Cabrera Infante, who inaugurated the event as the literary grandfather of those present, and Roberto Bolaño, who had recently surged as the elder brother we had not had, or as the missing link of our letters.

That night, after disserting in vain, as one might expect, we met in the balcony of the foundation's building to drink some tequila, as one might also expect. Tired of brainy reflections, we devoted our time to the most pleasant and classic aspect of literature: jokes, which would suddenly confirm themselves as the most rooted way of telling. The scene has been narrated by many of those present, Rodrigo Fresán, Edmundo Paz Soldán, Fernando Iwasaki, and Jorge Volpi. All of them did it after Roberto's passing, which occurred only ten days later. Only then, when we found out that Roberto Bolaño had left us, did we understand the true dimension of that crucial moment, the moment when Roberto, spontaneously, tequila in hand, decided to embark on the task of telling, in all the possible literary versions, a bad joke. He would laugh, he would have fun, he varied the joke without noting the silence, without realizing that we, a collective of supposedly Latin American writers, were experiencing an epiphany: the expression of a native-born author, of a classic. We did not know that it would also be his farewell, at the peak of his writing career, a glory that came late and that he could not enjoy for long.

When speaking about that moment, in front of those authors and in such a meeting, those who have told the anecdote, who are always different and often confronted, they are all—strange thing— in agreement. There was Roberto Bolaño, finally, as an agglutinative element, as the missing link between our literary grandparents, whom we admired, and us. After the necessary parricide, we, authors in our thirties had become orphaned, wondering where was that bridge, that missing link needed to establish, if possible, a line between great-grandparents such as Borges, the Boom grandparents, and us. Orphanhood had plagued us during the 1990s until at last, all of a sudden, Roberto Bolaño showed up.

But he was not only the missing link. He could also be the last dodo. Frequently, the most lucid Latin American criticism and the very conspiracy of new authors has described Bolaño as the last Latin American writer. As time goes by, I am more convinced that this is true. Bolaño gestated as a classic Latin American author: he lived the banana-republic, dictatorial Latin America; he knew all the American and peninsular variants of Spanish; he confronted his own literary forefathers; he was part of absurd groupings; he wrote, wrote, wrote. Who, among us, could say the same thing? Definitely none of us. While our fatherland continued to be our language and our library, Latin America had become an entelechy, a marginal matter in a hyperconnected and fragmented world, a foam of sensitive bubbles, but as close to the Orient as it was to Africa. This was not Roberto's experience, as it was not that of his predecessors. To be or to stop being Latin American was or would be, for twenty-first-century authors, a contingency. But it was not for Roberto Bolaño, José Emilio Pacheco, Sergio Pitol, or Octavio Paz.

This closing nature of Bolaño's opus has been well analyzed. And this is fine, since it is the way we see him in our readings.

Today, Bolaño is sold worldwide, he is turned in to the corruption of the US academy, exactly as what he was not or ever pretended to be: an outsider, a victim, a Bukowski, a drug addict, a drunk. Nothing bothered Bolaño more than indiscipline, victimism, the bookish selling of alleged political experiences. And neither was he marginal: he never was. On the contrary, he belonged and remained in the literary trend of the most powerful writing in Spanish of the last decades.

Like any other classic, Bolaño had a Cervantine vocation, and he was capable of ending the same traditions that he satirized. Continuation and rupture—that is the heritage of his oeuvre. On the one hand, he managed to bring to a halt the Borgesian novel, which had such a great and healthy impact throughout the world, and he managed to end the deep-seated habit of writing books whose protagonists were writers: to do so, he wrote an immense novel where all the characters are writers, dysfunctional, absurd, terrible, grotesque, but writers like any other.

On the other hand, he went beyond American roots and brought the detective novel to a sudden death. A novel like *2666*, where there are eight hundred deaths, four hundred detectives, and no one recognizes the guilty one. The lesson is Cervantine: to destroy in order to preserve, on the one hand, and to show that reality continues to exceed us. Juárez, Ciudad Juárez, is the city of the future. And Roberto, who is no longer with us, was able to see it: reality is writing the most enormous of detective novels, the new apocalyptic novel, the last romantic text, which will always be, like Bolaño, the missing link and, at the same time, the last dodo of a way of writing literature in our language and a way of being a Latin American writer.

RESOURCES

Chronology of Roberto Bolaño's Life_____

1953	Born in Santiago, Chile.
1968	Moves with family to Mexico City at age fifteen on the year of the Tlatelolco massacre. Soon drops out of high school, works as a journalist, and becomes involved in left-wing politics.
1971	Returns to Chile to help Salvador Allende build socialism. After Augusto Pinochet's coup on September 11, he is imprisoned for eight days and released by two prison guards who used to be his classmates. Meets the poet Roque Dalton and members of the Farabundo Martí National Liberation Front in El Salvador.
1974	Returns to Mexico City.
1975	Co-founds the *Infrarrealista* poetic group. Writes the poetry collection *Gorriones cogiendo altura* (*Sparrows Gaining Altitude*) with Bruno Montané, but it was not published.
1976	Writes Infrarealist manifesto. Publishes first poetry collection, *Reinventar el amor* (*Reinventing Love*).
1977	Travels to Europe.
1980s	Works odd jobs in Catalonia, Spain.
1981	Moves to the Catalan town of Blanes, Girona.
1984	Publishes his novel *Consejos de un discípulo de Morrison a un fanático de Joyce* (*Advice for a Morrison Disciple from a Joyce Fanatic*, 1984), coauthored with Antoni García Porta, for which they win the Ámbito

Literario de Narrativa Prize in Barcelona. Publishes *La senda de los elefantes* ([*The Elephants' Path*] published again in 1999 under the title *Monsieur Pain*).

1985	Marries Carolina López.
1990	After the birth of his son Lautaro, he decides to write fiction to support his family.
1992	Diagnosed with liver disease. Wins Premio de Narrativa Ciudad Alcalá de Henares (City of Alcalá de Henares Award for Narrative) and the Rafael Morales Award for poetry. Publishes poetry collection *Fragmentos de la Universidad Desconocida* (*Fragments of the Unknown University*).
1993	Begins to live exclusively from his activity as a professional writer. Wins the Premio de Novela Corta Félix Urabayen (Félix Urabayen Novella Award) for *La senda de los elefantes*. Publishes poetry collection *Los perros románticos* (*The Romantic Dogs*) and novel *La pista de hielo* (*The Skating Rink*).
1994	Wins the Premio Literario Ciudad de Irún (City of Irún Literary Award) for poetry with *Los perros románticos*.
1995	Publishes poetry collection *El último salvaje* (*The Last Savage*).
1996	Publishes *La literatura nazi en América* (*Nazi Literature in the Americas*) and *Estrella distante*.
1997	Publishes short-story collection *Llamadas telefónicas* (*Telephone Calls*), which is awarded the Premio Municipal de Santiago de Chile (Municipal Award of Santiago, Chile); the Premio Ámbito Literario de Narrativa (Narrative Literary Field Award); and the

Premio Literario Kutxa Ciudad de San Sebastián (Kutxa City of San Sebastián Literary Award) for his short story "Sensini."

1998	Publishes *Los detectives salvajes* (*The Savage Detectives*) and wins the Premio Herralde de Novela (Herralde Novel Award). His best friend, Mario Santiago Papasquiaro, dies. Returns to Chile after twenty-five years.
1999	Publishes *Amuleto* (*Amulet*). Wins prestigious Rómulo Gallegos Award and the Premio Herralde (Herralde Prize) for *Los detectives salvajes*.
2000	Publishes *Nocturno de Chile* (*By Night in Chile*), inspired by his trip to Chile the year earlier. Publishes poetry collection *Tres*.
2001	Publishes short-story collection *Putas asesinas* (*Murderous Whores*).
2002	Publishes *Amberes* (*Antwerp*) and *Una novelita lumpen* (*A Little Lumpen Novelita*).
2003	Dies of liver failure at a hospital in Barcelona. *El gaucho insufrible* (*The Insufferable Gaucho*) is published.
2004	*2666* is published. It receives the Premio Salambó (Salambó Award) for the best Spanish-language novel. *Entre paréntesis* (*Between Parentheses*) is published.
2006	*Diario de bar* (co-written with A. G. Porta) is published along with a new edition of *Consejos de un discípulo de Morrison a un fanático de Joyce*.

2007	Poetry collection *La universidad desconocida* (*The Unknown University*) and short-story collection *El secreto del mal* (*The Secret of Evil*) are published.
2010	*El Tercer Reich* (*The Third Reich*) is published.
2011	*Los sinsabores del verdadero policía* (*Woes of the True Policeman*) is published.

Works by Roberto Bolaño

Novels

La pista de hielo (*The Skating Rink,* 1993)

La literatura nazi en América (*Nazi Literature in the Americas*, 1996)

Estrella distante (*Distant Star*, 1996)

Los detectives salvajes (*The Savage Detectives*, 1998)

Amuleto (*Amulet* 1999)

La senda de los elefantes (*Monsieur Pain* 1984; written 1981–1982)

Nocturno de Chile (*By Night in Chile*, 2000)

Amberes (*Antwerp*, 2002; written 1980)

Una novelita lumpen (*A Little Lumpen Novelita*, 2002; written 2001)

2666 (2004; written 1999–2003)

El Tercer Reich (*The Third Reich*, 2010; written 1989)

Los sinsabores del verdadero policía (*Woes of the True Policeman,* 2011; written 1980s–2003)

Short Story Collections

Llamadas telefónicas (*Phone Calls*, 1997)

Putas asesinas (*Murderous Whores*, 2001)

Last Evenings on Earth (Selection of stories from *Llamadas telefónicas* and *Putas Asesinas*, 2001)

El gaucho insufrible (*The Insufferable Gaucho*, 2003; five stories and two essays)

El secreto del mal (*The Secret of Evil*, 2007; seventeen stories and two essays)

The Return (selection of stories from *Llamadas telefónicas* and *Putas asesinas* not included in *Last Evenings on Earth*, 2010)

Poetry Collections

Reinventar el amor (Editor. *Reinventing Love*, 1976)

*Muchachos desnudos bajo el arcoíris de fuego. Antología de la nueva
     poesía latinoamericana.* (Editor. *Naked Youngsters under the
     Fire Rainbow. Anthology of New Latin American Poetry*, 1977)

Fragmentos de la universidad desconocida (*Fragments from the
     Unknown University*, 1992)

Al este del paraíso (*To the East of Paradise*, 1995)

El último salvaje (*The Last Savage*, 1995)

Los perros románticos: Poemas 1980–1998 (*The Romantic Dogs*, 2000)

Tres (*Tres*, 2000)

La universidad desconocida (*The Unknown University*, 2007)

Other Books (Novels, Essays, Speeches, Interviews)

Consejos de un discípulo de Morrison a un fanático de Joyce
     (*Advice from a Morrison Disciple to a Joyce Fanatic*, 1984;
     novel co-written with A. G. Porta)

Entre paréntesis (*Between Parentheses*, 2004)

Roberto Bolaño: The Last Interview & Other Conversations (2011)

Bolaño por sí mismo. Entrevistas escogidas (*Bolaño by Himself*,
     2011)

Manifesto

"Déjenlo todo, nuevamente. Primer Manifiesto del Movimiento
     Infrarrealista." *Correspondencia Infra* (Oct./Nov. 1977):
     5–11. 4 May 2015. Web.

Bibliography

Anderson, Don. "Visceral Realism in Bolaño's Sea of Seeming." *The Australian.* 10 Jan. 2009.

Anderson, Sam. "Prose Poem: Roberto Bolaño's Brilliant, Messy, Everything Novel." *New York Magazine.* New York Media, LLC, 7 Nov. 2008. Web. 28 May 2015.

Andrews, Chris. *Roberto Bolaño's Fiction: An Expanding Universe.* New York: Columbia UP, 2014.

Bagué Quílez, Luis. "Performing Disappearance: Heaven and Sky in Roberto Bolaño and Raúl Zurita." *Roberto Bolaño, a Less Distant Star: Critical Essays.* Ed. Ignacio López-Calvo. New York: Palgrave Macmillan, 2015.

Ballvé, Marcelo. "The face in the mirror: Late Chilean novelist Roberto Bolaño was a chronicler of Latin America's dashed utopias." *San Francisco Bay Guardian.* SFBG, n.d. Web. 28 May 2015.

Banville, John. Review of *Amulet* by Roberto Bolaño. *The Guardian.* Guardian News and Media Limited, 11 Sept. 2009. Web 28 May 2015.

Bertsch, Charlie. "Literary Game." *Souciant.* Souciant, Inc., 3 Feb. 2012. Web. 28 May 015.

Birns, Nicholas. "Valjean in the Age of Javert: Roberto Bolaño in the Era of Neoliberalism." *Roberto Bolaño, a Less Distant Star: Critical Essays.* Ed. Ignacio López-Calvo. New York: Palgrave Macmillan, 2015. 131–48.

Boe Birns, Margaret. "666 Twinned and Told Twice: Roberto Bolaño's Double Time Frame in *2666.*" *Roberto Bolaño, a Less Distant Star: Critical Essays.* Ed. Ignacio López-Calvo. New York: Palgrave Macmillan, 2015. 67–84.

Bolaño, Roberto, Sybil Perez, & Marcela Valdes. *Roberto Bolaño: The Last Interview and Other Conversations.* Brooklyn, New York: Melville House, 2009.

"Bolaño-mania." *The Economist.* The Economist Newspaper Limited, 20 Nov. 2008. Web. 27 May 2015.

Boullosa, Carmen. "Interview with Roberto Bolaño." *Bomb* 78 (Winter 2002): 49–53.

Braithwaite, Andrés, ed. *Bolaño por sí mismo: entrevistas escogidas.* Santiago, Chile: Ediciones Universidad Diego Portales, 2006.

Camps, Martín. "Con la cabeza en el abismo": Roberto Bolaño's *The Savage Detectives* and *2666*, Literary *Guerrilla*, and the Maquiladora of Death." *Roberto Bolaño, a Less Distant Star: Critical Essays.* Ed. Ignacio López-Calvo. New York: Palgrave Macmillan, 2015. 105–27.

Castellanos Moya, Horacio. "Bolaño Inc." *Guernica: A Magazine of Art and Politics.* Guernica, 1 Nov. 2009. Web. 10 Aug. 2013.

Corral, Will H. "Roberto Bolaño: Portrait of the Writer as Noble Savage." *World Literature Today* 81.1 (Nov.–Dec. 2006): 51–54.

Deckard, Sharae. "Peripheral Realism, Millennial Capitalism, and Roberto Bolaño's *2666*." *Modern Language Quarterly* 73. 3 (2012): 351–72.

Deb, Siddhartha. "Foreword: On Roberto Bolaño." *Roberto Bolaño, a Less Distant Star: Critical Essays.* Ed. Ignacio López-Calvo. New York: Palgrave Macmillan, 2015. ix–xxi.

D'Erasmo, Stacey. "The Sound and the Führer." *New York Times Book Review.* The New York Times Company, 24 Feb. 2008. Web. 28 May 2015.

Derbyshire, Philip. "*Los detectives salvajes:* Line, Loss the political." *Journal of Latin American Cultural Studies* 18.2 (2009): 167–76.

Dirda, Michael. Review of *Nazi Literature In The Americas.* *The Washington Post.* The Washington Post, 2 Mar. 2008. Web. 28 May 2015.

Dove, Patrick. "The Nights of the Senses: Literary (Dis)orders in *Nocturno de Chile.*" *Journal of Latin American Cultural Studies* 18.2–3 (2009): 141–54.

Eder, Richard. "A Line Divides Art and Life. Erase It at Your Own Risk." *New York Times.* The New York Times Company, 12 Apr. 2007. Web. 28 May 2015.

Epler, Barbara. "Roberto Bolaño in the USA." *Archivo Bolaño 1977–2003.* Ed. Juan Insua. Barcelona: Centro de Cultura Contemporánea de Barcelona, 2013. 167–69.

Estrada, Aura. "Found in Translation." *Boston Review.* Boston Review, 1 Jul. 2007. Web. 28 May 2015.

Farred, Grant. "The Impossible Closing: Death, Neoliberalism, and the Postcolonial in Bolaño's *2666.*" *Modern Fiction Studies* 56. 4 (Winter 2010): 689–708.

Franco, Jean. "Questions for Bolaño." *Journal of Latin American Cultural Studies: Travesía* 18.2–3 (2009): 207–17.

Goldman, Francisco, "The Great Bolaño." *The New York Review of Books* 54.12 (2007): n.p. Web. 3 Jan. 2009.

Hoyos, Héctor. *Beyond Bolaño: The Global Latin American Novel.* New York: Columbia UP, 2015.

Kerr, Sarah. "The Triumph of Roberto Bolaño." *The New York Review of Books.* NYREV, Inc. 18 Dec. 2008. Web. 28 May 2015.

Kunkel, Benjamin. "In the Sonora." *London Review of Books.* LRB Limited, 9 Jun. 2009. Web. 28 May 2015.

Lesser, Wendy. "The Mysterious Chilean." *The Threepenny Review.* The Threepenny Review, Spring 2007. Web. 28 May 2015.

Levinson, Brett. "Literature and Proportion in *The Insufferable Gaucho.*" *Roberto Bolaño, A Less Distant Star: Critical Essays.* Ed. Ignacio López-Calvo. New York: Palgrave, 2015. 149–67.

Long, Ryan. "Traumatic Time in Roberto Bolaño's *Amuleto* and the Archive of 1968." *Bulletin of Latin American Research.* 29.1 (2010): 128–43.

López, Carolina. "Editorial Note." *Woes of the True Policeman.* By Roberto Bolaño.

Trans. Natasha Wimmer. New York: Farrar, Straus & Giroux, 2012. 249–50.

López-Calvo, Ignacio. Introduction. *Roberto Bolaño, A Less Distant Star: Critical Essays.* Ed. Ignacio López-Calvo. New York: Palgrave, 2015. 1–14.

_____. "Roberto Bolaño's Flower War: Memory, Melancholy, and Pierre Menard." *Roberto Bolaño, a Less Distant Star: Critical Essays.* Ed. Ignacio López-Calvo. Palgrave Macmillan, 2015. 35–64.

López-Calvo, Ignacio, ed. *Roberto Bolaño, a Less Distant Star: Critical Essays.* New York: Palgrave Macmillan, 2015.

López-Vicuña, Ignacio. "The Violence of Writing: Literature and Discontent in Roberto Bolaño's 'Chilean' Novels". *Journal of Latin American Cultural Studies* 18.2 (2009): 155–66.

Lyle, Erick. "On Bolaño's *2666*, Election Night in the Mission, and Truth and Reconciliation in the Obama Era from Bay Guardian 3/4/2009." *On the Lower Frequencies*. Erick Lyle/WordPress, 9 Mar. 2009. Web. 28 Dec. 2012.

Lynd, Juliet. "Writing from the Margins of the Chilean Miracle: Diamela Eltit and the Aesthetics and Politics of the Transition." *Post-Authoritarian Cultures. Spain and Latin America's Southern Cone*. Ed. Luis Martín-Estudillo & Roberto Ampuero. Nashville: Vanderbilt UP, 2008. 12–33.

Madariaga Caro, Montserrat. *Bolaño Infra 1975–1977: Los años que inspiraron Los* detectives salvajes. Santiago de Chile: RiL editores, 2010.

Mangel, Alberto. Review of *Nazi Literature in the Americas. The Guardian*. Guardian News and Media Limited, 6 Feb. 2010. Web. 28 May 2015.

Maristain, Monica. *Bolaño: A Biography in Conversations*. Trans. Kit Maude. Brooklyn: Melville House, 2012.

Medina, Alberto. "Arts of Homelessness: Roberto Bolaño or the Commodification of Exile." *Novel. A Forum on Fiction* 42.3 (2009): 546–54. Web. 6 Sept. 2015.

Miles, Valerie. "A Journey Forward to the Origin." *Archivo Bolaño. 1977–2003*. Barcelona, CCCB, 2013. 136–141.

O'Bryen, Rory. "Mourning, Melancholia and Political Transition in *Amuleto* and *Nocturno de* Chile by Roberto Bolaño." *Bulletin of Latin American Research* 0.4 (2011): 473–87.

_____. "Writing with the Ghost of Pierre Menard: Authorship, Responsibility, and Justice in Roberto Bolaño's *Distant Star.*" *Roberto Bolaño, a Less Distant Star: Critical Essays*. Ed. Ignacio López-Calvo. New York: Palgrave Macmillan, 2015. 17–34.

Page, Alan. "Natasha Wimmer on Translating *2666.*" *Vulture*. New York Media LLC, Nov. 2008. Web. 28 May 2015.

Prose, Francine "'Last Evenings on Earth,' by Roberto Bolaño: The Folklore of Exile." *New York Times Sunday Book Review*. The New York Times Company, 9 Jul. 2006. Web. 28 May 2015.

Pollack, Sarah. "Latin America Translated (Again): Roberto Bolaño's *The Savage Detectives.*" *Comparative Literature* 61.3 (2009): 346–65.

Richards, Ben. "Poets, pimps and prostitutes." *The Guardian*. Guardian News and Media Limited, 22 Jun. 2007. Web. 28 May 2015.

rodríguez freire, raúl. "Ulysses' Last Voyage: Bolaño and the Allegorical Figuration of Hell." *Roberto Bolaño, a Less Distant Star: Critical Essays*. Ed. Ignacio López-Calvo. New York: Palgrave Macmillan, 2015. 85–104.

Rohter, Larry. "A Chilean Writer's Fictions Might Include His Own Colorful Past." *New York Times*. The New York Times Company, 27 Jan. 2009. Web. 6 Sept. 2015.

Salas-Durazo, Enrique. "Roberto Bolaño's Big Bang: Deciphering the Code of an Aspiring Writer in *Antwerp*." *Roberto Bolaño, a Less Distant Star: Critical Essays*. Ed. Ignacio López-Calvo. New York: Palgrave Macmillan, 2015. 189–209.

Scherson, Alicia. Interview. "Meet the 2013 Sundance Filmmakers #44: Alicia Scherson Adapts Bolaño in 'Il Futuro'." *Indiewire*. Indiewire, 21 Jan. 2013. Web. 6 Sept. 2015.

Stavans, Ilán. Review. "Willing Outcast. How a Chilean-born iconoclast became a great Mexican novelist." *The Washington Post*. The Washington Post, 6 May 2007. Web. 28 May 2015.

Solotorevsky, Myrna. "Pseudo-Real Referents and their Function in *Santa Maria de las flores negras* by Hernán Letel and *Amuleto* by Roberto Bolaño." *Partial Answers: Journal of Literature and the History of Ideas* 4.2 (2006): 249–56. Web.

Tonkin, Boyd. Review of *Amulet*. *The Independent*. independent.co.uk, 16 Oct. 2009. Web. 28 May 2015.

Valdés, Marcela. "Alone Among the Ghosts: Roberto Bolaño's '2666.'" *The Nation*. The Nation, 19 Nov. 2008. Web. 28 May 2015.

_____. Interview. *Inside Higher Ed*. 16 Dec. 2009. Web. 28 May 2015.

_____. *Roberto Bolaño: The Last Interview and Other Conversations*. Trans. Sybil Pérez. New York: Melville House, 2009.

Varn, C. Derick. "Bolaño and beyond: An Interview with Juan E. De Castro on Contemporary Spanish Language Literature." *Former People: A Journal of Bangs and Whimpers*. C. Derick Varn & Steven A. Michalkow/WordPress, 30 Nov 2013. Web. 16 Feb. 2014.

Villalobos-Ruminott, Sergio. "A Kind of Hell: Roberto Bolaño and The Return of World Literature." *Journal of Latin American Cultural Studies* 18.2 (2009): 193–205.

Williams, Gareth. "Sovereignty and Melancholic Paralysis in Roberto Bolaño." *Journal of Latin American Cultural Studies* 18.2 (2009): 125–40.

Wylie, Andrew. "Bolaño Studies." *New York Times*. The New York Times Company, 5 Dec. 2008. Web. 29 May 2015.

Wu Ziru. "The Chinese Edition of Bolaño's *2666* Newly Released." *Global Times*. Global Times, 25 Dec. 2011. Web. 28 May 2015.

About the Editor

Ignacio López-Calvo is professor of Latin American literature at the University of California, Merced. He is the author of seven books on Latin American and US Latino literature and culture: *Dragons in the Land of the Condor: Tusán Literature and Knowledge in Peru* (Arizona UP, 2014); *The Affinity of the Eye: Writing Nikkei in Peru* (U of Arizona P, 2013); *Latino Los Angeles in Film and Fiction: The Cultural Production of Social Anxiety* (U of Arizona P, 2011); *Imaging the Chinese in Cuban Literature and Culture* (UP of Florida, 2007); *"Trujillo and God": Literary and Cultural Representations of the Dominican Dictator* (UP of Florida, 2005); *Religión y militarismo en la obra de Marcos Aguinis 1963–2000* (Mellen, 2002); and *Written in Exile: Chilean Fiction from 1973–Present* (Routledge, 2001). He has also edited *Roberto Bolaño, a Less Distant Star: Critical Essays* (Palgrave, 2015); *Magical Realism* (Critical Insights Series, Salem Press, 2014); *Peripheral Transmodernities: South-to-South Dialogues Between the Luso-Hispanic World and "the Orient"* (Cambridge Scholars Publishing, 2012); *Alternative Orientalisms in Latin America and Beyond* (Cambridge Scholars Publishing, 2007); and *One World Periphery Reads the Other: Knowing the "Oriental" in the Americas and the Iberian Peninsula* (Cambridge Scholars Publishing, 2009) as well as coedited *Caminos para la paz: literatura israelí y árabe en castellano* (Corregidor, 2008). He is also the coexecutive director of the academic journal *Transmodernity: Journal of Peripheral Cultural Production of the Luso-Hispanic World* and the co-executive director of the Palgrave Macmillan Book Series "Historical and Cultural Interconnections between Latin America and Asia."

Contributors

Nicholas Birns completed his PhD at New York University in 1992, with his dissertation being directed by renowned critic Harold Bloom. He subsequently taught at several schools in the northeastern United States, joining the faculty of the New School in 1995. He has been associated with the Australian studies journal *Antipodes* since 1993 as a review editor and was appointed editor-in-chief in 2001, serving in that capacity to this day. He oversees a staff of several other editors and managers and has broadened the scope of the journal to include Asian and Pacific Rim concerns and consideration of transnational and diasporic issues. The journal is now published by Wayne State University Press and indexed in JSTOR. Birns maintains a strong interest in Australian literature and publishes many articles and reviews on the subject. He has also conducted regular seminars and university courses on Australian literature. He has two important books forthcoming on Australia: *Contemporary Australian Literature* (U of Sydney P, 2015) and *Options for Teaching Australian and New Zealand Literature* (coedited with Nicole Moore and Sarah Shieff; Modern Language Association, 2016). He has also coedited *Vargas Llosa and Latin American Politics*; *The Contemporary Spanish American Novel*; and, forthcoming, *Roberto Bolaño as World Literature.*

José Javier Fernández Díaz received his PhD in 2014 from the University of Barcelona, where he works as an associate professor in the online Master of Advance Studies in Spanish and Latin American Literature. He also serves as head of the languages department in the Ausiàs March High School. Previously, he was content executive for the London Book Fair, where he championed projects such as the Comic Book Pavilion and the Translation Centre.

David Lau is a poet, essayist, and coeditor of *Lana Turner: a Journal of Poetry and Opinion.* He holds degrees from the University of Iowa Writers' Workshop and UCLA. His books of poems are *Virgil and the Mountain Cat: Poems* (UC Press) and *Still Dirty: Poems 2009–2015* (Commune Editions/AK Press). His poetry and essays have appeared in many different publications, including *Boston Review, Counterpunch, Los*

Angeles Review of Books, and *A Public Space.* He teaches writing and global issues at UC Santa Cruz.

Ryan Long is associate professor of Spanish at the University of Maryland. His research focuses on culture and politics in Mexico and Latin America, with an emphasis on the twentieth century. He has published articles on a range of topics, including the conflict in Chiapas, Mexican cinema, and a number of writers, including Bruno Montané Krebs, Álvaro Mutis, Ignacio Manuel Altamirano, José Gorostiza, Juan Villoro, Laura Esquivel, and Roberto Bolaño. His book, *Fictions of Totality: The Mexican Novel, 1968, and the National-Popular State*, was published in 2008 by Purdue University Press. He is currently working on two new book projects, one on Bolaño and another on the Swiss architect and one-time Bauhaus director Hannes Meyer, who lived and worked in Mexico from 1939 to 1949.

Ignacio López-Vicuña is associate professor of Spanish at the University of Vermont. He has written scholarly articles on Southern Cone authors and filmmakers, such as Roberto Bolaño, Néstor Perlongher, Edgardo Cozarinsky, and Raúl Ruiz. His work has appeared in *Latin American Research Review*, *Studies in Hispanic Cinemas*, and *Journal of Latin American Cultural Studies*.

Juliet Lynd is associate professor of Spanish and Latin American studies at Illinois State University. She has a PhD in Hispanic and Luso-Brazilian Literatures and Linguistics from the University of Minnesota and a BA in Hispanic Studies from Vassar College. Her published work on Roberto Bolaño appears in *Chasqui: revista de literatura latinoamericana* and in the volume *Estar en el presente: literatura y nación desde el Bicentenario* (Eds. Enrique Cortez and Gwen Kirkpatrick, Latinoamérica Editores, 2012). Keenly interested in various approaches to the political possibilities of literature, visual arts, film, and cultural studies from the twentieth century forward, her work on authors such as Cecilia Vicuña, Raúl Zurita, Diamela Eltit, Ariel Dorfman, and Ángel Escobar, has appeared in *PMLA*; *Mandorla: New Writing from the Americas/Nueva escritura de las Américas*; *Sirena: poesía, arte, crítica*; and *Hispanic Issues Online Debates*. She has collaborated with Vicuña to publish her poetry, which was censored in Chile in 1973 (*El Zen Surado* [Editorial Cataloña, 2013]), and on an additional forthcoming book on the *Tribu No* (the No Tribe), a marginal avant-garde poetry group operating in Chile before the coup and parallel in certain respects to Bolaño's Infrarrealist opposition to official culture in Mexico. Lynd is currently incorporating a chapter on Bolaño into a book-length study of the points of contact between literature and performance in Latin America, bringing Bolaño into dialogue with authors as diverse as Zurita, Eltit, and Vicuña.

Rubén Medina has been a faculty member of the department of Spanish and Portuguese at the University of Wisconsin-Madison since 1991. He is also a translator, a poet and one of the founders of Infrarealism. He specializes in Mexican and Chicano/a literature and culture, continental connections, film studies, and Mexican migration to the United States. In these areas of research he has published *Autor, autoridad y autorización: Escritura y poética de Octavio Paz* (Colegio de México, 1999); *Genealogías del presente y del pasado: Literatura y cine meXicanos* (Lima-Berkeley, 2010); and numerous articles in journals and books on masculinity, violence, modern and postmodern hybridity, global melodrama, Infrarealism, and neo-avant-garde movements. In poetry, he has published, *Báilame este viento, Mariana* (1980), *Amor de Lejos . . . Fools' Love* (1986), and four editions of *Nomadic Nation / Nación nómada* (2010, 2011, 2015). He received the National Endowment for the Arts Fellowship in poetry (1981) and other poetry awards. His poems have been included in over a dozen of Mexican, Latin American, Spain, and US Latino anthologies. In collaboration with John Burns, he published a major anthology of Beat poetry translated into Spanish, *Una tribu de salvajes improvisando a las puertas del infierno* (Mexico: Aldus, 2012). He recently edited *Perros habitados por las voces del desierto: poesía infrarrealista entre dos siglos* (Mexico: Aldus, 2014).

Brantley Nicholson is an assistant professor of Spanish and Latin American studies in the department of modern languages and cultures at Georgia College. He holds a PhD in Latin American culture and literary theory from Duke University. His work engages comparative American literary studies through the theoretical questions of globalization, cosmopolitanism and ethics. His most recent work consists of the edited volume "The Generation of '72: Latin America's Forced Global Citizens" and a special edition of *Cuadernos de Literatura*, dedicated to the contemporary Colombian author Fernando Vallejo.

Salvador Oropesa is professor of Spanish literature and world cinema, and department chair at Clemson University. He received his PhD from Arizona State University. He coedited, with Maureen Ihrie, *World Literature in Spanish: An Encyclopedia* (ABC-CLIO, 2011), a comprehensive three-volume encyclopedia on literature written in Spanish. His other books include *The Contemporáneos Group: Rewriting Mexico in the Thirties and Forties* (U of Texas P, 2003); *La novelística de Antonio Muñoz Molina: sociedad civil y literatura lúdica* (Universidad de Jaén, 1999); and *La obra de Ariel Dorfman: ficción y crítica* (Pliegos, 1992). His last book is *Literatura y comercio en España: las tiendas (1868–1952)* (Universidad de Málaga, 2014).

Ignacio Padilla has received twelve international awards for his narrative, dramas, and essays, which have been translated into fifteen languages. He is the author of the novels *Si volviesen Sus Majestades, Amphitryon* (Premio Primavera, 2000) and *Espiral de artillería and La gruta del toscano* (Premio Mazatlán de Literatura). In 2008, he won the Premio de Cuento Juan Rulfo in Paris. He has also published the essays "El diablo y Cervantes," "La vida íntima de los encendedores," and "La isla de las tribus perdidas." He lives in Querétaro, Mexico; is a member of the Mexican Academy of the Spanish Language; and is a professor at Universidad Iberoamericana.

Alicia Ramos-Jordán received her PhD from the world cultures program at the University of California, Merced, with the dissertation *Conspiradoras in the Contact Zone: escritoras chicanas y su obra en español, hacía una literature menor*. Her research is in the area of Spanish and US Latino literature, with a focus on Chicano/a literature written in Spanish and its relation to Hispanic literature. She is currently a Spanish language assistant at Trinity College, Cambridge University. She has taught courses in Hispanic literature at the University of California, Merced, and at California State University, Fresno. Her work has appeared in two edited volumes, *Cinéma métis aux États-Unis: représentations de la frontière*

Mexique/États-Unis and *South-to-South Dialogues between the Luso-Hispanic World and "The Orient,"* as well as in journals such as *Revista forma, Transmodernity*, and *Next*.

Traci Roberts-Camps is associate professor of Spanish at University of the Pacific. Her areas of specialization include Latin American women film directors, twentieth-century Latin American literature, Mexican women novelists, and feminist film and literary criticism. She is the author of *Gendered Self-Consciousness in Mexican and Chicana Women Writers: The Female Body as an Instrument of Political Resistance*. She has published book chapters and articles on a variety of Latin American women film directors, including Marisa Sistach, Dana Rotberg, María Novaro, and Lucía Puenzo. She has published book chapters and articles on novelists such as Rosario Castellanos, Cristina Rivera Garza, and Bárbara Jacobs. She recently finished a manuscript on Latin American women film directors from Argentina, Brazil, Chile, and Mexico.

Marco Valesi received his PhD in interdisciplinary humanities at the University of California, Merced, with the dissertation *Clean Wall, Voiceless People: Exploring Socio-Identitarian Processes Through Street-Urban Art as Literature*. He taught in the department of foreign languages at UC Merced. He is the editor of From Monadism to Nomadism: A Hybrid Approach to Cultural Productions and has published articles in Italian, Spanish, and English, which have appeared in *Cinéma métis aux Etats-Unis: représentations de la frontière Mexique/ États-Unis*; *South-to-South Dialogues Between the Luso-Hispanic World and "The Orient;"* One World Periphery Reads the Other: Knowing the "Oriental" in the Americas and the Iberian Peninsula*; and *Exploit: Come rovesciare il mondo ad arte.Distruzioni per l'uso*. He has also published articles in journals such as *Revista Forma* (Universitat Pompeu Fabra), *Transmodernity* (University of California); *Next-Strumenti per l'innovazione* (Università La Sapienza); and *On the Waterfront* (Universiyt of Barcelona). In 2015, he published the novel *Duri come i muri*. He currently teaches at the University of Parma, Italy, in the Web Communication and Social Media Master program.

Index

Butler, Judith 150

Cabrera Infante, Guillermo xv, 235
Camacho, Isaac Rosa 51
Caro, Monserrat Mandariaga 40
Carrington, Leonora 85
Carvajal, Diego 120
Carver, Raymond 142
Casanova, Pascale 132, 232
Casares, Adolfo Bioy 19
Cassady, Neal 143
Castellanos Moya, Horacio 62, 173
Castro, Anabella Pérez 17
Castro, Fidel 45, 79, 87, 88
Catana, Rafael 17
Cela, Camino José 16
Cercas, Javier 4, 23, 28
Cervantes, Miguel de 50
Chacel, Amaya 82, 83
Chao, Ramón 219
Ciardo, Luigi 209, 227
Civil War x, 40, 42, 43, 85, 87
Colosio, Luis Donaldo 77
comparative literature 48, 64, 131, 133, 250
Corral, Wilfrido H. 52
Cortázar, Julio 5, 10, 19, 40, 190
cosmopolitanism xii, 121, 130, 257
Cuban Revolution 36, 81, 88, 117, 174
Cura, Lalo 36, 81, 88, 117, 174

Dalton, Roque 23, 25, 114, 115, 169, 241
Damián, Álvaro 72
D'Annunzio, Gabrielle 230

Darío, Rubén 105, 115
Deb, Siddhartha 214
de Castro, Juan 5
de Gortari, Carlos Salinas 82
del Paso, Fernando 51
Deming, Zhao 53
Derrida, Jacques 82
De Sica, Vittorio 222, 232
de Vega, Carmen Pérez 27
Dick, Phillip K. 134
dictatorship x, 8, 12, 33, 38, 39, 43, 45, 46, 52, 82, 177
Donoso, José 19, 221

Echevarría, Emilio 77, 92
Echevarría, Ignacio 6, 20, 22, 48, 98, 132, 137, 190, 206, 232
Echeverría, Luis 41, 67, 81
economy of prestige 130
Edwards, Jorge 19
Elliot, T. S. 141
Ellis, Brett Easton 145
Eltit, Diamela 16, 250, 256
Enrigue, Álvaro 19
Enrique Vila-Matas 19
Epler, Barbara 51
Espinosa, Patricia 223
Espinoza, Manuel 63
Estrada, Ramón Méndez 17
exile xi, 34, 37, 38, 43, 46, 80, 84, 122, 155, 157, 160, 167, 180, 202, 225

Faber, Sebastiaan 84
fascism 43, 102, 108
Felipe, León 79, 80, 84, 87, 88, 91
Fellini, Federico 221, 222, 230, 232, 233, 234
Ferlinghetti, Lawrence 54

Williams, William Carlos 54, 138
Wimmer, Natasha 20, 48, 118,
     165, 187, 205, 206, 232,
     249, 250
World War II x, 15, 43, 59, 229
Wyler, William 222, 234
Wylie, Andrew 61

Yvancos, Pozuelo 136

Zambra, Alejandro 52, 60, 220